Exposed to the J-curve

Understanding and Managing Private Equity Fund Investments

Exposed to the J-curve

Understanding and Managing Private Equity Fund Investments

Ulrich Grabenwarter and Tom Weidig

Euromoney Books

Published by
Euromoney Books, a division of Euromoney Institutional Investor Plc
Nestor House, Playhouse Yard
London EC4V 5EX
United Kingdom

Tel: +44 (0) 20 7779 8999 or USA +1 800 437 9997
Fax: +44 (0) 20 7779 8300
www.euromoneybooks.com
E-mail:hotline@euromoneyplc.com

ISBN 1 84374 149 0

Typeset by Servis Filmsetting Ltd, Manchester

Printed in England by Hobbs the Printers

Contents

About the authors xii

Preface xiii

Introduction xv

Part I Private equity fund investments: an alternative asset class 1

Chapter 1: The private equity fund as the intermediary in an expert market 3
- The private equity fund as the intermediary 3
- Investing in private equity funds 3
- Risk levels of private equity investments 4
  - Direct investments 5
  - Private equity funds 5
  - Private equity funds of funds 5
  - Securitisation and structured products 6
  - Publicly traded private equity 6

Chapter 2: Why invest in private equity funds? 7
- Who should invest in private equity funds? 7
- Private equity as part of an alternative investment strategy 7
  - Institutional investors seek exposure to alternative investments 7
  - The attractiveness of alternative investments 8
- Reasons to invest in private equity funds 8
- Investing in private equity – a critical look 9
  - Challenging the reasons to invest in private equity funds 9
  - Disadvantages of investing in private equity funds 10

Chapter 3: The private equity fund industry 12
- Origin of the private equity fund industry 12
  - The formalised private equity industry takes off in the 1970s 12
  - The size of the private equity industry 12
  - Market prospects 13
- The main markets 14
  - The US market 14
  - The European markets 14
  - Asia Pacific and other emerging markets 15

The main private equity players 16
The fund manager or general partner (GP) 16
The fund investor or limited partner (LP) 16
Prospects 16

Chapter 4: The investment focus of private equity funds 18
The sub-segments of private equity – an overview 18
Characteristics and risk of venture capital and late-stage PE segments 19
Risk–return comparison 20

Chapter 5: Performance of private equity funds 21
Sources of return for private equity funds 21
Performance measurement in private equity 21
Finding a meaningful performance measure for private equity funds 21
The multiple 22
The internal rate of return (IRR) 23
Why public market performance measures fail 23
The public market equivalent (PME) 24
Problems with the PME 24
Vintage year-weighted performance? 25
Leaving out young funds due to the J-curve 25
The risk (or uncertainty in returns) of private equity funds 26
The public market concept of risk fails 26
Using the standard deviation as risk measure 26
The bias of the standard deviation as risk measure 27
Empirical studies of risk–return of private equity funds 27

Chapter 6: Asset allocation to and within private equity 32
Correlation between private equity and other asset classes 32
Why is correlation important? 32
What are the problems when determining correlation? 32
How strongly correlated is private equity to public indices? 33
Asset allocation to private equity 34
Standard asset allocation and its problems 34
How much capital to allocate to private equity funds? 34
Correlation between private equity funds of different investment foci 34
Asset allocation within private equity 35
Investing in a broad range of funds across several vintage years 35
Implementing the asset allocation goal 36

Part II Being a private equity fund investor 37

Chapter 7: Evaluating an investment opportunity 39
The set-up of a private equity fund 40
Evaluating an investment opportunity from a limited partner perspective 41

Private equity – a people's business 41
Business ethics in private equity 41
Professionalism – the backbone of the industry 42
Evaluating the market opportunity 42
The factors involved in evaluation 43
Market opportunities due to political or macroeconomic change 46
Generalist funds versus specialist funds 46
Evaluating the quality of a private equity fund's management team 47
Assessing a management team's track record 48
Evaluating the fund management individuals 52
Assessing the deal flow of a team 54
First-time teams versus experienced teams 55
What is the better choice? 55
Evaluating first-time teams 56

Chapter 8: Assessing terms and conditions – what to watch out for 57
Management fee structures 57
What does it cover? 57
Budget-based assessment of management fee levels 58
Step-down structures 58
Scaling fee levels to the fund size 58
Other partnership expenses 59
Broken deal expense 59
Set-up cost 59
Fee offset 60
Operating costs and capital invested 60
Investment periods and fund duration 60
Equalisation premia 61
Hurdle return – does it matter? 61
Catch-up mechanism 62
Two concepts 62
Alignment of interest and the sharing of profits 62
Carry distribution based on repayment of full contributed capital 63
Protection for limited partners in the case of overdistributions 64
Carry distribution based on repayment of full committed capital (full-fund-back concept) 65

Chapter 9: The legal documentation – how to protect your investment 68
The legal structure 68
Limited liability for limited partners 68
Tax transparency 69
Regulatory constraints 69
Cost efficiency 69
Creating an industry standard 69
Protective clauses 70
Key-man clauses 70

Removal clauses for cause and without cause 71
Defaulting investors 76

Chapter 10: Avoiding or managing conflict of interest 78
Conflicts of interest within the scope of a general partner 78
Exclusivity clauses 79
Overlapping investment activities 79
Conflicts of interest involving limited partners 81
Best market practice corporate governance 82
Limited partners' involvement in the management of the fund 82
Limited partners' place in the corporate governance of a fund 83

Chapter 11: Investment monitoring and crisis management 84
Warning signs in monitoring a fund investment 84
Unusually slow or fast investment pace 84
Quality of reporting 85
General partner's transparency on valuation 85
Lost investments 86
Reserve policy in early-stage funds 86
Stability of the management team 86
Decreasing commitment of co-investors 86
What if everything goes wrong? – How to react in a crisis 87

Part III Managing a portfolio of private equity fund investments 89

Chapter 12: The challenges of portfolio and risk management in private equity 91
Goals and tasks of portfolio management in private equity 91
The portfolio manager's goals 91
The portfolio manager's tasks 92
Identifying and reducing the risks of private equity fund investments 93
Undiversifiable risks 93
Diversifiable risks 94
Reducing diversifiable risks 96
Quantitative risk management in private equity 97
Reluctance towards the use of quantitative risk management practices 97
Trend towards more quantitative risk management 98
Applying risk management techniques to private equity 99
Implementation challenges 99
Challenges to modelling 99
Active portfolio management is difficult 99

Chapter 13: Information for risk and portfolio management 101
The information deficiency in private equity 101
Sharing of information and the agency problem 101

Pressure to disclose 101
Lack of information exchange standards 102
The demand for information exchange standards 102
Developing reporting and valuation guidelines 103
Overcoming the information deficiency 104
The importance of information management systems 104
The quality of information 104
Which information to trust? 105
Information from own funds 105
Information from personal networks 105
Information from private equity publications 106
Information from external sources 106
Private equity databases 106
Can private equity databases overcome the information deficiency? 106
VentureXpert (from Thomson Venture Economics) 107
Cambridge Associates 108
Venture One 108
Fund investors' portfolios 108

Chapter 14: Monitoring a portfolio 110
Portfolio measures 110
The importance and type of portfolio measures 110
Measures at portfolio level 110
Measures at fund level 112
Measures at company level 112
Monitoring diversification 112
Monitoring the value of the portfolio 114
The importance of valuation in private equity 114
Valuation methods for companies 114
Special considerations when valuing portfolio companies in private equity 115
How fund managers compute the NAV 116
The nature of the private equity NAV 116
Monitoring performance using a benchmark 117
Benchmarking the fund management team to its peer group 117
Do too many teams claim to be top quartile? 118
Is past performance a good indicator of future performance? 119

Chapter 15: Forecasting the future portfolio 120
Forecasting the distribution of future cash flows 120
The need for cash flow modelling 120
Important issues on the use of cash flow models for forecasting 121
Monitoring risk numbers 121
Forecasting the performance of the portfolio 122
Using the interim IRR 122
Improving the forecasting power of the interim IRR 122

Chapter 16: Steering the portfolio 124
General issues 124
Liquidity reserves 124
Overcommitment 125
Diversification 126

Chapter 17: Advanced cash flow modelling 127
Cash flow modelling 127
The importance to fund investors 127
Public disclosure 127
The challenges 128
High model risk 128
Cash flow patterns as a guide to fund investors 129
The pattern of fund cash flows 129
Studies on historical patterns 130
Different types of cash flow models 131
Models of a fund as a portfolio of direct investments 132
Model based on manager cash flow estimates 132
Model based on company grading 133
Non-probabilistic models at fund level 133
Simple approach 133
Takahashi and Alexander's model 134
Weidig's interim IRR model 134
Probabilistic models at fund level 135
Fitch Ratings model 135
Standard & Poor's model 135
Weidig internal age model 136
Partners Group model 136
Malherbe model 137
Kaserer and Diller model proposal 137

Part IV Alternative private equity investment vehicles 141

Chapter 18: Helping institutional investors to access private equity 143
The role of the alternative investments 143
Outsourcing 144
Exiting private equity 144

Chapter 19: Funds of funds 146
Advantages 146
Outsourcing 146
Larger networks 146
Accessibility 146
Increased diversification 147
Deal flow availability 147
Greater bargaining power 147

	Disadvantages	147
	Additional layer of fees	147
	Less control	148
	Illiquidity	148
	Hard to find perfect match	148
	Overcrowded market	148
	Selecting a fund of funds management team	148
	Ability to access the best fund management teams	148
	Investment strategies as differentiating factor	149
	Other selection criteria	150
	The risk profile of a fund of funds	151
Chapter 20:	Secondary transactions	152
	Motivation and considerations on the sell-side	152
	Reasons to sell	152
	Disadvantages to selling	153
	Motivation and considerations on the buy-side	153
	Advantages	153
	Disadvantages	154
	Outsourcing the investment into secondary transactions	155
Chapter 21:	Securitisation and structured instruments in private equity	156
	Securitisation of private equity funds	156
	Benefits	156
	Disadvantages	157
	Prospects	158
	Structured instruments and hedge funds	158
	Other products: publicly traded private equity	159
Chapter 22:	Conclusion	161
	Glossary	163
	Bibliography and further reading	178

About the authors

Ulrich Grabenwarter is head of division for Venture Capital Operations at the European Investment Fund (EIF), and responsible for a portfolio of nearly 100 private equity funds and €1 billion under management. Prior to EIF, he worked for several years at the European Investment Bank in the Directorate for Financing Operations in Germany and Austria, executing structured finance operations in the corporate and financial sector and private equity fund of fund investments. He was the personal adviser of the Austrian Management Board Member at EIB. He began his career at PricewaterhouseCoopers in the Audit and later Finance Consulting Department, specialising in derivatives for investment and risk management purposes including their use in hedge funds.

Dr Tom Weidig is the author of several works on private equity funds, funds of funds and the impact of the new Basel Accord. His study *The Risk Profile of Private Equity* has been publicised and endorsed by the European Venture Capital Association, and translated into German and French. He holds a Master of Science in Theoretical Physics from Imperial College London and a PhD from the University of Durham. He was a postdoctoral researcher at the University of Manchester, and a visiting researcher at Trinity College, University of Cambridge. Leaving physics behind, he then worked as a risk analyst in derivatives for the US investment bank Bear Stearns in London. He is currently an independent consultant, and also worked for the European Investment Fund researching and modelling private equity funds.

Preface

There are many books on private equity financing of companies and on the relationship between the entrepreneur and the managers of private equity funds, but none is written exclusively with the institutional or private fund investor in mind. However, fund investors face serious issues during the asset allocation and investment process, and want independent advice. Our book intends to fill this gap in the private equity literature: how can institutional and private investors safely invest in private equity? We approach this question with a review of the private equity fund industry and a description of all the relevant management issues of fund investments – both from an individual investment and a portfolio perspective – as well as discussing indirect investment vehicles such as funds of funds or securitisation notes.

We faced no easy challenge writing about a market where visibility is often reduced to the sales pitch of the market players or their quarterly reports. We base our judgement on our extensive professional experience and a review of over 600 publications. We tried to think independently and avoid following the many myths floating about in the industry. This book is the best we could do to give you the day-to-day view and the big picture on investing in private equity. If our book gives you a point of reference for your daily work and food for thought for an interesting discussion, we will have achieved our goal. Please feel free to contact us with your comments and suggestions for any improvement.

Whilst Dr Tom Weidig assumed the overall management of this project, this book is a joint and highly complementary effort on the part of both authors based on Uli Grabenwarter's hands-on experience in fund of funds investment management and Dr Tom Weidig's knowledge in quantitative and risk management techniques in private equity and beyond. Their complementary backgrounds are reflected in views exposed in Parts II and III, and combined in a general description of the private equity industry in Part I and a discussion of alternative investment instruments for private equity in Part IV.

This book would not have been possible without the strong support we received from others. First, we would like to thank our families, especially Véro and Farrah, for their many sacrifices in quality of life during the time we spent on writing this book. Special thanks also go to Andreas Kemmerer and Robert Blotevogel for their valuable assistance during the literature review and feedback. We also thank the editors at Euromoney Institutional Investor Plc, Elizabeth Gray, Charles Harris and Johanna Geary for their continuous support and constructive feedback along the process. Finally, we would like to thank the following people, who have proof-read the drafts or provided us with valuable comments, in alphabetical order: Bjorn Born, Paul Hauffels, Michael Moise, Professor André Prüm, Laurent Schummer and Matthias Ummenhofer. The European Venture Capital Association and their chief economist Dr Didier Guennoc were kind enough to provide us with data and permission to use their glossary.

We should like to thank Thomson Financials (VentureXpert database), EVCA and PwC for their permission to publish graphs based on their data. We primarily use their data to demonstrate long-term trends between individual markets, sectors and stages, and the dynamics of the industry but not to give up-to-date statistics. The data is up to an appropriate cut-off date, in most cases up to 2003, but sometimes earlier where necessary. For example, for the discussion of historical performance, we eliminated all funds less than five years old, as early performance figures related to such investments would be largely meaningless due to the typical return pattern of private equity funds. It is also important to realise that data collection in private equity has a significant time lag of more than six months and without a guarantee of complete coverage. Readers interested in the most recent data in private equity for general statistics, historical performance or cash flow modelling should consult one of the databases discussed in Part III.

We should also like to thank the Luxembourg Fonds National de la Recherche for their financial support under FNR/04/MA4b/06.

If you are interested in accessing the electronic summary of our literature review of over 600 publications, please contact weidig@quantexperts.com. The literature review is based on information provided by QuantExperts. An extended bibliography can be found at www.ssrn.com.

Introduction

At the heart of private equity lies a simple concept: the need of a privately held company to raise capital for an ambitious business plan, which is too risky for a bank loan and too big to be self-financed. On the other side of the spectrum is the institutional or high net worth investor who provides capital to private equity, among other asset classes, in the hope of achieving a better risk-adjusted return. The private equity fund is the intermediary between the company in need of capital and the generalist investor in need of private equity expertise. It is a collective investment scheme managed by a team skilled in private equity financing using the capital of several investors. This book is about the issues investors face when investing in private equity funds, either directly through fund investments or via alternative instruments such as funds of funds, securitisation notes, listed products or secondary transactions.

For institutional investors, such as insurance companies, pension funds, banks or foundations, and high net worth individuals, Part I provides the necessary background information to decide on whether to make private equity a part of their broad asset allocation. The private equity fund acts as the intermediary in this specialist asset class as investors rarely undertake direct private equity investments in companies. Investors hope to further diversify an existent portfolio of more traditional asset classes such as debt and public equity instruments, and to enhance the overall performance of their investment activities. Only after carefully considering the benefits and drawbacks of private equity should an investor allocate capital either to private equity funds, as shown in Parts II and III, or by indirect exposure through specialist funds of funds or other investment vehicles, as described in Part IV.

Chapter 1 introduces the private equity fund, the intermediary through which investors gain access to private equity, and the different ways to invest in funds. The investors' reasons to go into this specialist asset class are described and critically reviewed in Chapter 2. Then, Chapter 3 shows how widely available an investment opportunity the organised private equity fund industry has become: its explosive growth, its size, the worldwide markets and the main players. After this global perspective, Chapter 4 elicits the different possible investment foci of private equity funds, from seed to special situation investments in companies. As historical performance of private equity is crucially important for the investor, Chapter 5 deals with the tricky issues surrounding the performance measurement of funds, and the empirical studies of risk–return. Finally in Part I, Chapter 6 discusses how much capital an investor who has decided to invest in private equity funds should allocate to private equity and its sub-segments.

Part II extensively deals with the challenges fund investors face when investing in a private equity fund. It chronologically follows the full investment process of fund investors, from the identification of an investment opportunity to the monitoring of active investments. Chapter 7 provides an overview of the main parties in a fund structure: the fund investors, also commonly called limited partners (LPs) and the fund manager, typically referred to as the general partner (GP). It also offers guidelines for the due diligence process and the assessment of an investment opportunity, including the evaluation of the market potential and the selection process of a successful management team. Chapter 8 deals with the main terms and conditions fund investors should be familiar with when investing in a private equity fund and deals with the incentive structure for GPs under various distribution mechanisms. Chapter 9 discusses basic principles of the legal structuring process and explains useful protective measures fund investors should consider in the legal documentation to limit their downside risk. Chapter 10 deals with conflict of interest situations fund investors may be exposed to when investing in private equity funds and provides concrete advice on how to avoid or manage conflict of interest of various parties. Finally, Chapter 11 provides useful guidance on how to monitor fund investments, what early warning signs to watch for and how to react when investments get off track. This book cannot replace hands-on experience but it gives fund investors a comprehensive overview of key success factors and efficient tools to manage downside risk that should prevent them from making costly mistakes.

Part III discusses the issues fund investors face in private equity portfolio and risk management, and hopefully provides their portfolio managers with useful tools and ideas on implementation. Novel issues arise when an investor holds a portfolio of fund investments: how to plan liquidity for a portfolio with commitments to several funds of different vintage years? How to assess the value of their unrealised investments? How to measure performance of the portfolio? How to project returns? What conclusion to draw for future investments? Portfolio and risk management techniques become crucial to steer a private equity portfolio of fund investments, and to ensure the implementation of a long-term investment strategy. The new tasks of portfolio management deal with the fund investments at the portfolio level, and are complementary to the interactions of the investment manager with the fund, such as team selection and due diligence, as described in Part II.

To begin, Chapter 12 discusses the goals and tasks of portfolio management. A main challenge is to apply quantitative risk management techniques, and to diversify away or manage the many types of risks that the investor faces in private equity. Chapter 13 then describes the type of information needed and available for portfolio and risk management, and discusses how this information should be collected, stored and handled systematically. Based on the gathered information, Chapter 14 proposes how to aggregate information in a meaningful way, and includes a discussion on how to monitor diversification and valuation of the portfolio. However, an investor not only needs to know about the current state of the portfolio, but also about the future projection. Thus, Chapter 15 deals with the nature of cash flows of private equity funds, and how the prediction of cash flows leads to liquidity planning and portfolio performance projection. In Chapter 16, the information gained from portfolio monitoring and forecasting feeds into deciding on the future set-up of the portfolio. This portfolio steering is also useful for overcommitment strategies and liquidity reserves. Finally, Chapter 17 is an advanced and technical review of cash flow models that are vital to portfolio forecasting.

Part IV explores other private equity investment vehicles as an alternative to a private equity fund investment. Many investors either lack the expertise, the capital or the willingness to confront the challenges of directly managed fund investments, as described in Parts II and III. Alternative investment vehicles allow investors to access different risk profiles, to outsource the tasks of an LP holding a portfolio of funds, and also provide more flexibility in terms of liquidity, for example, in exiting fund investments in private equity.

Chapter 18 begins with an overview of the alternative investment vehicles of private equity, and focuses on the key concepts behind the main products. Chapter 19 introduces the private equity fund of funds, which is the most important alternative investment vehicle in private equity, and lists its distinguishing features such as access to and selection of fund managers. Chapter 20 reviews secondary transactions, the most common instrument providing liquidity to investors who seek to exit fund investments. On the buy-side, secondaries provide investors with an opportunity to quickly build up a mature and diversified portfolio of fund investments and can be a useful tool for proactive portfolio management. Finally, Chapter 21 introduces securitisation notes and structured instruments to invest in private equity, as well as reviewing publicly traded private equity by discussing the advantages and disadvantages of listed private equity vehicles. While securitisation notes may become a serious alternative to secondaries for investors who partially or fully want to divest their private equity exposure, structured instruments, such as hedge funds involving private equity components, have emerged to provide access to private equity with a tailor-made risk profile.

Part I

Private equity fund investments: an alternative asset class

Chapter 1

The private equity fund as the intermediary in an expert market

The private equity fund as the intermediary

Private equity arises from the need of a privately held company to raise capital for an ambitious business plan. Private equity financing of companies supports many different business strategies, for example: to develop new products and technologies, to expand working capital, to make acquisitions, to strengthen a company's balance sheet, and to resolve ownership and management issues in a family succession, or a management buy in or buyout. However, this book is not about private equity financing per se, but only about how the institutional investor can gain exposure to private equity financing. Institutional investors investing in private equity through private equity funds is the overriding theme of this book.

Private equity is an expert market, where the right skills, experience and resources are vital to succeed. The private equity fund is the intermediary that provides institutional investors with a safe access to the asset class. The fund management team has the right skills and experience to undertake direct private equity investments in companies, called the portfolio companies, on behalf of the fund investors, who have equipped the fund with the necessary capital resources. The objective is to sell the portfolio companies after a few years of value development for a higher price, and to generate profit for the fund's investors.

Investing in private equity funds

Exhibit 1.1 shows how institutional investors gain exposure to private equity financing on a company level. By far the most important access channel is to directly invest in funds which

Exhibit 1.1

Different ways to invest in private equity funds

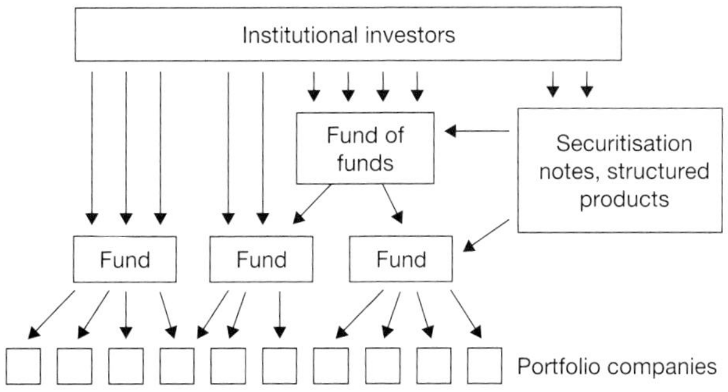

Source: Authors' own.

themselves invest in companies. Depending on their needs and constraints, some investors choose to invest in a private equity fund of funds, which then in turn invests in private equity funds. About 20 per cent of the capital provided to funds come from funds of funds.[1]

Other ways of accessing private equity are gaining popularity but are still niche investments. The institutional investor can go via other alternative investment vehicles such as securitisation or structured products, but again the capital ends up in the hands of fund managers. Finally, the investor can gain exposure to private equity by buying fund or fund of funds investments second-hand or investing in a secondary fund of funds. The different types of investments are not only different ways to access private equity funds but they also have very different risk profiles.

Risk levels of private equity investments

Investors often perceive private equity as a risky asset class. This is certainly true for direct investments in companies. Especially in the venture capital segment, the total loss rate of private equity direct investments is very high. On the other hand, successful venture capital investments return many times the invested amount. However, investments in private equity funds are far less risky than one direct investment. Institutional investors always invest in several private equity funds to gain exposure to a range of portfolio companies where the gains on a few would more than compensate the losses on others. Other investors do not have the skills or resources to directly invest in a sufficient number of funds, and choose funds of funds or other alternative vehicles.

Exhibit 1.2 illustrates just how different the risk profiles of investments in a company, in a fund and in a fund of funds are. It shows the return distribution of US venture capital direct, fund and fund of funds investments. The horizontal axis indicates the return expressed as a multiple of capital invested, and the vertical axis gives the frequency of investments with a given multiple. For example, about 30 per cent of all direct investments have a multiple of zero, which is effectively a complete loss of the capital invested, but no total loss for a fund or fund of funds investment. And around 10 per cent of all fund investments have a multiple of less than one, that is, they return less than the capital invested. However, a fund of funds

Exhibit 1.2

The return distribution of US venture capital direct, fund and funds of funds investments

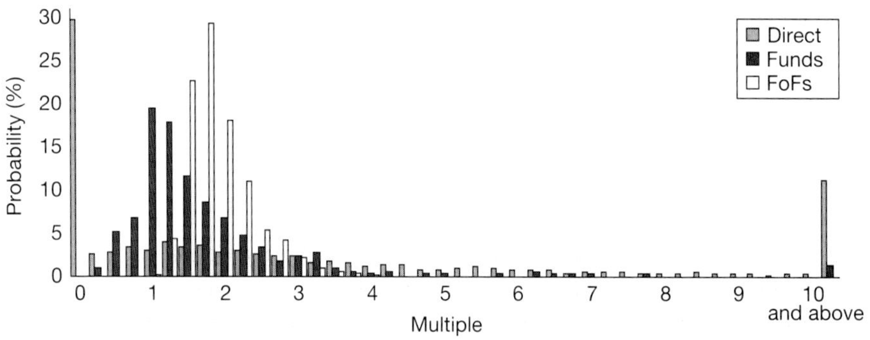

Source: Weidig and Mathonet (2004).

investment nearly always returns the capital invested. To conclude, private equity might be a risky asset, but a private equity investment is not necessarily so.

Direct investments

Private equity funds undertake risky direct investments. The rewards on a single direct investment can be high, and so can the pitfalls. Exhibit 1.2 shows that the return distribution of a direct venture capital investment is highly skewed and very spread out. Around 30 per cent of all direct investments result in a total loss, but more than 10 per cent generate high profits and return more than 10 times the capital invested. Of course, these extreme high multiples vary between different segments of private equity, and are lower for buyout investments, for example. Nevertheless, investors should only commit all their capital in one direct investment if they want to gamble. If investors believe in the superiority of their selection skills and their ability to add value they should invest in several direct investments to achieve a much better risk–return ratio than for a single investment. Their potentially superior skills would generate a higher average return and the diversification effects reduce the risk of extreme losses but also reduce the upside potential of their portfolio return. If investors are not sure whether they have the appropriate skills, resources or risk appetite for direct investments, they would be better to seek exposure to private equity through indirect investment instruments such as funds, funds of funds or structured products. This is the case for the vast majority of institutional investors.

Private equity funds

A fund is a collective investment scheme that invests in between 10 and 30 portfolio companies. It is far less risky than a direct investment, because it is very unlikely that all direct investments in a fund's portfolio perform badly or result in a total loss. Exhibit 1.2 shows that unlike for direct investments the returns of fund investments are centred around a peak, with still a significant tail of high returns but very few extreme losses. The fund portfolio induces significant diversification effects compared with a direct investment. A fund investment is not as risky as a direct investment, but the risks are not negligible. If investors have good selection skills and monitoring resources, as related to funds, and sufficient capital to build a diversified portfolio, they should invest in funds. The skills necessary for successful fund investments are described in Parts II and III. However, if investors do not possess the necessary skills to manage the risks associated with fund investments or do not have enough capital to build a diversified portfolio of funds, they should invest in a fund of funds, or structured products.

Private equity funds of funds

Funds of funds typically invest in more than 20 funds, which then have several hundred direct investments in portfolio companies. Funds of funds offer a far better diversification of risks, are much safer, and their managers typically have a wide market view and access to well-established funds. Exhibit 1.2 shows that the return distribution of a fund of funds looks similar to an index of an efficient public market; it has a symmetric distribution, not too pronounced fat tails and no total losses. The hundreds of portfolio companies do not go bankrupt together, but the high returns and total losses from these direct investments balance out. Even the probability to lose any capital seems small. (For a discussion of funds of funds see Part IV.)

Securitisation and structured products

Collateralised fund obligations (CFOs) are one example for the securitisation of a portfolio of private equity funds. The securitisation effectively transforms the risk of a private equity fund of funds into various layers of different degrees of risk. These different risk layers are then sold as bonds to investors who choose the appropriate one according to their risk appetite. The individual tranches are typically rated by rating agencies, often starting with an AAA for the most senior debt layer. Often the capital of the bond benefits from a guarantee by a monoline insurer. CFOs may serve multiple purposes and not only be used to invest in private equity but also to decrease exposure to private equity by selling assets into a CFO deal.

Another example of structured products in private equity are funds or funds of funds raising capital for their investment activity by issuing a bond that pays interest and may provide a limited participation in the fund's or fund of funds' profits. (Securitisation and structured products are discussed in Part IV.)

Publicly traded private equity

Another interesting alternative vehicle is publicly traded private equity (PTPE), for example: listed companies whose core business is private equity, quoted investment funds and specially structured investment vehicles. These entities are often evergreen funds that have raised capital from the public market, and reinvest proceeds from exits. They cater for investors that cannot hold unlisted products or need more liquidity. Thus in terms of liquidity and transparency, they are less risky but at a cost, as they typically trade below their net asset value. The market price reflects the market's judgement on their fair value, minus an illiquidity discount. Still, it is difficult to judge the risk profile of publicly traded private equity instruments on the basis of their market price evolution, because most products are infrequently traded. (These products are discussed further in Part IV.)

---

1 According to the European Venture Capital Association (EVCA) statistics provided to the authors.

Chapter 2

Why invest in private equity funds?

Who should invest in private equity funds?

Investment consultants recommend private equity to investors with long-term strategies such as pension funds, endowment funds and insurance companies mainly because a well-diversified portfolio of private equity fund investments requires a commitment of at least 10 to 15 years without easy and cheap exit routes. Moreover, private equity investors should carefully choose the right investment vehicle according to their skills and experience, and the size of their capital allocation.

Private equity is an expert market, and many institutional investors prefer or have to rely on intermediaries who provide specific expertise. The private equity fund is the most common intermediary. However, even fund investors need a good understanding of the private equity fund industry, and should only go into private equity funds if they have sufficient capital to hold several fund investments – that is, more than US$50 million – and the right know-how, infrastructure and people in place. Thus, for the brave, wealthy and skilled ones, investing into private equity funds may be the preferred choice. But for investors who are new to the asset class, a more prudent approach through a fund of funds or structured instruments may be advisable. This is also true for smaller investors who are unable to diversify with several funds or who cannot afford the necessary resources.

Private equity as part of an alternative investment strategy

Institutional investors seek exposure to alternative investments

The fundamental reason why institutional investors now invest in private equity is that alternative investment strategies have become part of their overall investment programme. Institutional investors typically only managed a broad publicly traded portfolio, but now invest up to 15 per cent of their portfolio in alternative investments such as hedge funds, real estate and private equity.

Alternative investments[1] are probably best defined by what they are not, namely traditional investments: publicly traded stocks and bonds, and their derivatives. Three groups can be identified: alternative strategies such as hedge funds that have a specific strategy to exploit market imperfections; alternative assets which include physical assets (such as real estate, land, art and coins), private equity and securitised products; and traditional alternatives such as high-yield bonds. While major differences between various categories of alternative assets prevail, there is a common underlying theme: these alternative investments are typically not traded in an efficient, transparent and liquid market. And there are few regulations, seemingly endless opportunities for the clever and lucky ones, and vultures for the inexperienced.

The attractiveness of alternative investments

The popularity of alternative investments is due to the investors' desire and hope to further diversify their portfolio, and harness potentially extraordinary return opportunities in these non-traditional markets. Public markets are now so efficient that public fund managers have a hard time to beat the index that everyone can buy, but in alternative markets the experienced and clever can achieve superior returns, or so the claim goes. This is true for all alternative markets, but especially for private equity. Private equity is a financing tool at crucial stages of a company's life, be it a new venture, a succession issue or entering a new market. The suitable skill-set of the fund manager to provide support in mastering the challenges at the inflection points in the life of a company may benefit the company and generate considerable returns.

Furthermore, alternative investments are very different to the traditional asset classes, and have notable diversification benefits. Returns in hedge funds and real estate are driven by factors that are sufficiently different to stocks and bonds. The diversification case for private equity as opposed to hedge funds or real estate is, however, weaker, because the value and return potential of private equity investments in companies is moving with the public markets to some degree. Venture capital partially defies this argument as it bases the value potential primarily on innovation. The development and feasibility of a new product such as a novel drug or a new computer chip has no direct relationship to the public markets.

Finally, alternative investments are generally riskier, and should imply a higher return as compensation for higher risk-taking. Private equity-backed companies seek financing at critical stages of their development. The success in mastering these challenges is decisive for investors' returns. This constitutes additional uncertainty and hence risk for investors, which is compensated by a risk premium built into the return on private equity investments.

Reasons to invest in private equity funds

Investors need to make sure that the exposure to private equity funds improves the risk-adjusted return of their overall portfolio. Pure commercial return objectives are usually driving the investment decisions of institutional investors, but sometimes within regulatory constraints. Some pension funds may, for instance, be limited in the scope of their geographic diversification or in their choice of investment vehicle. Such constraints add to the complexity for institutional investors in making their investment decisions.

Potential investors should carefully consider the following possible arguments in favour of private equity[2] and challenge their validity in the context of the investor's specific situation.

Long-term historical outperformance

The long-term historical fund return outperforms against the public markets, which is seen as a compensation for extra risk-taking and low liquidity. Many studies – mostly based on Thomson Venture Economics data – quote an average internal rate of return of between 10 and 15 per cent, depending on the period, sub-segment and method of sampling. Public stock indices lie in the region of 5–10 per cent time-weighted return.[3]

Expertise leads to superior returns

A private equity fund manager can act as a true stock picker, choosing from hundreds of business plans. Superior expertise will lead to above-average return. Managers of a public fund need to hold similar stocks to their peer group. This gives them little discretion in deciding on a specific investment strategy.

Diversification benefits

A private equity allocation gives diversification benefits because private equity is a different asset class and, to some extent, follows different value creation patterns than public stock markets. Diversification improves the overall risk-adjusted return of a portfolio. This benefit is especially true for early-stage venture capital, which is less related to the stock market than later-stage and buyout investments.

Untapped developing markets

Private equity is still a relatively untapped market, especially in parts of Europe and emerging markets such as the Asian markets. Thus, there is an enormous growth potential, although a growing market does not necessarily create superior returns.

Access to insider information

A private equity investor has access via the fund manager to legitimate insider information, which allows the manager to better assess the viability of a business plan. On the stock market, a public fund manager needs to rely on the not-very-detailed quarterly reports to judge the potential of a company and the market price typically incorporates all publicly available information. Influence over management and flexibility of implementation is much greater for private equity investors. They hold a significant minority or majority share of the company, and often serve on the board of directors. Thus, they have the ability to actively influence management and add value. Public fund managers rarely have such powers, as they only hold a small percentage of a company's stocks.

Investing in private equity – a critical look

Challenging the reasons to invest in private equity funds

Before getting into private equity, the investor should challenge and validate the above proposed reasons to invest in the asset class. This is no easy task due to a lack of data and research arising from the opaqueness of private equity. In fact, there are no straightforward answers without qualifiers, and some research findings are even misleading due to the use of inappropriate methods. The two main reasons for investing in private equity, namely good risk-adjusted returns and diversification, are not self-evident.

Is there long-term historical outperformance?

It is not evident that the long-term historical average outperforms the public market on a risk-adjusted return.[4] One recent study suggests that private equity funds underperform with respect to the risk they carry.[5] Many other studies disagree with this view as discussed in 'Empirical studies of risk–return' in Chapter 5. Also, the picture certainly looks different for various stages, countries or time periods.[6] Finally, there is also a tricky debate on how to measure the performance of a fund, which is discussed in Chapter 5. The public markets use a different performance measure, namely the time-weighted return, and not the internal rate of return or multiple.

Diversification benefits might not be significant

There are substantial arguments on what diversification benefits private equity may provide. Diversification benefits may not be very exciting, because there is a clear relationship between public markets and private equity. Some studies have found close-to-zero correlations, but these might be flawed. A detailed discussion on correlation issues and diversification benefits is provided in Chapter 6.

Disadvantages of investing in private equity funds

Apart from questioning the reasons proposed to go into private equity, investors must also be aware of some disadvantages of private equity.

Management cost

Private equity is an expensive asset class. Investors need to pay considerable fees to the fund management team: management fees and up to 20 per cent participation on profits, the so-called carried interest. In addition, fund investors have increased internal resource requirements and costs to set up a fund investment programme in terms of infrastructure and human capital. Indirect fund investors who go through alternative structures such as funds of funds or structured instruments pay additional fees to the fund of funds manager or the arranger of the structured deal.

Lack of liquidity

Private equity fund investments are long-term investments, typically over 10 years. An investor cannot sell the fund investment quickly and at fair value, because the private equity market is not very liquid. This makes changes in the asset allocation very difficult.

Resource requirements and diversification issues

An investor needs to have a considerable amount of money to invest in private equity in order to achieve a meaningful diversification of risk. Due to a minimum required commitment for fund investments of typically US$1–5 million, an investor with only US$5 million to invest can only gain exposure to one or two funds, which is a poorly diversified investment. Thus, investors need at least US$50 million to have a somewhat diversified portfolio of about 10 funds. Indirect investment vehicles offer access to a diversified investment at a lower entry level, typically starting from US$1 million, but at the cost of extra fees.

Required expertise

Fund investors need to be convinced of their expertise, experience and dedication. The requirements and efforts of selecting and monitoring a collection of limited partnership investments are intensive, as Parts II and III demonstrate. A lack of expertise in private equity is far more dangerous than in a public market, where everyone can hold the index and achieve the average market performance. In private equity, lack of expertise may lead to significant underperformance.

Blind pool investment

Finally, investors in private equity funds do blind pool investing. They leave the decision to the fund managers, and generally have no say in selecting the investment.

Advantages:
- Historical average between 10% and 15% IRR
- Higher returns than public market
- Diversification benefits
- Skilled and experienced fund managers can achieve superior returns
- Many untapped markets
- Access to legal insider information

Disadvantages:
- Risk–return studies are not clear-cut
- Performance comparison to public markets difficult
- Higher returns only due to higher risk and illiquidity premium
- Exit markets depend on public markets
- Costs for fund and fund of funds structure
- Long-term illiquid investments in an opaque market
- Need for considerable capital
- Need for considerable expertise
- Blind pool investing

---

1 For an introduction, see for example Miller (1998) and Jaeger (2004).

2 See EVCA (2004a) on 'Why and how to invest in private equity'.

3 Frei and Studer (2004) quote the performance of the MSCI World Index with 6.3 per cent and of the S&P500 with 9.3 per cent over the past 10 years.

4 According to Gottschalg, Phalippou and Zollo (2004).

5 Gottschalg, Phalippou and Zollo (2004) say that their 'analysis indicates that private equity funds underperform under conservative assumptions about the risk they carry. Such performance is perplexing and we cannot reject the possibility of mispricing by so thought sophisticated institutional investors'.

6 For example, European venture capital funds seem to have underperformed with respect to European buyout funds, despite the fact that venture capital fund returns are more volatile and investments carry more risk. See Weidig and Mathonet (2004) for more details.

Chapter 3

The private equity fund industry

Origin of the private equity fund industry

The formalised private equity industry takes off in the 1970s

The first private equity funds were created in the United States and the United Kingdom in the middle of the last century.[1] However, there were few such formal private equity structures in the following years, and they were mostly marketed to individual investors rather than to hesitant institutions. Direct investments by individual investors, affectionately called business angels, foundations, universities and charities dominated the private equity industry well into the 1970s.

Regulatory changes were key to the growth of the industry. Relaxations and clarifications of investment constraints imposed on banks and pension funds opened up the gate for vast additional capital channels. For example, the 'prudent man' rule in the United States prohibited pension funds from allocating significant amounts to high-risk assets such as private equity, and was relaxed in 1979. Similarly, some years earlier in 1971, the United Kingdom gave its banks greater investment flexibility. These events paved the way for these institutional investors to enter the private equity industry, and forced the fund managers to move toward professional standards.

In the 1980s, another milestone was the easier access to private equity for a non-expert investor either via a fund of funds, a consultant or gatekeeper.[2] The investors were suddenly able to effectively outsource the management of fund investments to specialised firms, and eliminate the need for expertise on the side of the investor. Together with the infamous internet hype of the 1990s and a low inflation environment, the private equity markets exploded and reached a climax of US$200 billion invested worldwide in 2000. The following slowdown produced a healthy slimming-down and consolidation of the industry. Exhibit 3.1 shows the impressive growth of the private equity industry during the 1990s and a noticeable decline afterwards in western Europe, and similar patterns were played out in North America and Asia Pacific.

The size of the private equity industry

The modern organised private equity industry is a far cry from the sporadic, localised and informal private equity financing of the past. It has passed the threshold to become a firmly established market of more than a US$100 billion raised globally every year and bears all its landmarks: a great number and many types of investment vehicles; many investors with plenty of capital and long-term investment strategies; well-defined legal structures and regulations; constant information exchange; independent research by academics; and an understanding of underlying dynamics.

In the aftermath of the internet boom, the investment levels have come down after the dramatic increase in private equity investments over the 1990s, but they have consolidated

Exhibit 3.1

Evolution of private equity fundraising in Europe, 1990–2003

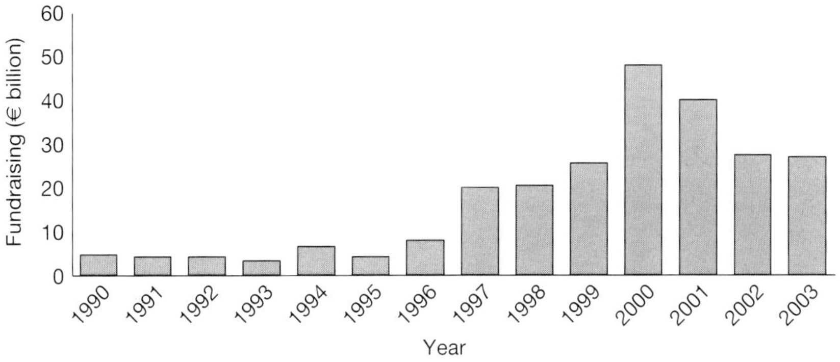

Source: EVCA/PwC.

Exhibit 3.2

Distribution worldwide of private equity in 2003

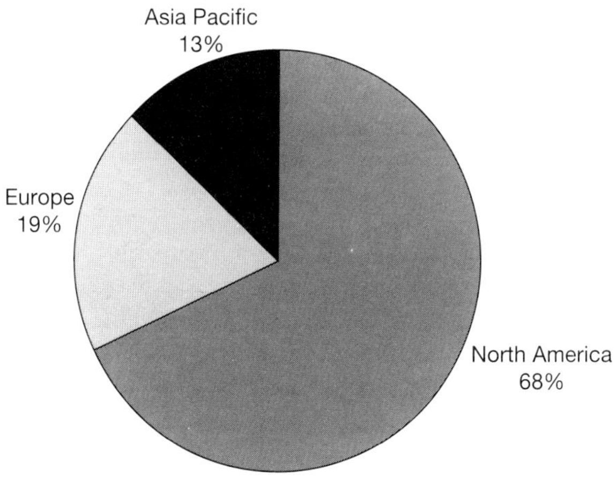

Source: PwC/3i 'Global Private Equity 2004 Report'.

at a level significantly higher than at the beginning of that decade. Private equity is now well established. In 2003, more than US$150 billion had been invested worldwide in private equity, representing 0.5 per cent of the world's GDP. A significant amount went to buyouts with US$120 billion.[3] North America is by far the largest market with US$110 billion (or 68 per cent of the worldwide market) invested, followed by Europe with US$30 billion (or 19 per cent worldwide) invested and Asia Pacific with US$20 billion (or 13 per cent worldwide). (See Exhibit 3.2.)

Market prospects

The industry is still evolving in many ways, and will become more and more connected to the capital markets. Several structured instruments now exist that put private equity on the radar screen of smaller wealthy investors. Institutional investors will press further for converging standards, especially in reporting and valuation. They will also constantly question the benefits of private equity. Private equity will become more liquid via secondary funds, publicly traded private equity companies and other structures. Quantitative risk management will take hold and this will improve the modelling of cash flows and understanding of the dynamics of funds. Surely, investment banks will enter the market, as they spot arbitrage opportunities that can be exploited due to a more liquid and quantitative market. Finally, even if the private nature of private equity financing can never be overcome, the industry will eventually confine it to black boxes that the capital markets can trade.

The main markets

The success of private equity investments in individual markets is strongly dependent on macroeconomic parameters, social aspects and the regulatory environment. The most developed markets in the United States and the United Kingdom are very much driven by an equity culture. In these markets private equity investors have good exit opportunities either via initial public offerings (IPOs) or trade sales. Their deal flow is rich due to very active research and development from universities and corporations, an entrepreneurial attitude and an entrepreneur-friendly regulatory environment. Continental Europe is catching up, based on strong scientific research, but is suffering from the lack of exit channels and an entrepreneurial culture that has relied upon bank loans rather than private equity financing. In emerging markets great efforts are undertaken to create the right framework for a flourishing private equity industry as the importance of this industry for economic development is undisputed.

The US market

The most developed private equity market is without doubt the US market. This market has a long tradition and private equity has become an integral part of the institutional investors' asset allocation. The US market has mature investors both at the level of institutions and private individuals. It has a highly developed and knowledge-based economy, ample research and strongly developed financial markets providing the ground for a well-diversified private equity industry with a high degree of specialisation at the level of private equity funds.

The depth of the US market is unmatched in other parts of the world. In 2003, the US venture capital market was roughly 10 times bigger then the European market, despite comparable sizes of the two economies.[4] The US market also shows much stronger resistance to setbacks in the industry, such as the bursting of the technology bubble in the late 1990s. Certainly the US market also contracts in adverse market conditions but investors' interest revives much quicker once the general market climate improves.

The European markets

In the European market downturns tend to last longer because the market lacks maturity and institutional investors lack confidence to maintain a long-term view. In Germany, for instance, insurance companies' commitment to private equity dropped from US$1 billion in 2001 to US$280 million in 2003. A prolonged period of losses such as those experienced in the post-technology hype period still causes sizeable European investors to permanently withdraw or to resume investment activity only when the returns for private equity have returned to stable positive territory. This behaviour may seem logical at first glance, but it is detrimental to investors' returns in a cyclical industry such as private equity. It ultimately may lead to situations where investors invest in the boom period and divest during recession. Of course, such behaviour cannot yield attractive returns.

In the European markets, the UK market is probably the most developed one and comparable to that of the United States. It is characterised by a stable investor base providing strong support to both the venture capital and the buyout segment. Many pan-European funds also operate out of offices in London. Scandinavia has established itself as an attractive market, especially in the venture capital-backed information technology segment, based on the clusters around global market leaders in the communications industries. Other European markets such as France and Germany still show a high vulnerability in periods of market downturns and lack long-term commitment from domestic institutional investors.

The southern European markets, although gradually catching up with the European average still show sizeable similarities with emerging market characteristics such as large fragmentation of the industry, little specialisation and little vertical depth in covering the various sub-segments of the private equity spectrum. While markets such as the United Kingdom show a fairly balanced distribution of investments across venture capital and late-stage private equity segments, Spain shows a strong overweight of expansion-stage financing, accounting for almost 75 per cent of all investments in 2003[5] with little activity in the buyout segment. Eastern Europe has seen isolated success stories, especially in the development capital and buyout segment with a handful of successful investment firms having emerged since 1990.

Asia Pacific and other emerging markets

Russia has shown spectacular results in a broad range of private equity segments. In the Middle East, Israel has developed a strong venture capital activity benefiting from close ties to the US market. In the Asian and Pacific regions, India, Singapore, Japan and Australia have developed sizeable venture capital activities, with US$18 billion invested in 2003.[6] In the Asian markets, which are growing considerably and often have a great potential in innovative technologies, governments are making great efforts to create more private equity-friendly legislation, tax regimes and currency exchange rules. However, creating a regulatory environment is not enough: education, political stability, reliable jurisdiction and social acceptance of private equity to finance economic growth and innovation must follow. Identifying the progress an economy has made on this path is one of the biggest challenges in assessing investment opportunities in emerging markets. It is vital to assess the political risk and legal risk dimension associated with an investment and to judge whether the return potential of an investment promises an adequate compensation for taking on these additional risks. Hence, while the emerging private equity markets offer good investment opportunities, an intimate knowledge of these markets is required to achieve investment success. In many cases, investment returns in emerging markets are the result of a fund manager's ability to exploit market imperfections such as poor transparency of information or incomplete financial markets lacking leverage for expansion financing.

The diversity of geographically different markets exposes investors to a great variety of macroeconomic, regulatory and political risks. Investors should therefore diversify their portfolio geographically to be less vulnerable to macroeconomic changes in the various markets, for example, by investing in several funds focusing on different countries or in a global fund of funds.

The main private equity players

The fund manager or general partner (GP)

For management team members, launching a private equity fund is a major decision in their professional career. Not only are they normally required to commit a sizeable portion of their personal wealth to the fund in order to contribute to the fund manager's share in the fund's commitments, they also need to have a long-term perspective with respect to their involvement in private equity. A fund has a lifetime of 10 years and more, and it may take a long time for private equity fund managers to see the pay-off from their financial and professional efforts spent on a fund. It is this long-term commitment from investment professionals in the private equity industry, and the high requirements on their skill-set, that justify the relatively high salary levels in this industry.

The fund investor or limited partner (LP)

Limited partners are the oxygen of the private equity industry. They provide the capital required to carry out the investment strategy of a fund. Without them, there would be no GPs and hence no organised private equity industry. Although the origins of private equity go back to wealthy private individuals who, through business angel-type investments, funded the first venture capital-backed companies, the investment activity of large institutional investors carries today's industry. The main players in the market are pension funds, insurers, funds of funds, banks, government agencies, corporate investors, foundations and family offices. Their weight in relative terms varies depending on the markets. In Europe, banks have a much bigger share in the funding of private equity funds, about a quarter as opposed to no more than 5 per cent in the United States. In the United States, pension funds are by far the most dominant funding source.

Over the past decade, funds of funds have worldwide become an important source of capital, with a share of up to 20 per cent. Exhibit 3.3 shows the share of capital provided by different investors in Europe. The differences in the composition of funding sources are certainly linked to the risk–return profile of private equity in specific markets. In the United States, private equity has substantially and systematically outperformed public equity and become an indispensable element in the asset allocation even for absolute return strategy-driven investors such as pension funds. In the European market, the picture is slightly different. Private equity, and in particular venture capital, are still maturing and have struggled in the past to outperform lower-risk asset classes. Hence, the incentive to invest in private equity was less for institutional investors who cannot afford to gamble in their asset allocation. In these markets it was predominantly banks that provided funding to the industry, often through captive funds that did not always have a pure financial return-driven investment strategy but also served as part of a broader banking product portfolio.

Prospects

Market conditions change and so does the composition of the institutional investors providing funding for private equity in various markets. The Basel Committee, made up of all important central banks worldwide, is working on a new regulatory framework called the New Basel Accord. It is likely to increase capital charges for private equity and make it more

Exhibit 3.3

Breakdown of private equity investors in Europe, 2003

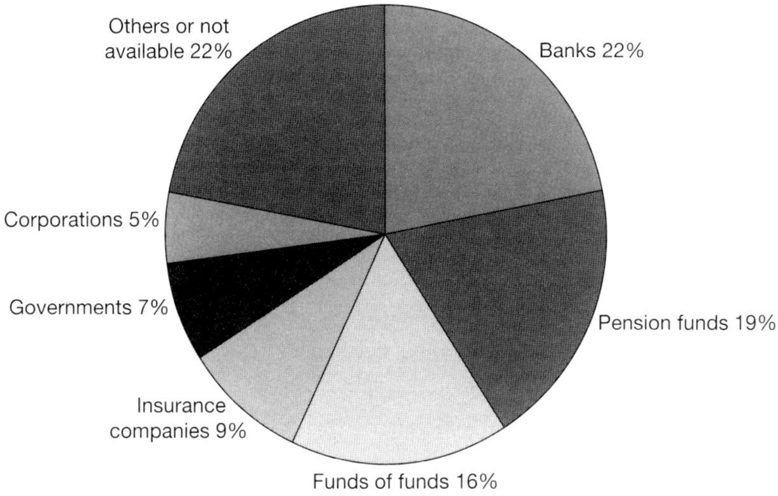

Source: EVCA/PwC.

expensive for banks to invest. However, it is unclear what impact these new rules will have on the enthusiasm of banks to invest in private equity, especially in Europe where banks provide a quarter of all capital. Pension funds face the challenge to meet absolute return targets on their investment activities and need to look for alternative asset classes to enhance performance. Legislative changes make the global investment in private equity more accessible for institutions that so far have been subject to stringent constraints on their investment policy. The number of funds of funds are increasing and enlarging their portfolio of investment products, giving private individuals access to private equity. Structured products are coming to market giving investors a tradable instrument for investing in private equity and allowing them to choose from products that are tailored to their risk appetite.

These trends go towards a true globalisation of the industry, which will benefit all participants. It will enhance the flexibility of investors in their asset allocation, consequently improve their ability to diversify risk, thereby allowing them to achieve better risk-adjusted returns. This effect ultimately will increase the amounts allocated to private equity, and make it a globally interlinked asset class.

1 See for example Fenn, Liang and Prowse (1995) and Gompers and Lerner (1999) for an historical view.
2 A gatekeeper takes over many tasks of a fund investor. See glossary.
3 According to the PwC/3i *Global Private Equity Survey* (2004).
4 According to PwC/3i *Global Private Equity Survey* (2004).
5 According to EVCA *Yearbook* (2004).
6 According to PwC/3i *Global Private Equity Survey* (2004).

Chapter 4

The investment focus of private equity funds

The sub-segments of private equity – an overview

Private equity fund managers have a wide range of sub-segments available in which they could invest, but they typically focus on one specific segment in accordance with their skill-set and experience. In its broadest, and now most commonly used, sense private equity encompasses all equity investments in non-public companies with a series of sub-segments ranging from seed to pre-IPO financing. This definition is also the one this book uses.

Private equity can be split into venture capital and the sub-segments targeting the late development stages of private equity-backed companies such as development capital, capital for management buy in (MBI) and management buyout (MBO), and pre-IPO financing. It also includes special situation financing such as investments in turnaround situations or succession situations in family-owned companies. The late-stage private equity segments also comprise investments in mezzanine debt financing, a form of subordinated debt, where the debtholder can enhance the return through equity-linked features such as conversion rights, warrants or options. Exhibit 4.1 shows the percentage of total amount invested into the different segments across North America, Europe and Asia Pacific in 2003. The buyout segment featured prominently in part because venture capital investments declined after the high-tech bubble of the late 1990s.

Each segment in private equity has its unique features and risk profile. The boundaries between them, however, are sometimes blurred. The main distinguishing factor between the various sub-segments of private equity can be seen in the origin of value creation from the investor's point of view. While venture capital investors base their investment rationale strongly on the success of a new business concept and/or innovative product and its market potential, later-stage private equity investments build their business case more on expanding the market share of a company by marketing the company's existing product portfolio in existing or new markets. Thus the skill-set of investors being successful in private equity varies depending on the sub-segment of private equity they target. For venture capital investments, especially in the technology sectors, a strong knowledge base in targeted technologies is indispensable, development-stage investments require a stronger focus on organisation building and marketing

Exhibit 4.1

Investment focus of funds, 2003

	North America (%)	*Europe (%)*	*Asia Pacific (%)*
Early-stage (incl. seed and start-up)	4	7	2
Late-stage/expansion	14	26	47
Buyout	82	67	51

Source: PwC/3i 'Global Private Equity 2004 Report'.

skills, while the replacement capital-focused investment strategies in MBO/MBI-type transactions derive their value creation potential often from financial structuring skills.

Characteristics and risk of venture capital and late-stage PE segments

Venture capital refers to equity investments made for the launch, early development or expansion of a business. It comprises the sub-classes seed financing, start-up financing and expansion financing. Seed financing typically refers to the financing provided for research and the development of an initial business concept. The start-up segment targets companies in the development phase of their product up to the initial marketing. In this phase, companies may have some revenues from cooperation agreements but typically have no commercial revenues. The expansion phase segment finally provides finance for the marketing of the product. Companies in this phase have significant revenues although they may still be cash burning.

Venture capital investments are riskier than later-stage private equity investments from various perspectives. Companies financed through venture capital are typically not self-sustainable at the time of investment. Especially in the seed and early-stage phase they are often cash burning. Their aim is to develop a product with a market potential that later in the company's life hopefully outweighs the losses accumulated in the early years of existence. During this development phase, venture capital-financed companies are exposed to a series of risks that are ultimately borne by the venture capital investor such as:

- technology risk – the company's product or service may prove to be unviable or obsolete by the time it is marketed;
- timing risk – competitors might come up with a similar or identical product in a shorter time;
- refinancing risk – the company may be unsuccessful in getting the funding required to bring its product to the market; and
- risk of lacking management quality – these companies' business concepts often depend on a deep, sometimes scientific, knowledge of the products underlying technology. The departure of key individuals may put an end to the company's development potential.

Refinancing risk, in particular, is a crucial risk from the perspective of a venture capitalist as the cash need of such portfolio companies is often difficult to plan. For companies developing products with a long time to market, for example, in certain segments of the biotech industry, it is often impossible that one single investor provides the financing for the company until it is self-sustainable. These companies are typically not suitable for leverage as they cannot serve debt due to their cash burning and cannot provide collateral for debt. Therefore, venture capital investors need to attract other venture capital providers to finance their portfolio companies. If unachievable, a company might become bankrupt despite its potentially promising product. Many venture capital funds experienced this phenomenon in the aftermath of the internet boom period when a lack of exit opportunities through IPOs and trade sales required massive additional funding at the level of portfolio companies to keep them afloat. Consequently, due to a lack of own reserves for follow-on financing requirements of their portfolio companies, many funds lost a substantial part of their portfolio or needed to accept external financing for their portfolio companies at valuations that destroyed the return potential for their fund.

The risks described above are typically less pronounced in the later-stage private equity segments. With the exception of special situation investments, such as turnaround deals, portfolio companies are typically cash-flow positive and can be leveraged through bank debt.

Companies in this later-stage segment normally have a more predictable market potential and the business planning has fewer unknown elements. This is why in times of high economic uncertainty and poor stock market climate, the buyout segment often sees a substantial increase of interest from private equity investors as shown above in Exhibit 4.1.

Risk–return comparison

In the various sub-segments, value is created in different ways, and affected by different macroeconomic drivers. Therefore, the sub-segments exhibit quite different behaviour in terms of cyclicality, risk as volatility and levels of returns. As a result, they perform independently of each other to a considerable degree, which leads to a diversifying effect for a portfolio containing a mix of investments in different sub-segments. Exhibit 4.2 shows the historical average and standard deviation of performance of both venture capital and buyout funds for Europe and the United States.

In the past, later-stage private equity has shown more stable return patterns, hardly ever providing negative return rates to investors. Venture capital is traditionally more volatile even when disregarding the extremes of industry cycles such as the technology hype in the late 1990s. In prosperous years, venture capital is able to outperform buyout investments by a sizeable margin, in bad years venture capital investments can yield significant losses. Assuming capital market efficiency, venture capital investments should, on average, outperform buyout investments, compensating venture capital investors for the higher risk reflected in the higher volatility of their returns. The more mature and efficient private equity markets, such as the United States, show this pattern of risk–return distribution between various sub-segments of the asset class. In Europe and emerging private equity markets, the case is less clear. Here, buyout funds managed to outperform venture capital over longer periods suggesting an inefficient risk–return allocation between various sub-segments, as shown in Exhibit 4.2.

Investors should diversify across segments in order to decrease their exposure to the cyclical nature of some sub-segments of private equity and to market inefficiencies in the risk–return allocation between such segments. Therefore, a fund investor should invest in several funds targeting different sub-segments of private equity. Considering the great differences in skills required from fund managers in order to be successful in a specific sub-segment, risk diversification results are better for investors investing into a larger number of specialised funds with different investment foci than for investors investing into a small number of funds, each targeting a great variety of sub-segments of private equity.

Exhibit 4.2

Performance of segments

		Europe (%)	*United States (%)*
Venture capital	Average IRR	7	22
	Standard deviation	27	56
Buyout	Average IRR	16	13
	Standard deviation	28	25

Source: PwC/3i 'Global Private Equity 2004 Report'.

Chapter 5

Performance of private equity funds

Sources of return for private equity funds

Investors will only commit capital to private equity funds if they expect a better return on a risk-adjusted basis. In an efficient market, investors are compensated for taking undiversifiable risk, that is, an unavoidable degree of uncertainty of the future value of an investment. The higher the intrinsic uncertainty of the future value of an investment, the higher the average return over the long term. Therefore, an investor must accept more risk to get higher average returns. For example, an investor buying AAA-rated government bonds should expect at least the risk-free return. Bonds of countries with lower credit standing or corporate bonds have higher yields, reflecting the higher default risk. Furthermore, investing into stocks of a given company is even riskier and carries an additional risk premium for the investor as equity is subordinated to debt. Public markets are near-efficient markets. Investors cannot hope to beat the market, because information is quickly absorbed in the market price and small inefficiencies cannot generally be exploited due to transaction costs. The only way to get higher risk-adjusted returns is to have more information than the market, that is, insider information.

What about private equity? Intuitively, a private equity investor should get a higher return than for quoted equity to compensate the much lower liquidity of their investment. Furthermore, private equity investors have reason to claim a risk premium because their companies are in riskier stages of their development. Apart from the prospect of outperforming public equity through higher risk-taking, the private equity investor has the possibility to enhance their risk-adjusted average investment return by exploiting market inefficiencies. This opportunity does not exist in efficient public markets, where not even skilled investors can beat the market index consistently over the long term after deduction of transaction costs. Private equity is not an efficient market, and fund managers might be able to get higher risk-adjusted returns through legal insider information. Therefore, many investors put considerable efforts in selecting the best teams, also called top quartile teams, that seem to systematically outperform the market average through their superior skills in investment selection and value creation.

Performance measurement in private equity

Finding a meaningful performance measure for private equity funds

How do these conceptual arguments on risk and return of asset classes translate into reality? The challenge is as basic as finding measures that allow a meaningful comparison of performance of individual asset classes. In measuring investment performance in private equity, the cash flows of a fund are what is most important to investors: it is the money that leaves and returns to your pocket that counts! However, cash flows from two different funds are difficult to compare. Each fund has many cash flow transactions with different amounts and timing over an at least 10-year period. Therefore, the investor needs a measure that summarises all pieces of cash flow information into a single meaningful number. This process inevitably leads to an approximation of reality. There is loss of information, because the cash flows cannot possibly be reconstructed from knowledge of this single number derived from the measure. In other words, the same number could have arisen from many different collections of cash flows.

The two most important return measures are the internal rate of return (IRR) and the multiple. These measures also exist as interim return measures where the fund is not liquidated yet and the fund's estimated net asset value (NAV) is used as theoretical residual payout of the fund at the time of the performance calculation. Then, the return measures could be net returns, that is, from the perspective of the limited partners or gross returns on the fund, that is, only based on the cash flows between the fund and its portfolio companies, excluding any costs originating from running the fund.

The following sections discuss the concept of multiples and IRR as performance measures for private equity investments. The theoretical basis of IRR and multiple calculations is provided and challenges in comparing these measures to public stock market performance indicators are described in detail. These are vital elements in an investor's asset allocation process, as discussed in Chapter 6.

Further practical applications of IRR and multiple as performance measures in private equity are discussed in the context of track record analysis in Chapter 7 in the section entitled 'Realised and unrealised investment performance: hard and soft facts', and in Chapter 14 in the section entitled 'The nature of the private equity NAV'.

The multiple

The multiple is the simplest measure and expresses what multiple of the invested (or drawn down) money has been returned. It is calculated as follows:

$$\frac{\text{Total distributions}}{\text{Total drawdowns}}$$

For example, if a fund manager draws down 100 and distributes 200 back, the multiple will be two.

The multiple describes how effective the investment was in terms of returning money to the investor, but completely neglects the time dimension. It does not ask how time-efficient the fund has invested, whether the investment took one or 10 years. The multiple is a simple mathematical formula, and conceptually and practically easy to work with. However, it is still non-linear, which means that the multiple of the cash flows of a portfolio of funds is not the average multiple of the cash flows of all funds in the portfolio. The interim multiple is used for funds that have not yet been liquidated and is simply total distributions plus NAV, as a proxy for the future distributions, divided by the total drawdowns. Finally, the multiple is also often called TVPI as total value per paid-in, a term which is used by Thomson Venture Economics.

The internal rate of return (IRR)

The internal rate of return (IRR) is the most commonly used performance measure in private equity. The IRR does not indicate how much money a fund has made, but how time-efficient the fund has invested, that is, the shorter the investment period for a profitable investment, the higher the IRR. Furthermore, the IRR is money-weighted in the sense that cash flows of higher amounts contribute a greater part towards the IRR value. The IRR is the value of the discount rate that makes the net present value (NPV) of all cash flows zero. The formula for the IRR then is as follows:

$$\sum_{n=1}^{n=L} \frac{C_n}{(1 + IRR)^{t_n}} = 0$$

where C_n = the nth cash flow at time t_n
L = the total number of cash-flow events
IRR = the discount rate that makes the left-hand side of the equation zero.

The IRR is in units of t. For example, if the unit of t is one year, the IRR is the annualised IRR. During the life of a fund, the final IRR is often estimated by the interim IRR from the fund's past cash flows and the remaining value of the fund's assets as the last cash flow at the evaluation date. Typically, the value is set equal to the reported NAV. The IRR is a tricky measure to work with, both conceptually and mathematically. For example, the simple case with one drawdown of −100 in year zero, and three distributions of 100 in years one, two and three leads to the following equation:

$$\frac{-100}{(1 + IRR)^0} + \frac{100}{(1 + IRR)^1} + \frac{100}{(1 + IRR)^2} + \frac{100}{(1 + IRR)^3} = 0$$

For which value of IRR is the left-hand side of the equation zero? There are no obvious explicit solutions, and a computer algorithm needs to find that numerical value of the discount rate, that is the IRR, that makes the NPV of the cash flows, that is the left-hand side, equal to zero. In this case, the solution is an IRR of around 84 per cent. In a few cases, there are no values of IRR that make the left-hand side equal to zero or there are two or more such discount rates.[1] The IRR is also highly non-linear. For example, the pooled IRR of two funds, pooling all their cash flows, is not equal to the average IRR of the two funds, and unlike with the multiple there is no formula to determine by how much the two values differ. Due to all these issues, the IRR is not an easy measure with which to work, and this makes it very difficult to use the IRR in any model. Finally, further applications of the IRR concept are discussed in Chapter 7 in the section 'Realised and unrealised investment performance: hard and soft facts' and in Chapter 14 in the section entitled 'The nature of the private equity NAV'.

Why public market performance measures fail

Unfortunately, the IRR is not the standard return measure for investments in the public market. This fact makes it very difficult to compare the performance of private equity with the performance measures used for a stock or bond index such as the time-weighted return (TWR). Why is the private equity industry not using the time-weighted average like public indices?[2]

Essentially, the TWR computes the annual return for each year, but this is not really possible for a private equity fund due to a lack of market prices. In private equity, the annual return is difficult to calculate, because the unrealised portfolio does not have a transparent and objective market price. Thus, the difference in the net asset values from the beginning of the year and the end of the year plus the cash flows in between would need to be used. But this NAV is not a fair value estimate of a portfolio of private equity investments: it is set at the discretion of the reporting fund managers, biased by infrequent revaluation and the underlying portfolio cannot be sold to test the accuracy of the valuation used. Another essential aspect is that the IRR would be unfair to the public fund managers, because they have no control over when cash comes to or leaves the fund, whereas private equity managers can time their investment and exits. The investors of a public fund can withdraw or invest at any time of their choosing. However, the IRR is influenced by the timing of cash flows, and only a private equity fund manager has some freedom over the timing of its investments and exits. Exactly the same is true for the amount of cash invested, which a public fund manager cannot control. The TWR looks at the percentage return regardless of how much was invested, whereas the IRR is capital weighted and gives more weight to periods with more capital invested.

The non-applicability of the TWR to private equity has caused significant confusion and the industry has sought more appropriate measures. The fundamental issue boils down to comparing the fund cash flows with a cash flow for investments in a public index with the same constraints and timing. Another crucial issue is that the IRR only measures the efficiency of the manager's investments during the time of investment, but not over the fund's whole life. The private equity fund investor has opportunity costs, because the investors need to hold capital in liquid low-return investments to respond quickly to drawdown calls, and live with the unpredictable timing of receiving the distributions. The effective return from the fund investor's perspective is therefore lower.

The public market equivalent (PME)

In 1996, Lond and Nickles proposed a new measure called the public market equivalent (PME or Index Method) by asking: what would be the return had you invested or sold the same amounts in a public market? Thus, every drawdown is matched by an equal investment in the index, and every distribution by an equal sale of the index. The cash flows of the fund and the PME are the same, but the difference comes from the remaining value in the PME. Here is an example: US$100 are drawn down by the private equity fund for an investment and thus US$100 are invested in 100 shares of a stock index, assuming US$1 per share. Later, the private equity investment is sold for US$150, and thus index shares worth US$150 are sold. If the share price of the index is US$2, then 75 shares are sold. Even though the fund is now liquidated, the PME still has 25 shares, which are worth US$50. Thus, the cash flows are the same until the end of the fund, but the difference comes from the PME value due to the relative performance of the public index. A positive value shows that the PME performed better, and a negative balance that the PME performed worse. The PME IRR is then computed from the cash flows plus the remaining PME value.

Problems with the PME

The PME still depends on the NAV for non-liquidated funds. As not all investments are exited, some residual unrealised value is in the portfolio. Then, a private equity investment outperforming the index can produce a negative final value for the investment in the PME, in which case the divestment can only be done running a short position. Coming back to the example from the last paragraph: if the investment had been sold not for US$150 but for US$250, the PME would have needed to sell shares worth US$300. However, if the share price of the index is again US$2, then the PME needs to sell 150 shares but only has 100 shares. Thus, the PME has to run a short position of 50 shares, that is it borrows 50 shares from the market. Apart from these issues, the IRR of the PME cash flow is sometimes undefined.

There are now several different versions of the original idea that try to address these challenges. For example the PME+ approach[3] tries to avoid running short positions by multiplying the distributions by a coefficient so that the PME and the PE NAV have the same value. Its author, Rouvinez, admits that: 'the cash flow patterns are not exactly matching . . . [but] is mitigated by the fact that at least timing, in-flows and a fixed proportion of outflows are the same, which seems to be the minimum that can be relaxed to fix the benchmark.' Finally, Kaserer and Diller (2004) use yet again a different PME: they do not sell the shares in the index corresponding to the value of the fund distribution but reinvest distributions of the fund into the index.

Vintage year-weighted performance?

The number of funds in each vintage year, that is the year the fund started investing, is not constant. An important issue, which is often overlooked, is whether the investor should really look at the vintage year-weighted historical average and not at the simple historical average fund return. Investors only want to know what they should expect of funds starting next year, which is not the average of all historical funds, but rather the average of all vintage years' average return. This distinction is important as the next vintage year could be any of the last vintage years. However, the simple historical average does not treat vintage years equally, and overemphasises vintage years with more funds. This subtlety does make a difference in return figures, because the late 1990s' vintage years had many more funds than any other vintage years before and after, and their performance might distort the real return potential. Thus, the return figures should ideally be the average of every vintage year's average because the simple average is unattainable. However, many studies do not seem to take this fact into account, which could result in a difference of several per cent of IRR.

Leaving out young funds due to the J-curve

Another obstacle towards studying historical fund performance is the J-curve effect of the fund performance. The performance of an active fund is calculated using the past cash flows and the NAV, because there are still unrealised company investments that have not yet been exited and therefore did not produce a distribution cash flow. In the first years, the fund portfolio value often is at cost, that is at the value it was purchased, while set-up costs and management fees reduce the fund's NAV. Thus, the value of the fund investment from the perspective of the fund investor is virtually always negative in the first years of their existence. This situation normally gradually improves as the portfolio is revalued and companies are sold. Therefore, the performance figures of new funds do not contain any useful information. They are an underestimation of their real value and should therefore not be part of the sample for empirical studies. There are two methods to exclude young funds, but the choice on exactly how to apply them are somewhat arbitrary. The first one is by age: for example, to take all funds older than four years,[4] which roughly corresponds to the end of the investment period, or to take even more years.[5] The second method[6] is to take all funds that are past their investment period and are nearly liquidated, as indicated by a ratio of the NAV divided by the total drawdowns below 10 per cent or 20 per cent. This measure reflects the percentage of unrealised value left in the fund. However, this procedure might also create a systematic bias by including some funds from a recent vintage year and excluding others. Overall, all approaches seem reasonable, but the simplest is to use all funds older than four years.

The risk (or uncertainty in returns) of private equity funds

The public market concept of risk fails

When looking at risk–return considerations, there are two questions that every investor needs to ask: what is the risk-adjusted historical return for private equity? Is it above the public equity risk-adjusted return due to a priced-in illiquidity premium? The concept of 'risk-adjusted' is not easily applicable to private equity. For publicly quoted investments, the risk-adjusted return is usually the Sharpe ratio. This ratio is the return divided by the volatility, where the volatility is the standard deviation of a time series of market prices. Thus, the risk-adjusted return is the return earned per unit risk within a set time period and frequency of observations. However, for private equity the notion of volatility is slippery. There are no time series of market prices for a volatility. The funds' NAV is no replacement for a market price, because the value of a company is initially set to its purchase price, and is not determined by trading. Moreover, the value changes infrequently, which causes the volatility, that is fluctuation over time of the value to be artificially low.

For example, a public stock price constantly reacts to new information and might go up and then down in a quarter, whereas the private equity NAV is only adjusted once in these three months with no fluctuation between two valuation dates. Hence, at the end of the observation period both the public stock investment and private equity investment may show the identical value as at the beginning of the observation period but the public stock has more fluctuation, that is more volatility because it first went up and then down before returning to its original price. On the other hand, the private equity NAV did not show any fluctuation, because it is only priced once every quarter, not recognising that the value of the underlying assets might have moved considerably between two valuation dates.

Using the standard deviation as risk measure

One alternative to the volatility is to define private equity risk as the standard deviation of the distribution of returns over a sample of funds. This standard deviation is simply the degree by which individual fund returns deviate from the average return of the sample. It is then possible to replace the volatility in the denominator of the Sharpe ratio by the standard deviation of the sample, that is, the new risk–return measure is now the return divided by the standard deviation.[7] This measure is appropriate to compare risk–return relationships between sub-segments within private equity, but not for comparison with the public Sharpe ratios.

The Sharpe ratio uses risk as the volatility of a market price and not as the standard deviation of all fund returns. A comparison within the asset classes is useful for the fund investors or fund of funds manager to distinguish between the historical attractiveness of different market segments, such as US venture capital or European buyout, because the investor can see which segment has a higher historical risk-adjusted return value and, for example, invest more in this segment. Finally, Thomson Venture Economics uses a similar measure, namely the inverse of the measure. Their coefficient of variation, which is the standard deviation divided by the return, is however flawed, because it becomes infinite or very large for a perfectly reasonable scenario, that is zero average return. This effect does not happen for the measure proposed here as it only becomes infinite or very large for an unrealistic and artificial scenario, namely the standard deviation of the sample being zero. Therefore, this measure appears preferable to the approach proposed by Thomson Venture Economics.

The bias of the standard deviation as risk measure

However, the use of the standard deviation as risk measure is also not without problems. As the standard deviation computes the total deviation of all individual fund returns from the average return, outliers increase the value dramatically due to their extreme deviation from the average. Exhibit 1.2 in Chapter 1 in the section 'Risk levels of private equity investments' illustrates nicely that the multiple distribution of funds has long tails with outliers such as a few extreme winners or total losses. As a consequence, the standard deviation is artificially high due to extremely rare examples of funds with unusually bad or good performances. To obtain a more realistic result, the investor should think about excluding them from the risk–return computation. A professionally managed fund cannot have an extremely low performance, because it is very unlikely to invest only in extremely badly performing companies. For an extremely low performance, something out of the ordinary such as severe incompetence or fraud must have happened. If done professionally, team selection, due diligence and monitoring should significantly reduce such avoidable downside risks. Thus, the investor might want to focus on the typical fluctuations as a measure of risk and not include the extreme downside risk which could be reduced with good practices.

Empirical studies of risk–return of private equity funds

There are now several empirical studies on risk–return. Unfortunately, they mostly rely on VentureXpert data for fund performance, or on much smaller samples from large funds of funds. These issues are discussed in the 'Private equity databases' section in Chapter 13. The situation is certainly not ideal, because a potential VentureXpert bias is the bias of these studies, and the smaller funds of funds samples are too small to be wholly representative. Moreover, no study seems to have analysed the bias of the underlying sample in real depth. Nevertheless, although the data situation is not ideal, the findings of these studies are important in the sense that they finally do shed some light on the private equity fund performance and cash flows, even though grey areas remain.

Different studies have looked at different time periods, filtered out young funds in different ways, and have used different return measures and datasets such as US venture capital or European buyout. Thus, somewhat paradoxically, there are plenty of findings but a meta-analysis,[8] in the sense of reaching a consensus across all studies, is ambiguous. Exhibit 5.1 lists all the key articles with a short description of the key findings to allow the investors to pinpoint the research most relevant to their area of interest. Overall, most studies suggest

Exhibit 5.1

Risk–return

Reference	*Data source*	*Data sample*	*Data period*	*Data level*	*Data correction*	*Results*
Cochrane (2005)	Venture One	17,000 US venture capital financing rounds	1987–2000	Company	Correction for survival bias	59% annual average (arithmetic) gross return / alpha of 32%
Das, Jagannathan and Sarin (2002)	Venture Economics	57,000 financing rounds in US venture capital and buyout	1980–2000	Company	No correction as data comes from funds	1.1 average multiple for late-stage / 5.1 average multiple for early-stage / performance depends on industry, stage, financing amount, valuation, market sentiment
Kupperman and Griffiths (2001)	Venture Economics	400 US and European venture capital funds	1980–1994	Fund	Only liquidated funds	The average private equity manager does not beat the public market / US funds higher return / return distributions are similar
Kaplan and Schoar (2003)	Venture Economics	Over 1,000 US private equity funds	1970–1997	Fund	No funds younger than five years	Funds that outperformed tend to outperform again / average fund excess return but varies with benchmark period / VC fund returns vary with public index more than buyout funds
Ljungqvist and Richardson (2003)	Private fund of funds	73 US private equity funds (mostly buyout)	1981–1993	Fund cash flows	Liquidated	20% IRR / private equity generates an excess of 5–8% to the aggregate public market
Peng (2001)	Venture One	13,000 US venture capital financing	1987–1999	Index	Use of econometric methods to counter bias	Annual geometric average return of 35.21% / high return / high volatility / high correlation

Exhibit 5.1 (Continued)

Risk–return

Reference	*Data source*	*Data sample*	*Data period*	*Data level*	*Data correction*	*Results*
Schmidt (2004)	CEPRES database from Venture Capital Management (VCM)	1,500 financing rounds worldwide	1970–2002	Fund cash flows	No correction as data comes from funds	Looks at optimal asset allocation
Gottschalg, Phalippou and Zollo (2004)	Venture Economics	500 funds	1980–1995	Fund	Nearly liquidated	Average performance of private equity funds is lower than the performance of the market portfolio
Kaserer and Diller (2004)	Venture Economics	200 European funds	1980–1995	Fund	Nearly liquidated and using public market equivalent	IRR of 12.7% / overperformance to bond index / 2 out of 3 datasets have an underperformance to equity index
Weidig, Kemmerer and Born (2004)	Venture Economics	1,600 US and European venture capital and buyout funds	1983–1998	Fund of funds	Generated from fund data, no funds younger than four years	Spread of return decreases significantly due to diversification
Burgel (1999)	BVCA	188 UK funds	1980–1998	Fund	No fund younger than one year, bias possible as funds were asked	14.3% IRR overall / performance cyclical / higher risk–return for later-stage
Chen, Baierl and Kaplan (2002)	Venture Economics	150 venture capital funds	1960–1999	Fund	Liquidated	VC has an annual arithmetic average return of 45% / annual compounded average return of 13.4% / high standard deviation / zero correlation (suspicious)

Exhibit 5.1 (Continued)

Risk–return

Reference	*Data source*	*Data sample*	*Data period*	*Data level*	*Data correction*	*Results*
Jones and Rhodes-Kropf (2003)	Venture Economics	1,250 US funds	1980–1999	Index	No fund younger than four years	Fund investors do not earn positive alphas on average / buyout funds have a value-weighted IRR of 4.6% and venture capital funds an IRR of 19.1%
Quigley and Woodward (2003)	Sand Hill Econometrics	13,000 US private equity financing	1987–1999	Company	Use of econometric methods to counter bias	Lower returns than public index and low correlation
Website of Cambridge Associates	Cambridge Associates	Over 2,000 funds	1986–2004	Index	No special corrections	10-year net IRR is 11%
Gockeln (2003)	CEPRES database from Venture Capital Management (VCM)	3,000 portfolio companies of 228 private equity funds	1990–2003	Fund cash flows	Only liquidated and from funds	Annual geometric returns of 30% for EU sample / 25% for US sample
Moskowitz and Vissing-Jorgenson (2000)	Survey data	On all private equity regardless of company size	1989–1998	–	Use of econometric methods	Risk–return significantly lower than public equity

Source: QuantExperts.

that private equity funds have an historical average IRR of between 10 per cent and 15 per cent. This numerical value compares favourably against public index returns, but again it is hard to compare directly for the various reasons described above. Private equity seems to give more return with more risk, but it is more difficult to judge the case of the risk-adjusted return due to the problematic concept of risk in private equity. Contradicting this positive to neutral view, Gottschalg, Phalippou and Zollo (2004) write that their 'analysis indicates that private equity funds underperform under conservative assumptions about the risk they carry. Such performance is perplexing and we cannot reject the possibility of mispricing by so thought sophisticated institutional investors'. To summarise, the debate on risk–return is ongoing, and no definite conclusions can be drawn.

---

1 See, for example, Martin (1995).
2 This issue is also discussed in Thatcher (2003), Rouvinez (2003) and EVCA (2004b).
3 As introduced by Rouvinez (2003).
4 Weidig and Mathonet (2004).
5 Gottschalg, Phalippou and Zollo (2004) and Chen, Baierl and Kaplan (2002).
6 Kaserer and Diller (2004).
7 Weidig and Mathonet (2004).
8 See detailed reviews of all past literature in Gottschalg, Phalippou and Zollo (2004) and Cumming and Walz (2004).

Chapter 6

Asset allocation to and within private equity

Correlation between private equity and other asset classes

Why is correlation important?

The strength of the relationship, that is the correlation, of private equity to other asset classes is important to asset allocation because the diversification effect of adding private equity to a portfolio consisting of other asset classes increases the lower the correlation. In general, the less correlated assets are within a portfolio, the lower the risk of the portfolio because low and high performances happen independently of each other and cancel out each other. Thus, if private equity were less correlated with other assets within a bigger portfolio, a greater capital allocation to private equity would make sense. The discussion of correlation is conducted on two different levels: based on conceptual arguments, for example, the exit price level of portfolio companies is influenced by the stock market and the correlation between private equity and public markets therefore must be strong; and on empirical numerical evidence, for example, looking at the historical correlation between a private equity index and a public stock market index such as the Dow Jones and concluding that the correlation between the two is low. For investors, this discussion is important as they want to know whether the diversification effect from adding private equity to a portfolio of publicly traded stocks is high, or, if this is not the case, whether the risk-adjusted return on their overall portfolio improves. If the case for neither of the two is convincing, investing in private equity is not useful.

What are the problems when determining correlation?

What is the correlation between private equity and a public index? The question appears to be clear, but its meaning is less easily understood: is it the correlation between direct investments and the index, or between a private equity index and the public index? For example, a private equity investor cannot hold an index of private equity, but can only invest in several private equity funds, whereas public equity investors can hold the index. Thus, a correlation study between a constructed private equity index and a public index is not directly relevant to the investor as the investor can only invest in a small part of the available private equity funds.

But there are additional issues with correlation. First, returns on private equity funds are measured using internal rate of return (IRR) or multiple; public market products use time-weighted return (TWR). Thus, they use two different return measures, which makes it meaningless to compute a correlation between the two time series. In theory, a volatility of private equity could be computed using the TWR where the inputs are the quarterly reported net asset values (NAVs) plus the cash flows in between. As explained above, changes in NAV are artificially low due to infrequent updates and the conservative valuation methods. Any correlation computation will therefore reveal a low relationship to public indices. Second, even in public markets, the study of correlation is viewed with suspicion. Correlation typically fluctuates substantially and changes dramatically with the period of sampling. Hence the saying: 'Lies, volatilities, and correlations'. Moreover, during a severe downturn or market crash all asset classes become much more correlated. Third, there are two ways to approach the question of correlation, namely whether it is correlation of the cash flows or the overall return. However, the overall return, that is the fund's IRR or public market equivalent (PME), might be less correlated. A fund manager typically invests over the first five years and divests over the last years, and the returns between two direct investments is less correlated when the first happens in year one and the second in year five than for the same year. This effect might become important and reduce the correlation with the stock market.

How strongly correlated is private equity to public indices?

Many early studies claim a low or moderate correlation, but their methods are flawed. These studies mainly use the two well-known private equity indices from Cambridge Associates and from Thomson Venture Economics, which create time series based on the drawdowns, distributions and the NAV of the unrealised investments. And, as shown before, the volatility is artificially low, which leads to an artificially low correlation. This view is supported by Singer, Staub and Terhaar (2003), but also by Gompers and Lerner (1999) who authoritatively state that: 'Many institutions . . . have increased their allocation to venture capital and private equity in the belief that the returns of these funds are largely uncorrelated with the public market . . . But there appears to be many linkages between the public and private equity market values. Thus, the stated returns of private equity funds may not accurately reflect the true evolution of value and the correlations reported by Venture Economics and other industry observers may be deceptively low. To ignore the true correlation is fraught with potential dangers.'

Even without looking at empirical evidence, amount and timing of distributions should be correlated to the stock markets. A boom in the stock market means better opportunities for successful IPOs, more cash in the pocket of trade buyers and higher valuations for companies. Several academic studies[1] have looked at the relationship between exits and the stock market, and find a significant correlation. The market conditions affect the decision to go public, and the exit opportunity.

To summarise, the distributions of a fund are clearly affected by the markets. Thus, investors should expect that when the stock market goes down, distributions will also dry up, though possibly with a time lag of a few months.[2] Still, even if distributions dry up during a downturn, the value of the portfolio company might not have been lost but postponed with an exit a few years later. This realisation leads to the question of whether the fund performance is less correlated because it is the aggregated performance of 10 to 20 portfolio company investments spread over 10 years. The bad and good periods might cancel out each other to some extent.

Finally, several researchers have tried to overcome the problem with correlation due to infrequent valuation, and devised several methods. They all find non-zero moderate to high correlation between a corrected private equity index and a public index.[3]

Asset allocation to private equity

Standard asset allocation and its problems

The standard procedure for asset allocation was first proposed by Markowitz, and is based on maximisation of the risk-adjusted portfolio return. The general idea is twofold: first to estimate for each asset class its future return and risk and the correlation between the asset classes using historical data, and then to find the appropriate weighting for each asset class that makes the risk-adjusted portfolio return maximal. In essence, the bigger a weight the asset class has in the optimal portfolio the higher must be its risk-adjusted return and/or the lower its correlation with other asset classes. The approach is conceptually very instructive to understand the dynamics of asset allocation; that is in the world of mathematical finance, until reality kicks in during implementation. There are many problems with the approach:[4] returns are often not distributed (which goes against Markowitz's assumption), extreme events are not included, correlation between asset classes is not stable, especially in a market crisis, lack of liquidity and marketability is completely ignored, and estimation of historical data is problematic. These issues already apply to publicly traded assets!

How much capital to allocate to private equity funds?

To be absolutely clear, there is no and never will be a definite answer to this question. The Markowitz approach is very useful in the sense that the investor understands the main dynamics on constructing an efficient portfolio. However, its implementation for liquid products is difficult to get right, and very difficult for illiquid products. Rather than being obsessed by numbers, the investor should take a step back and look at the big picture.[5] To start with, the question is not about digits behind the comma, but rather: should there be no allocation, between 5 per cent and 10 per cent, or more? Investors with no long-term investment horizon should not allocate capital to private equity. Most institutional investors with the appropriate long-term investment horizon who have concluded that private equity exposure improves their risk-adjusted portfolio return should be able to invest from 5 to 15 per cent of their assets in private equity. This recommendation is in line with the current allocations by institutional investors.[6] A quantitative analysis in the style of Markowitz might tilt the balance between a smaller share of between 5 per cent and 10 per cent, or a share of between 10 per cent and 15 per cent.

Correlation between private equity funds of different investment foci

An investor not only needs to look at the correlation to the public markets, but also at the correlation between different segments of private equity. Again, such a study is difficult to undertake, because there are no real indices for each segment such as public indices. Private equity indices do exist that consider all drawdowns, distributions and NAVs, but no investor can invest in this way. Therefore, investors should look at the correlation between returns of private equity funds and different investment foci. The question is: how correlated are the performances of funds that start in the same year with funds of the same market segment and funds of other markets?

The following study[7] provides an example. The analysed market segments are both from the United States and Europe, and comprise early-stage venture capital funds

Exhibit 6.1
Correlation

	European early-stage (%)	*European mid-market (%)*	*US early-stage (%)*	*US mid-market (%)*
European early-stage	**41**	8	10	11
European mid-market	8	**38**	13	9
US early-stage	10	13	**50**	11
US mid-market	11	9	11	**40**

Source: Weidig using VentureXpert data of funds to 2000.

and mid-market funds composed of late-stage venture capital and small to medium-sized buyout investments. There are 10 correlations of markets possible (four within the same markets or market segments and six between different markets). Exhibit 6.1 shows the results of this correlation study. The correlation within the markets is greatest and around 40 per cent, and is small between markets. This result shows that there are indeed different market segments that move relatively independently of each other. A further interpretation of the findings is tricky, because the strength of the correlation varies with the sampling period, but does not change the qualitative statement made. Further, investors should be aware that even though there seem to be significant diversification benefits for a mixed portfolio regarding the overall returns and risks, the distributions from the different market segments are very likely more strongly correlated, that is if the stock market goes down, all distributions dry up.

Asset allocation within private equity

Investing in a broad range of funds across several vintage years

Once investors have fixed the asset allocation to private equity, often within the allocation to alternative investments, they need to decide how to implement this part of their global long-term investment programme. The first implementation issue arising is the allocation of capital to various private equity sub-segments and vintage years to ensure a well-diversified portfolio. But like the asset allocation to private equity, it is no easy task to convincingly construct the portfolio with an optimal combination of different subtypes such as: venture capital and buyout, US, Europe and emerging markets, technology and traditional sectors, and across several vintage years. The investor also faces a new issue, namely investment constraints. For example, a portfolio might be diversified across vintage years but not across stages and sectors, because a balancing for stage and sector might make it impossible to have an equal amount of high-quality funds per vintage year.

There are no fixed rules on how much to allocate to different sub-segments. Generally, the private equity fund investor should invest in funds across a broad range of regions, vintage years, sectors, managers and stages. Of course, some investors might decide to exclude some market segments due to meagre historical risk-adjusted returns, foreign private equity due to unwanted currency risks, or technology funds due to high Nasdaq index exposure.

Implementing the asset allocation goal

Thus, implementation of a chosen asset allocation is not straightforward and far more tricky than for a portfolio of liquid assets. Essentially, the private equity fund investor needs to master two important tasks:

- select high-quality investments and make sure that the fund investments are well-structured and monitored, as shown in Part II; and
- ensure the efficient implementation of the private equity investment programme by balancing and monitoring the portfolio while ensuring sufficient liquidity and diversity, as shown in Part III.

Some institutional and high net worth investors do not want to take on these tasks and choose to invest in funds indirectly. They should consult Part IV for a discussion of alternative investment vehicles.

---

1 See, for example, Gompers and Lerner (1999).
2 See Weidig, Kemmerer and Born (2004).
3 See EVCA (2004b), Peng (2001) and Quigley and Woodward (2003), and Gottschalg, Phalippou and Zollo (2004).
4 See, for example, Swensen (2000).
5 Nevertheless, EVCA (2004b) and Schmidt (2004) have taken on these challenges, and came up with asset allocation weights: 5 per cent for venture capital and 8 per cent for buyout funds.
6 See, for example, Blaydon, Wainwright and Hatch (2003), Singer, Staub and Terhaar (2003), and EVCA (2004b).
7 Study undertaken by Weidig for this book.

Part II

Being a private equity fund investor

Chapter 7

Evaluating an investment opportunity

The private equity fund is the key intermediary structure to connect investors with the entrepreneur. The process leading to the creation of a fund typically involves a group of individuals with complementary backgrounds and skills who form a management team and create a private equity management firm. They propose a private equity fund to potential private equity investors via a private placement memorandum in which they spell out their investment strategy for achieving superior returns to their investors. The potential investors review the proposal, and conduct a due diligence to form their view on the attractiveness of the investment opportunity. In doing so, the investors select the fund investments that eventually form their portfolio. Once an investor has come to a positive assessment on the investment opportunity proposed, the management team and the investors negotiate the exact structure of a fund vehicle and the terms and conditions that govern their relationship. On the basis of this understanding, the private equity fund is created. The private equity fund can be established under various jurisdictions and the fund vehicle can have a broad range of different legal forms.

As discussed in Chapter 9, the choice of a specific investment vehicle largely depends on the specific regulatory and tax requirements of individual investors. These vary greatly with many special purpose structures under various jurisdictions, especially in the European Union (EU). Discussing each of those structures is virtually impossible and not the purpose of this book. This book aims at dealing with the fundamentals of the relationship between investors and fund managers, which is largely independent of the investment vehicle ultimately chosen by the investors. If reference is made to the terms limited partnership, limited partner and general partner in this book it is because the limited partnership structure is by far the most widely used investment vehicle in private equity, as it offers great flexibility in defining corporate governance structures for a fund and provides a tax-efficient set-up for a wide range of investors. As a consequence, the terms limited partnership, limited partners and general partner in private equity have become synonyms for fund, fund investors and fund managers respectively. In line with this market practice, and for simplification purposes, these terms will also be used in the same way in following sections, which extensively describe the relationship between the fund manager and investors in a private equity fund.

A typical fund structure using the example of a limited partnership is shown in Exhibit 7.1. In this set-up, the management team creates a legal entity called general partner (GP) through which it acts as the manager of the partnership. Investors then join the partnership as limited partners (LPs), committing a certain amount of capital to the partnership. They are called limited partners, as their liability for the partnership's obligations is limited to the amount of their respective capital commitment. The general partner theoretically has an

Exhibit 7.1

Typical fund structure

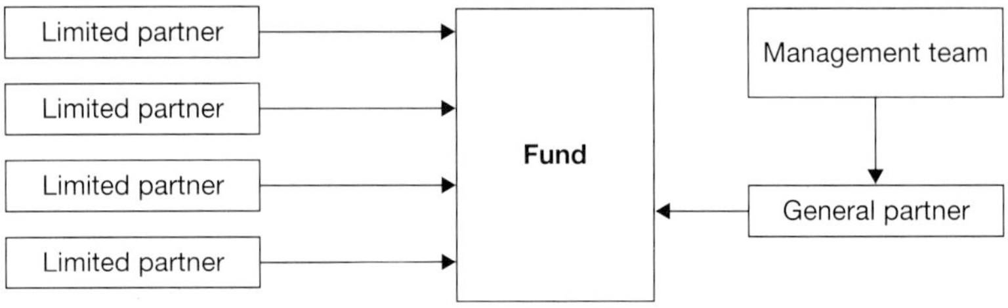

Source: Authors' own.

unlimited liability for any claims on the partnership but the management team typically limits its liability through the choice of the legal form of the general partner.[1]

The set-up of a private equity fund

LPs commit to invest in a fund as a blind pool, which means that, at the time of commitment, they do not know into which portfolio companies their money will be invested. They also do not normally participate in the investment decision process, which is part of the responsibility of the GP.[2] The management team also often commits capital to the fund to give LPs greater comfort through aligned interest in managing the fund's assets. This contribution of the management team to the fund's committed capital can be done through the vehicle of the GP or through another special purpose vehicle. It varies in size but typically amounts to about 1 per cent to 3 per cent of the total fund size.

Once sufficient capital commitments have been received to execute the fund's investment strategy, the investment activity starts. The GP draws capital from the LPs' and GP's commitments to undertake investments in the portfolio company and to cover the operating cost of the partnership. In addition to the set-up costs, operating expenses for the partnership also include the management fee, audit fees, legal fees and administration costs. The management fee is the GP's remuneration for the day-to-day management of the partnership. The investment period, which goes over three to five years, is the time given to the GP to put the LPs' money to work by investing in a diversified portfolio of promising portfolio companies. Once a fund is fully invested, the management fee basis normally decreases, taking into account that the GP then typically earns a management fee on a successor fund and allocates part of its resources to the investment activity of the new fund while divesting the portfolio of its previous fund. The return of a fund is generated through its exit proceeds which the GP realises after, hopefully, having added value to the portfolio companies over time by giving advice on the development of the company in many areas such as strategic positioning, financial structuring, organisation building, marketing, recruitment of key individuals and searching for additional sources of financing. To align the interest between the GP and the LPs, the GP typically receives a share of up to 20 per cent of the fund's profits. This variable part in the GP's remuneration is called carried interest and should be the main incentive for the GP to manage the fund.

Evaluating an investment opportunity from a limited partner perspective

Investing in a private equity fund poses multiple challenges to a limited partner and the decision to invest has far-reaching consequences. Unlike investments in public equity, the decision to invest in a fund cannot easily be reversed. Hence, making the right choice in selecting a fund investment is crucial. Also, private equity lacks transparency on available investment opportunities, individual teams' investment performance, and market regulation and supervision on quantity and quality of information disclosed to investors. On the other hand, being able to judge the risks and opportunities, and, more importantly, being able to evaluate and negotiate the rights needed to efficiently protect their interests are key success factors for limited partners in investing in private equity funds. Therefore, the selection of successful fund investments requires a rather specific skill-set.

Private equity – a people's business

What makes an investor sufficiently skilled to safely enter this asset class? A textbook can never replace practical experience. This is especially true in an industry such as private equity where few hard facts are available to support an investment decision. Private equity is a people's business and sometimes a degree in psychology may be as useful as a master in finance in the selection process of promising investment opportunities. This book does not claim to provide a recipe for success. No book could. But the following sections aim to shed light on the working relationship between LPs and GPs. They explain what it takes to become a limited partner and provide a tool-set for investors to orientate themselves in this opaque asset class, give advice on how to avoid costly mistakes and list the tricks of the trade that can make a difference.

Business ethics in private equity

Reading through the next sections may leave an impression that private equity is an industry that sails close to the wind, with regard to the law. If there is any doubt on ethics in this industry, the feeding ground will be its opaque nature. In an opaque industry such as private equity and especially in emerging markets, the line between legal insider information obtained from a powerful network and a competitive advantage obtained through outright corruption is often blurred. Informal ties offering privileged treatment to some parties at the expense of others are common and again the line between legality and fraud is often unclear. There is no perfect protection for limited partners in private equity funds against intended misleading information, omission of crucial information or even fraud. Unfortunately, the private nature of the industry provides fertile soil for such attempts at the expense of insufficiently skilled limited partners. This has particularly been true for the period of the technology hype in the late 1990s when the prospect of quick profits on companies with little or no real substance attracted many novice investors to private equity. Some did not fully understand how and why money was made in this industry, they merely saw that money was made. Promising offers of GPs were plentiful. Unfortunately, many of the GPs were not much more skilled than the investors they persuaded to invest in their funds. The fall was predictable and deep. Investors lost a lot of money on GPs that preferred to maximise the lifetime of their revenue stream rather than the value of their investors' assets. Many of these investors have learned from this experience, others have not returned to private equity since. This is unfortunate because this asset class is better than the judgement of those disappointed investors that were drawn in during the technology hype.

Professionalism – the backbone of the industry

By its nature, the industry can never be without risks, but a joint effort from fund managers and investors can lead to standards that strike a fair deal between the parties. Fund managers must accept that the professional behaviour and transparency they display to their investor base is an investment in their long-term reputation and that of their industry. Investors must thoroughly understand the dynamics of the industry to allow them a level dialogue in defending their interests. For the institutional investors, this may mean building up substantial resources to deal with the risks associated with this investment class, and these resources may not have a short-term pay-off. However, they are vital to cap the downside risk and avoid financial losses. Institutional investors unable or unwilling to deploy the required resources should rather seek an indirect channel to private equity through professionals such as funds of funds investors, or abstain from the industry all together.

Evaluating the market opportunity

Private equity is a heterogeneous asset class, with many different market segments across stages, sectors and regions. There is little information available that can guide an investor on market opportunities. The opaqueness and low liquidity of the market create market inefficiencies. However, investment opportunities exploiting these inefficiencies through arbitrage are rare for many reasons.

- Correlation between the performance of individual investments is low making it difficult to establish predictable relative return patterns between individual investments, which could be exploited through arbitrage.
- Investment cycles are long, implying a sizeable lead time before the performance of an individual investment becomes reasonably predictable.
- Investments are not easily tradable to change the asset allocation within the asset class at short notice.
- There is no market transparency on the performance of individual funds and management teams. Such transparency would result in investors only funding the most successful GPs of the industry and deprive unsuccessful teams of their funding source. Even strongly underperforming management teams may be around for 10 years due to their one successful fundraising.

Hence, the selection process segregating the survivors from the underperformers takes time. Against this background, selecting winning market strategies is a difficult task for limited partners.

In the absence of clear guidance, investors need to look at factors that foster or hinder investment success. These factors vary with the sub-class of private equity, but many are linked to the macroeconomic environment. The development state of an economy clearly correlates with the emergence of investment opportunities in various market segments.

In particular, the development of financial markets in an economy has a major impact on the prospects of private equity investments.

Market efficiency in pricing risk increases with sophistication of financial markets. Some GPs may argue in their investment strategy that market inefficiencies create investment opportunities, especially in emerging private equity markets, as long as the prospects for economic growth are good. They argue that in markets with exceptional economic growth, companies need additional equity to finance their own expansion. Eventually, companies with critical mass would seek expansion through buy-and-build strategies, where companies achieve growth by acquiring competitors. On the other hand, market opaqueness on the supply of private equity and incomplete financial markets would give GPs greater bargaining power, more choice in the deal flow and better entry valuations. All this would lead to a higher return potential for private equity funds. Empirical evidence appears to contradict this view. The development of private equity in Portugal and Spain after their accession to the EU, or in the Central and Eastern European region in the run-up to EU membership, may serve as an example. Despite spectacular economic growth rates well above the EU average, these markets failed to deliver superior returns. Investors' interest in Spain and Portugal remained poor for many years after their accession. Spain and Portugal acceded to the EU in 1985 but even 15 years later their ratio of private equity investments as a percentage of GDP was only half the value of the EU average. Central and Eastern Europe (CEE) countries have also shown similar behaviour in anticipation of their accession: once the enthusiasm in the early 1990s over the change in the political regimes in the CEE countries was gone, investors' interest in the region dropped sharply. Over the period 2002 to 2004 only one private equity fund in CEE managed to raise its target fund size within the initially set fundraising period.

The factors involved in evaluation

So what are the factors needed for an LP to assess a market opportunity for private equity investments? Which investment strategy works best in a specific geographic area? The following sections aim to provide guidance to potential LPs on how to derive conclusions from macroeconomic indicators on private equity investment opportunities in a given market.

The size of the market as an indicator

For a first assessment, the structure and maturity of the private equity market in an economy can serve as a valuable indicator. The number of private equity investment firms, the amounts raised by these players, or private equity investment as a percentage of GDP are key indicators. Exhibit 7.2 illustrates these values for 2003 and various markets.[3]

Private equity is an asset class where commercial investors seek to achieve superior returns. Markets with low return perspectives would hence not attract the interest of institutional investors. Markets with good return opportunities attract the most money. Hence, the volume of private equity funding raised for a given market is an indicator of investment opportunities. Exhibit 7.3 shows funds raised and funds invested in 2003 in various markets.[4]

However, this indicator should never be taken as a standalone criterion. Herd behaviour is a common phenomenon in financial markets and may lead to providing too much money

Exhibit 7.2

Private equity investment as percentage of GDP, 2003

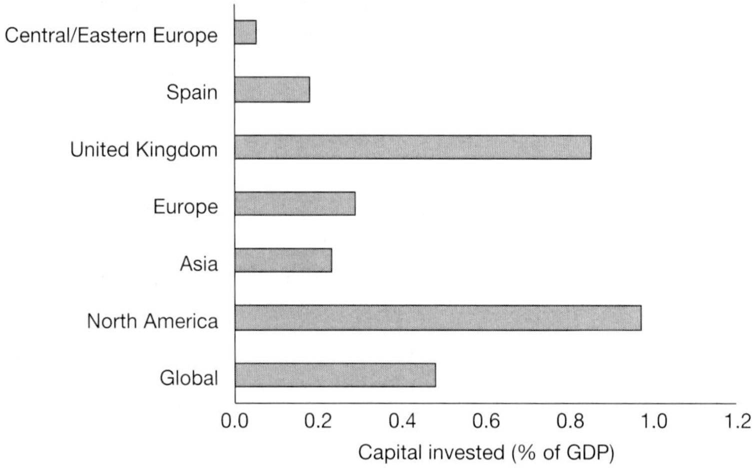

Source: PwC/3i 'Global Private Equity 2004 Report'.

to a market with too little deal flow. This may eventually have a disastrous effect on the investment return, as fund managers are tempted to deploy capital into poor-quality investments or overpay for investments in an overly competitive environment.

Information on private equity activity in various markets has become more available over the last decades. Private equity and venture capital associations publish such information on a regular basis and make benchmarking between countries and regions possible.

The specialisation of the market as an indicator

Another reliable indicator for the maturity of a specific private equity market is the communicated investment focus of investment firms. In developing economies, funds are more

Exhibit 7.3

Funds raised and funds invested in different regions in 2003

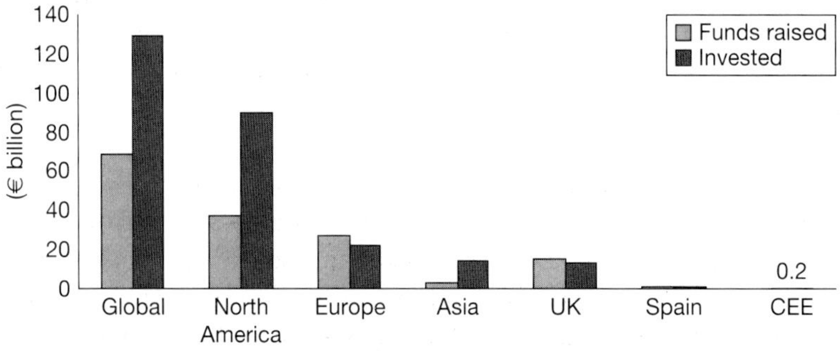

Source: PwC/3i 'Global Private Equity 2004 Report'.

generalist and focus on late-stage companies, which are self-sustainable, cash flow positive and have limited refinancing risk. Immature economies are therefore more targeted by generalist-type funds investing across a wide range of sectors and market segments, rather than specialist funds such as specific technology funds, because specialisation in a fund's investment strategy requires sufficient deal flow in specialist sectors.

The emergence of venture capital therefore can be taken as an indicator for maturing private equity markets. Venture capital-type investments emerge in large numbers only in economies that have the basic ingredients of a knowledge-based economy and have sufficient research and development activity with a commercial potential. In this context, applied research activity needs to be distinguished from basic research, which is linked to pre-commercial scientific work. The more a perceived investment opportunity is linked to a specific investment strategy, the more information is needed to assess the deal flow potential. In the technology venture capital investment segment, this may require the assessment of research clusters, patent application activity, research activity of technology-oriented multinational companies and so on. For example, Silicon Valley has traditionally had a very high level of technology-focused venture capital fund activity, because its ICT industry cluster has generated ample deal flow with attractive return opportunities. Similarly, venture capital investment activity with a strong technology focus in western Europe has emerged first in countries with a strong research base and solid technology clusters. Examples of European clusters are the Cambridge area in the United Kingdom, the Munich area in Germany, and the Scandinavian region with global technology leaders in communication technologies.

The sophistication of the financial market as an indicator for private equity prospects

The sophistication of capital markets in a given market is a further valuable indicator for private equity prospects. The more developed the capital markets in a fund's geographic focus, the more likely there are suitable exit channels for private equity investors, a prerequisite for the return potential of a fund. Indicators for the maturity of capital markets are stock market activity, total market capitalisation, liquidity of the market, merger and acquisition and IPO activity but also more basic indicators such as the simple availability of debt financing for corporations. Debt finance is a valuable tool for private equity firms to enhance return by leveraging their deals in the late-stage segment of private equity (buyout deals). Furthermore, debt financing is a competitor to equity financing in an economy and hence promotes the arbitration of risk and return across individual market segments: where debt is not available, more expensive private equity serves to finance expansion. As equity investors seek equity-like returns, unavailability of debt financing will lower entry prices for equity investors.

The historical risk–return profile as an indicator of market maturity

Finally, the historical or perceived future risk–return profiles are also an important aspect in deciding on the attractiveness of a market segment. The profiles vary considerably for sub-classes according to specific markets and their degree of development. There may be markets with very sound returns in the buyout segments, but poor performance in venture capital-type investments. This was, for example, the case in Europe where buyout funds have historically outperformed European venture capital on a risk-adjusted basis, while

Exhibit 7.4

Risk–return of venture capital and buyouts, Europe vs United States

	Europe (%)	*United States (%)*
Venture capital		
Average IRR[6]	7	22
Standard deviation	27	56
Buyout		
Average IRR	16	13
Standard deviation	28	25

Source: Based on Venture Economics data.

US venture capital delivers the highest returns, reflecting the higher risk in this market segment. As shown in Exhibit 7.4, based on historical fund data up to vintage year 2000, buyout investments in Europe delivered a superior return to venture capital investment despite an apparently comparable risk level, while in the United States the riskier venture capital segment outperformed buyout investments.[5]

This distortion could have been due to less-experienced GPs in Europe and typically poorer exit opportunities both through IPOs and trade sales for European technology companies.

Market opportunities due to political or macroeconomic change

In certain markets, specific opportunities may also arise from a temporary phenomenon often linked to political change or major changes in the tax or legal environment. Examples for such special situation strategies are funds focusing on privatisation deals (for example, in CEE after the fall of communism in the early 1990s) or small-scale MBO funds targeting succession situations in economies with a high density of family businesses. In CEE the political changes in the aftermath of the fall of communism led to a shift from centralist economies to market-driven economies. The first step was a wave of privatisation of state-owned industries. Certain countries such as Poland set up special privatisation funds to get this process started. In other countries the American Enterprise Funds, launched with the support of the US government, were the main drivers. For a decade, the CEE countries saw many transactions where private equity supported the transition of entire industries to a market-based business model.

Generalist funds versus specialist funds

None of the above can give LPs a guarantee for identifying a viable market opportunity. But assessing them individually and looking at the overall picture helps assessing the general prospects for private equity investment in general and specific sub-segments in particular in a given market. They certainly help the investor in deciding between a specialist and a generalist fund, which should be based on the maturity of the target market and not on diversification considerations at fund level.

Generalist funds might claim diversification benefits. However, investing in specialist funds does not necessarily inhibit diversification across industry sector and stage because a fund investor can easily diversify by investing in specialist funds focusing on different sectors or stages. Actually, the choice largely depends on the assessment of what best captures the market opportunity. The more mature a market is, the stronger the variety of deal opportunities, the greater the importance of specialised skills in the selection and management of private equity deals, and the more sensible the creation of specialist funds. Therefore, in immature markets, generalist-type funds are the prevalent fund type while sophisticated markets with a high degree of innovation will show a greater density of specialist funds.

Evaluating the quality of a private equity fund's management team

After the assessment of a market opportunity, crucial questions arise for a limited partner.

- How to select the right team to exploit this opportunity?
- How to find the teams that go after such opportunities?
- How to compare different teams?
- How to assess their relative past performance?
- How to distinguish lucky winners from teams with superior skills?
- How to assess the stability of a team?
- How to assess a team's deal flow potential?
- How to evaluate first-time teams?

Assessing an investment opportunity is judging the coherence of a business case with respect to a promising deal flow, the right skill-set of the team to exploit an opportunity through a convincing investment strategy, and a reasonable fund size in relation to the market opportunity and the resource requirements for a suitable management team. There is no point in investing in a team with a fund size that is unsuitable for the investment focus or where the operating costs will absorb too big a share of the committed capital due to a fund size below critical mass.

Especially for first-time limited partners, assessing a management team is a challenge. Experienced market players already know the markets, and the key players with their relative strengths and weaknesses. They have networks of co-investors with whom to compare notes on their assessment of individual funds and GPs. They also follow the market carefully and can anticipate what teams are coming to the market for fundraising and at what time. This also gives experienced investors a competitive advantage in getting the first choice of investment opportunities.

Often, the best-performing funds are not openly fundraising at all but propose their funds only to a restricted and pre-selected group of investors. They have a fairly stable investor base, grown over several generations of funds, with whom they have a privileged relationship. Such GPs are almost certain of the support of their current investors and the turnover in their investor base is low. Getting into such funds is hence almost not a matter of choice but of invitation and very difficult to achieve for first-time limited partners. Establishing long-term relationships with skilled GPs is one major reason why institutional investors often support promising first-time teams. They consider their investment as an entry ticket to a long-term relationship with a, hopefully successful, GP. In doing so, they deliberately take the higher risk resulting from the team's limited joint track record and unproven investment strategy, and base their investment case on their assessment of a team's deal-sourcing capacity and perceived skill-set to convert these opportunities into superior returns for their investors.

Evaluating the quality of a management team is the most important success factor in a fund investment that the fund investor can actively control. There is no business plan on which fund investors can base their assessment. The investors need to judge the capabilities of a team to select companies in which the team can create value in such a way as to generate superior returns. There are few hard facts available to judge the team. Even for experienced teams that have raised and returned a series of funds, little meaningful information is available to conclude on the future success of a team with an acceptable degree of certainty. Assessing the quality of a first-time team is even more challenging, as no common track record is available and neither is there evidence on whether their business strategy can be put into practice.

The following chapters outline tools that may help LPs to bridge the uncertainty in the decision-making process for a private equity fund investment, keeping in mind that there is no general rule and the tools exposed are meant to provide ideas for an approach that may decrease the rate of error rather than being a recipe for success.

Assessing a management team's track record

Assessing a fund management team's track record is about gathering proof on a team's investment skills by looking at a management team's past transactions. Past investment activity may include many things. Ideally, a management team would have an investment track record from a previous fund, with a defined amount of capital available for investments in individual portfolio companies, a defined fund life and easily identifiable cash flows from investments in and realisations of individual portfolio companies.

Often, however, the track record assessment may be more complicated:

- past activity may include investments in portfolio companies from various funds;
- the team composition may have changed;
- part of the track record of some team members may not be verifiable because it is based on investments in companies with a former management team for which it is difficult to obtain detailed data; and
- past investment activity may even be based on business angel-type investments in companies on which little formalised information is available.

All this is just a small glimpse of the difficulties LPs may face in looking at a fund management team's track record. Whatever the track record of a team comprises, LPs need to look at individual transactions with portfolio companies to get tangible information for the assessment of a team's investment performance. In a second step, LPs then have to combine the arithmetic results from an analysis at the transaction level with a more global analysis of a team's past investment activity.

The following sections provide a framework for a limited partner's analysis of a team's track record. It starts with the transaction-based performance analysis and adds views on how the quantitative results of a performance analysis can be enhanced with a qualitative assessment that may help to conclude on whether a team's past success was by luck or by design and what relevance it has for a proposed investment strategy.

Realised and unrealised investment performance: hard and soft facts

The logical way to track record analysis is to look at the hard facts first: realised and unrealised overall performance is a quick and rough way to gauge how well the team did in its past investment activity. Internal rate of return (IRR) and multiples are the most common investment performance measures.[7] The multiple indicates what the investor's absolute cash increase was on a specific investment, and the IRR adds a time dimension, taking into account how long capital was put to work to generate the investment return.[8] However, both are incomplete views of the return of an investment, they should complement each other and detailed analysis should follow. A high multiple on an investment may look much less impressive if the holding period of the asset was very long. Similarly, a high IRR on an investment that was realised after a few months only may have added little wealth in absolute terms.

When looking at performance figures, investors should always obtain for each portfolio company the dates and amounts of investment and divestment from the manager and re-perform the IRR calculations both on the individual investments and the overall portfolio. There are many ways to calculate an IRR, and the fund managers do not always give the most conservative one. For example, there may be several percentage points of difference between the IRR of the portfolio (based on the aggregated cash flows of all investments) and the average IRR of all investments (based on the IRR of each investment weighted with its cost as a percentage of the overall portfolio cost). If the fund manager always chooses the higher of the two, the overall IRRs could be overstated by as much as 3 per cent to 5 per cent. It is equally useful to ensure that cash flows are based on actual cash flows and dates and not pooled per month quarter, semester or even year. This could introduce a bias to the dataset that makes comparison meaningless.

Gross IRR versus net IRR: the implication of management cost

Calculating the IRR on a GP's individual investments and overall portfolio (generally referred to as the gross IRR) is a good start, but another dimension is relevant to assess the investment performance of a team: the management cost. At the end of the day it is the cash-on-cash return to investors that matters most. This net IRR is calculated on the cash flows drawn from and returned to investors over the lifetime of a fund and is hence net of any operating cost of a fund. Analysing the difference between the gross IRR on a portfolio and net IRR to investors can be very revealing, as a big difference points towards several important issues for which an investor should watch out:

- slow investment pace: a slow investment pace increases the gap between gross IRR and net IRR, as during the investment period the management fee is typically paid on the committed capital, independently of how much capital is effectively put to work;
- high level of expenses charged to the fund on top of the management fee: set-up fees, administration expenses, broken deal cost and structuring cost are the most prominent items to watch in this respect; and
- excessively long investment periods: hidden extensions of the investment period may occur before the first closing by starting to invest from sponsor resources and constituting a 'live pipeline' of investments which then are transferred to the fund against charge of a management fee from the date of the first investment onwards. In other cases, the investment period is extended with the consent of investors because the money could not be placed in time.

Unrealised investments

Except for first-time teams, the management team has ongoing unrealised investments during the fundraising. Actually, many teams have less realised than unrealised investments.

Therefore, looking at the overall unrealised portfolio is a substantial part of the track record analysis. An investor should carefully look at the valuation methods. In Europe, the EVCA valuation guidelines are the norm, and professional management teams generally follow them. In the United States, GAAP standards are applied, which in the context of highly judgemental valuation of unquoted companies are often of limited use.[9]

Whatever the valuation method used, the most important aspect investors should understand is the valuation methodology used, and they should check whether it is applied consistently over time. In the absence of a liquid market for private equity investment, any valuation methodology that accurately reflects the value of a portfolio company can only do so by pure coincidence. However, looking at the evolution of valuations over time may give valuable insight into how the individual portfolio companies are doing compared with the initial investment case.

Larger funds of funds have a further tool to assess valuations proposed by the GP, as they often are indirectly invested in the same company through two or more funds, and hence can compare the approach of different GPs to valuation and the development pattern of individual portfolio companies.

Assessing unrealised investment performance of venture capital funds

Particular issues arise when evaluating unrealised track records of venture capital funds investing in technology companies. In such cases, evaluating the track record is virtually impossible without specific industry know-how, which only few LPs can afford having as an in-house resource. Large funds of funds have biotech and ICT experts in their own staff, who assess the potential of portfolio companies that are part of a team's unrealised track record. Their task is to assess the time line needed to develop such companies into interesting exit candidates and the risks for them to fail along this way. The complexity of such assessment is comparable with the investment decision in the first place and is subject to a high degree of uncertainty. This is also why teams with an exclusively unrealised track record in very specific niche sectors face big challenges in raising a successor fund and are often just considered first-time teams by institutional investors.

Looking for a team's systematic pattern of success

Once the analysis of past realised and unrealised performance track record and the value assessment of unrealised investments is done, investors should have a rather detailed understanding of value drivers in a fund's portfolio and the contribution of individual deals to a team's investment performance. Such a good foundation allows them to engage in the second layer of a thorough track record analysis which is the assessment of drivers of a team's investment success. The key question is whether a team is successful by luck or by design, and whether the past overall investment performance comes from one lucky winner or is on the result of a systematic pattern of success? This question is particularly important when an investment track record has been built up in a hype period where virtually everybody managed to deliver decent returns.

In search of a systematic pattern of success, investors should first get a concrete understanding of the distinctive factors in a team's investment strategy. They should try to identify which selection criteria the team applies, what return-specific investment rationale they have in making a deal, how they monitor and influence these success factors, and how this compares with the value realisation they achieve at exit. In a second step, the investor would evaluate the team's past investment performance against these factors, and judge whether a consistent causal relationship, as opposed to a random correlation, between the success of an investment and the key factors in a team's investment strategy exists.

To do so, investors should ask for investment memoranda of past deals on a sample basis. They typically include an investment rationale for the deal and key objectives in creating value with a portfolio company. A first assessment could be whether the team had the lead in a specific deal. The track record may be impressive in numbers but if a team has not contributed anything but money, investors should better become an investor in the fund that has actually done the real work on the deal unless they believe in the fund manager's ability to systematically join syndicates on successful deals. The following are other questions which can be asked.

- How did the team source the deal?
- What position did it have in the negotiation?
- Did it have syndication strategies?
- If yes, were they appropriate for the type of deals it invested in?
- If the investment rationale states a convincing management team in the portfolio company, did it have to change management during the investment period?
- Have identified milestones be met?
- Has it accurately assessed and understood the risks associated with the investment?
- In the case of venture capital investments, has the cash reach defined by the team at the time of investment been accurate?
- When did it take action if things deviate from plan?
- How does it take action?
- How does the team decide whether to keep investing or pull the plug?
- Did it proactively identify the exit route, that is was it driving the exit or did it rely on being approached?

The core question is whether there is a clear investment strategy and whether the team sticks to it. Evidence for this can only be derived from the discipline a team shows in selecting, structuring, developing and exiting its individual investments. Opportunistic investment strategies may deliver sound returns but might not give a lot of comfort for future return perspectives. If investors invest in GPs, they will not only hope that GPs make money on their investment but also require that the GPs know why they make money. A powerful tool to assess this issue in due diligence processes is to ask for exit memoranda. Professional GPs typically have a final assessment in which they make a critical analysis of a deal's history at its exit. They will evaluate their investment criteria on the basis of completed deals themselves in order to draw conclusions for the future. Professional teams are not satisfied by a successful deal, but they seek to know why a specific deal has been successful, and whether they rightly anticipated these factors in their initial investment decision. Likewise they want to know what went wrong in their initial assessment in the case of underperforming deals, and draw for themselves conclusions for the future.

Investors should do the same final assessment. Often one disastrous investment tells the investor more than five success stories. It is therefore worth looking at lost investments of a team, and see what they tell about the key features of a team's investment strategy.

- Has it opportunistically neglected its investment criteria?
- Did the investment criteria prove to be wrong?
- Did it misjudge its own criteria?

Finally, an investor should also assess the downside protection the team negotiates in a deal, such as adjustments to their entry valuation in the case of an underperformance of the investee company, priority pay-out at the exit, rights to trigger an exit (drag-along and tag-along rights), protection against dilution in future financing rounds and similar. It gives an insight on how diligent a team is in anticipating worst-case scenarios, how big their negotiation power is, and whether they find the right balance between securing the best possible return for the fund whilst keeping the management of the portfolio company motivated.

Investors should also look at the role of the individual team members to put the track record in perspective. Which individual had what role with respect to the different stages of a deal? A successful track record will be worth nothing if the key person responsible for the success has left the team. Getting a view of the relative contribution of team members to the investment success is also a valuable input for defining which team members are vital resources for the fund's investment activity. Investors should judge on whether individuals, who are key to the success of the fund, are likely to be around in five to 10 years' time, or whether they have plans to shift their interest to something else. If key people are likely to retire over the lifetime of the fund, the question will be whether succession plans are in place, and whether the team accepts the designated successors. Professional GPs seek to keep their team strong, during the evolution of the fund, and to expand management resources as the management activity of the GP increases. They are adding key individuals over time with the consent of LPs in order to make the fund's investment activity less vulnerable to unforeseen departures of key individuals and succession situations. In any case, it is useful to have safeguards in the fund's legal documentation to ensure appropriate replacement both in quantitative and qualitative terms for key people that leave a management team. This can for instance be achieved through clauses governing key-man events as discussed in Chapter 9, in the section entitled 'Key-man clauses'.

Finally, investors should assess the relevance of the track record for the investment focus of the fund in which they intend to invest. Often GPs tend to change investment strategies depending on fundraising perspectives, and ignore the fact that they are moving away from a market segment that matches their initial skill-set. Investors should be aware of this risk. A team that has done a great job in seed and start-up financing will not necessarily perform in the buyout segment and vice versa.

Evaluating the fund management individuals

Evaluating management individuals has two objectives: assessing their individual skills, and getting a view on how they can fit into the management team. It is difficult to say which of the two is more important. Once an investment is made, changing a team or individual team members is complex, finding replacements is difficult and time-consuming, and artificially setting up management teams involves high risks. Also, making changes to a management team distracts management attention from its investment activity which can have a major impact on the investors' return: in private equity one really bad year can forever destroy the investment performance of a fund.

Checking the background of fund management individuals

Assessing individual team members' professional skills appears manageable. CVs provide their career history. They are verifiable and can be cross-checked through references provided by the team member. Professional investors also use their personal networks in the industry to assess individuals and their reputation of integrity. Referencing is a very useful tool in checking on team members' background beyond their professional reputation, and gives insight into their personal integrity. In an industry such as private equity where mutual trust needs to compensate for lacking transparency, this is of key importance.

Investors should also assess the personal impact the individual can make in the investment cycle. LPs should try to get a feel for concrete knowledge of individuals that is relevant for private equity investments and more specifically for the investment focus of the proposed fund. Sometimes, individuals may be highly qualified for a specific investment strategy but cannot get a fund raised in the sector of their core competence because of general market conditions. Or, successful teams in a specific segment decide to change their investment focus in order to be able to raise bigger funds. LPs should be alert to such phenomena and proactively analyse these aspects as GPs in such cases are very unlikely to be outspoken on their true intentions.

Assessing the chemistry within a management team

Assessing the chemistry within the team is even more complex than assessing the individual. A common objective such as raising a fund can convert individuals into great actors pretending perfect harmony in a team. But, from an investor's point of view, the objective is not fundraising but 10 years of dedicated investment management performance. Individual interviews are the most powerful check. They can serve to sound out the motivation of individuals to work in private equity, the financial dependency they have on the success of the fund they want to manage and their views on the functioning of the team of which they are part. Often questions on the development strategy of a management firm best reveal the diverging views of individual team members on the functioning of a team. They also may make leadership or succession issues apparent. The latter are of utmost importance in view of the long lifetime of fund investments.

A useful approach is also to extend the one-to-one interviews to the organisational layer below the senior investment professionals. This may well be the most informative insight an investor can ever hope to get. Second layer team members may be less used to being exposed to this type of interview and less skilled in avoiding tricky territory than their senior partners. They also provide a more neutral view on who plays what role in the team, informal leadership structures, and specific strengths and weaknesses of top layer individuals. Assessing their quality is also important, as they are generally very involved in the day-to-day investment activity, even if they are invisible in the fundraising process.

To complete the view obtained from interviews with team members, investors should also seek direct dialogue with a few managers of the companies in which the team has invested. This opens another perspective on the type of value-added that the fund managers provide, and on the level and quality of cooperation. This type of conversation with managers of portfolio companies only makes sense without the presence of the fund's management team.

Distribution of carried interest within the management team

An additional element that may help assessing the coherence of teams and the relative weight of individuals is a close look at the distribution of carried interest in the team. Investors grant a management team a sizeable portion of the fund's profits as an incentive for achieving outstanding investment performance. However, in doing so, investors should ensure that the split of the profit share granted to the general partner effectively reaches those team members that are considered key individuals for achieving investment performance. Often senior individuals in the team who actually are no longer involved in the daily activity of the fund management take a major portion of the carried interest. An uneven distribution of performance incentives may however lead to tensions in the team and, in extreme cases, even to the departure of valuable team members who may get financially more attractive offers in the market. Looking at the distribution of carried interest is therefore not only a valuable indicator for the hierarchy of power within the team, it is also an important element to watch for the long-term stability of a fund's management team.

Drawing conclusions

Summarising the results of the due diligence on a management team feels like reflecting on a candidate after a recruitment interview. But there is one major difference: candidates that are hired after a recruitment interview do have a trial period during which the employer can correct any mistakes in the assessment made. For fund investments, once the commitment is made, correcting a decision is cumbersome, time-consuming and costly. That is why investors should take any doubts they may have seriously. Often openly confronting teams with doubts that emerge from such team assessment brings useful clarifications that simplify the investment decision, either way. If the investors do not feel comfortable with the key aspects of team stability and chemistry between team members, they should not invest. There are already too many cases out there in the market where investors have invested in the glorious past of a team without a future.

Assessing the deal flow of a team

Quality of a management team also derives from its ability to generate a lucrative deal flow. Sources of insight into a team's deal generation capacity are manifold: to start with an investor should look at the deal pipeline, check the deal log, look at historical deal records in terms of numbers of deals logged and the selection rate along the investment process. It is important to know whether teams led their deals or were merely followers. The internal documentation of investments along the investment process often reveals the source of a deal and the role the team has played in sourcing the deal. Questions may include the following.

- Is it a referred deal in the context of a syndication?
- If yes, what is the weight of a team in the syndicate?
- Was the deal proactively sourced?
- Did it come through the team's network? Is the network exclusive?
- How big is the share of auctioned deals in the pipeline or in the portfolio?
- On what grounds did the team win the auctioned deals?[10]
- Did it compromise on the price?
- Or did it compromise on terms and conditions?

If most past deals have been sourced through auctions, the team probably has little lucrative proprietary deal flow and may lack the necessary networks. Auctioned deals with little downside protection may also be a sign of a deal flow problem, indicating that a team compromises on investment standards for the sake of getting money invested.

An investor should look at the deals that the team has not managed to close but would have liked to. Investors should enquire why a deal has been lost to a competitor. If it is on terms and conditions, this is not necessarily bad. It may indicate good investment discipline by the management team. However, investors should cross-check the credibility of explanations given through their own independent research and check to whom the team has lost deals, and what their performances were. Large funds of funds have again a comparative advantage as they have easier access to such information through their network or even through their own portfolio. Frequently, they are invested in several competing teams in a specific market and follow the investment activity through their portfolio investments. Less-experienced investors may seek access to databases that monitor the deal activity in specific markets and that become increasingly complete and reliable.

First-time teams versus experienced teams

What is the better choice?

Whether first-time teams or established teams are the better choice is an ambiguous question. Intuitively, experienced teams should deliver better returns. Not only do they have more explicit private equity experience, but they were also successful in the past and as a consequence raised follow-on funds. But is past success a good indicator for future success?[11] There appears to be a trade-off between experience and performance for fund managers that have returned successfully several funds and earned substantial carried interest on them. There is a distinct risk that the management has no performance incentive at all any more as they got rich on the past funds and continue their business just for fun. An investor may invest in a management team with several key senior individuals, who only sell a fund but are not the people to manage it. They will have a young, and potentially inexperienced, management team working below them. The senior people may take the biggest share in the carry for only one contribution to the fund, which is showing their face in the fundraising process. Investors may actually end up with a virtual first-time team, even though they believe that they have just invested in one of the most experienced teams on the market. Therefore, it is of utmost importance to evaluate the incentive structure of a team in detail and to try to find out in interviews who is doing what in the team.

The most powerful tool is again to interview team members at the level of senior partners minus one and managers of portfolio companies who can say who is really involved in the business. Then, investors should also know how much money the senior managers are putting into the fund and where it comes from. The more the team puts up from their own resources, the more they are devoted to the management of the fund. However, sometimes, rich senior key individuals require their young staff to put up money in unreasonable amounts that go beyond their financial resources, and make them totally dependent. Senior managers often offer a guarantee to these individuals to allow them to make a more sizeable commitment on a leveraged basis. This does not serve the purpose of the fund. Not only do such structures potentially jeopardise the existential basis of management individuals, but they also bear the risk of artificially keeping together a team that turns out not to be able to function any longer. In the worst case this may even lead to people becoming desperate in a situation of low performance of the fund, and they may try to make up for their personal losses through illegal action such as fraud. Both scenarios are a rather unpleasant prospect for an investor in a fund.

On the other hand, being a first-time team does not mean having no relevant experience in private equity. Often individuals from established teams spin out from their previous management firm to set up their own management firm for which they recruit people from a wider range of industries. Such spinouts are generally a healthy evolution as it spreads knowledge on private equity, increases competition, and creates new investment opportunities for LPs.

Evaluating first-time teams

A first-time fund represents a big question mark, because there is no track record of investments and evidence for a stable long-term team. Thus, the due diligence focus for a first-time team is much more on the skills and experience that the individual team members can bring along. Assessing a first-time team requires a much deeper understanding from the LP on what skill-set is required for the proposed investment strategy of a fund. Depending on the fund focus, relevant experience can include serial entrepreneurs, turnaround managers, M&A managers, researchers and many more. It is also important to ensure that the entire skill-set of team members complements itself. Putting together teams with a mono-dimensional background is a frequent weakness of first-time teams. This is especially true for teams that spin out of consultancy firms. Such teams may claim a very broad background, but often have little operational experience to offer.

---

1 Typically GPs are established as limited liability companies with the minimum amount of capital authorised under the respective legislation.
2 In some markets there are residues of fund structures where investors participate in the investment decision process through investment committees. These structures increasingly lose ground and the dominant model is the Anglo-Saxon approach where the investment and divestment decisions of the fund are at the sole discretion of the GP.
3 Data from EVCA, Moneytree and PwC/3i.
4 Data from EVCA, Moneytree and PwC/3i.
5 Based on Venture Economics data.
6 Refer to Part I, Chapter 5 for a detailed discussion of the concept of IRR as a performance measurement tool in private equity.
7 Refer to Chapter 5 in Part I for a detailed discussion of the concept of IRR and multiples as performance measurement in private equity.
8 See also the Chapter 5 section entitled 'Performance measurement in private equity'.
9 This is particularly relevant in the genuine venture capital segments, where portfolio companies often have little to no revenues, are cash burning and peer companies are virtually impossible to find.
10 Auctioned deals are deals where an entrepreneur, often with the help of a consulting firm, seeks equity from funds by tendering the deal publicly or among a selected group of fund managers. The objective is to increase competition among the fund managers and to improve the conditions offered to the entrepreneur.
11 According to Frei and Studer (2004), the empirical evidence is not clear-cut. But, for example, Kaplan and Schoar (2003) find that follow-on funds do better.

Chapter 8

Assessing terms and conditions – what to watch out for

Once investors have formed a positive view on a market opportunity and a team's capability to exploit this investment opportunity for superior returns, the next crucial question arises: what is the cost for the investor to gain access to this investment opportunity? In terms of management cost, private equity is the most expensive asset class. There is no other market segment where asset managers take several per cent per year of the managed capital to pay the running cost of their business. There is also no other asset class where managers take away such a large share of the profits that they generate as part of a performance-oriented remuneration.

If these generous terms for asset managers are an accepted market standard in the private equity industry, it will be because this market segment is capable of generating returns that on average outperform any other asset class. But precisely because fees and other operating costs of a private equity fund are so sizeable, the definition of terms and conditions for a fund investment is crucial and may have an impact of several percentage points on the net return to investors. There are many myths in the market on what the right level of management fee is, what set-up cost a fund may incur, what fees may be charged on top of the management fee for a private equity fund and so on. No standard has really emerged, and the final set-up is still very much the result of a negotiation between general partners (GPs) and limited partners (LPs). However, the following sections describe the rationale behind key commercial terms of a fund investment and may help LPs to define a line of argumentation for the negotiations with the GP.

Management fee structures

What does it cover?

There is a simple rule for management fees: they should cover the running costs of the fund. Fees should not make the team rich or the carried interest loses its incentive. Especially in cases of poor market conditions where carried interest is out of reach for the team, excessive management fees can be an incentive to artificially extend the lifetime of a fund, for example, by keeping investing in companies that are bound to fail. This is why continuous monitoring of the investment and exit performance of a team in funds, where there is no chance for the team to earn carried interest and little prospect for raising a follow-on fund, is a must to cut losses on poor investments. Also, excessive surpluses on the management fee earned by the GP reduce the value for LPs of having the GP investing in the fund. In such situations, there is a distinct risk that the GP refinances its commitment to the fund out of the management fee and ultimately has actually no own money at risk. This gives the GP a free option on an additional portion of the fund's profits without providing any alignment of interest between the GP and the LPs.

Budget-based assessment of management fee levels

In assessing the fee structure of a fund, an investor should look at the budget of the management firm, and make sure that the fee structure fits the investment activity of the fund. Some strategies such as early-stage technology investments require a very widespread skill-set in the team, which may mean bigger teams to be financed by the management fee. In other segments, such as mezzanine funds, the required skill-set is more focused on financial structuring skills which may be achievable with smaller team sizes. When analysing the budget of a GP, the LPs should have this in mind. Also the budget should include the fee income from all management activities of the GP, including fees from previous funds that the manager continues to earn for divesting these portfolios while building up the portfolio of a new fund. The remuneration for the key individuals makes up a good portion of the management fee, and therefore a check on salary levels and benchmarking them against the industry is important. An experienced investor will know the salary levels, others might want to refer to co-investors or a recruitment agency.

Typically, the fee is a percentage on commitments during the investment period and on invested capital during the realisation period. As regards the percentage rate to be applied, there is no market standard, no matter what the GP is saying. In the 1990s there was a perception that 2.5 per cent on committed capital during the investment period was the generally acceptable flat rate. If it ever was the case, it certainly no longer is. GPs have understood that the running cost of a fund has become a matter of competitiveness in the fundraising process and have started to justify their cost structure in their investment memoranda.

Step-down structures

Some GPs propose fee structures that follow a step-down pattern during the divestment period, that is the fee level of each year during the divestment period amounts to a percentage of the previous year's fee. They argue that such fee structure gives them stability in planning their resources required for managing a fund, independently of whether they succeed in raising a successor fund. Investors should assess the cost pattern of such structures against a fee structure that is linked to the invested capital assuming a divestment profile typical for a fund with a comparable focus. Such scenario analysis could use the cash flows from a team's previous funds and run various models of fee structures. Generally, fee structures with step-down patterns tend to result in higher fees but the difference to a structure based on the invested capital may not be material in certain cases. If a step-down structure appears acceptable, a clause should still exist to adjust the fee for the case where the actual fee level ends up being in no relation to the underlying investment activity, for example, a high fee for a portfolio with only a couple of investments left to divest. This is particularly relevant for structures that foresee a floor for the level of the management fee, independently of how much of the portfolio is left to divest.

Scaling fee levels to the fund size

An important aspect is also to put the fee in relation to the real fund size. Teams during fundraising normally propose a minimum, a target and a maximum fund size, called hard cap. These amounts can differ considerably. If the management fee is a flat percentage based on commitments irrespective of what are the achieved size of commitments at final closing, this will lead to substantial differences in the management fee level. GPs typically base their budgets on the fee income derived from the minimum fund size. However, if the fund closes at its maximum size and there is no adjustment to the percentage rate for calculating the management fee, the GP will drastically increase its income level with a sizeable portion as a net profit for the GP. Professional teams therefore scale their fee level to the size of the fund and reduce the applicable percentage rate to determine the management fee according to the fund size achieved at final closing. In doing so, they are obviously also taking into account possible additions to the management team that are needed to deal with the increased fund size.

Other partnership expenses

During due diligence, LPs should get a clear understanding on which types of expenses are covered by the management fee and which items may be charged to the LPs in addition to the management fee. The level of due diligence cost that has been capitalised by the team for previous investments provides a good indicator on what type of investment expense is borne by the team out of its management fee and what share is outsourced to third parties. Generally, the rule should be that a team, on top of the management fee, may only charge due diligence costs for specific expertise in relation to an investment to be made, such as legal advice, financial audits of the investee or specific industry expertise if required. Investors should carefully analyse the outsourcing behaviour of a team with respect to due diligence cost. Who does it select? What are the selection criteria? What service does it typically require? How does it split costs with syndication partners? All these questions give valuable insights into the way a team operates on a daily basis.

Broken deal expense

An important item to address is the handling of broken deal expense, which relates to costs incurred by the GP for transactions that did not materialise. The GP often attempts to charge this cost to the fund, which appears questionable as the GP controls what resources are used at what stage in a due diligence process. A typical formula for broken deal expense suggests that such cost is borne by the fund once the investment analyses of a deal have reached a certain stage, for example, once the investment proposal has passed to the investment committee of the fund. At this stage, aborting deals is generally either beyond the influence of the GP or, in the case where disagreement on fundamental terms of the deal prevails, in the best interest of the fund.

Set-up cost

Another typical cost item to look at are set-up fees for the fund. These fees comprise legal costs for drafting the fund documentation and negotiation costs of lawyers, incorporation costs and similar. Typically set-up costs should be limited as a percentage of commitments. For large funds, a cap in the form of a maximum absolute amount should be introduced. Typical levels for set-up costs are up to 1 per cent of commitments for small to mid-sized funds (up to US$100 million), decreasing gradually to around 0.5 per cent for bigger funds. Some GPs also try to introduce fundraising expenses such as placement agent fees in the set-up costs of a fund. This approach appears questionable and LPs should challenge such practice. Why should LPs who invest in a fund support the cost of marketing of the GP? After all, it is the GP's business that is at stake.

Fee offset

Finally, investors should require full offset of any fee earned by the GP from any of the fund's portfolio companies against the management fee paid by the fund. The management fee compensates the team to provide hands-on support, and the team should not be paid a second time for the same service by the investee, no matter how valuable the service of the GP may be to the investee. GPs may argue that charging a fee for the services rendered to the investee is appropriate as an educative measure to make the value-added provided by the GP tangible for the management of the investee company. Even if true, this should not result in an additional revenue stream for the GP. Double income on the same service may very quickly lead to conflict of interest: the team may eventually continue to invest in a portfolio company not due to the significant return perspectives but rather to secure an ongoing fee income from the portfolio company.

Operating costs and capital invested

To gauge the approach of the GP to managing the cost structure of a fund, investors could cross-check with their track record analysis the gap between gross IRR and net IRR. Deriving the NAV of a fund from cash flows is a useful tool here: the aggregated profit and loss items since the inception of the fund are deducted from the cumulative net cash flows from investors to the fund. Individual cost items such as management fees, set-up expenses, audit fees, legal expenses and so on can then be expressed as a percentage of capital drawn from investors and provide a good view on the relationship between capital put at work in deals and the burn rate of the fund for its own operating expense. This exercise is highly recommended to investors to better understand the cost dynamics of their investment. The results may be surprising for investors not familiar with the dynamics of the economic parameters of a private equity fund, and are very revealing indeed.

Investment periods and fund duration

Another parameter with a significant influence on the cost structure of a fund investment is the definition of the investment period and the fund life. Investors should ensure that the investment period fits the fund focus and size of the fund. Often teams raise funds excessive in size of commitments to boost their management fee income. Once the fund is raised they then have difficulties in deploying the capital in promising deals. This can either lead to channelling money to less attractive deals in an attempt to get the fund invested or to a request to investors to extend the investment period of the fund. During this time, management fee accumulates on the committed capital, but only a fraction of the capital is put to work. This practice has a major impact on the net performance of the fund and is easily seen by analysing the gap between gross IRR and net IRR of a fund. As management fees during the investment period are typically calculated on the committed capital, any extension of the investment period adds significantly to the cost burden of the fund, which needs to be recovered before the fund can generate a return to investors.

For the same reason, the investor should ensure that the end of the investment period triggers an adjustment of the management fee. Generally, investment periods are defined as a certain number of years (typically three to five) after the closing of a fund. However, if the fund is fully invested, or if the GP has raised a follow-on fund and the investment activity in the current fund is reduced to follow-on investments only, there appears to be no reason to continue paying the full management fee for the funds investment activity. Therefore, contracts should foresee clauses that lead to an adjustment of the management fee level once the investment period of a fund has ended. What formula is suitable for what fund is assessed on a case-by-case basis, with the objective to ensure the right balance between adequate resources to professionally manage the fund and a reasonable cost structure for the fund.

The same applies to decisions on an extension of the fund's lifetime if, after the initially agreed lifetime, the fund is not fully divested. Typically, investors have to consent to an extension of the fund duration. This is also the right moment for reviewing the fee structure and adjusting it to the actual resource requirements to fully divest the fund.

Equalisation premia

Fundraising typically takes place in several closings, because the management team can often not raise enough capital in a short period of time. However, the investment activity of the fund usually starts with the first closing. Investments are made and expenses incurred between first and subsequent closings. The equalisation payment's objective is to put all investors on an equal footing as if they all had participated in the first closing. In paying the equalisation amount, subsequent investors acquire a share in the portfolio built up since the first closing. Typically, only cash realisations prior to a subsequent closing are not redistributed among subsequent investors as they did not participate in funding them. For the rest, subsequent closings typically assume cost valuation for existing investments. To avoid valuation issues to the benefit or detriment of first-closing investors, the time span between first and final closing should not be too long and generally should not exceed a period of 12 months.

The equalisation amount is typically increased by a premium to compensate first-closing investors for the cost of capital incurred on drawdowns between the first and subsequent closings. In the fund's legal documentation, this premium is normally expressed as a percentage of interest to be paid by new investors on the equalisation amount. Unless the fund needs the equalisation amount contributed by new investors for investments or covering costs, such amounts are normally distributed to the investors of previous closings. The equalisation premium, compensating investors for their cost of capital incurred in advancing capital on behalf of subsequent investors should, in any case, be distributed to the investors from previous closings. Typically, equalisation premia are based on variable short-term interbank rates plus a mark-up of 2 per cent or 3 per cent.

Hurdle return – does it matter?

There is a lively discussion in the industry on whether or not there should be a hurdle return for private equity investors. The hurdle return is a preferred return for investors in the fund to be paid prior to the manager getting its carried interest. Concepts of this preferred return are often referred to as cost of capital for investors having provided the funding for the fund's investment activity on which the manager earns its profit share.

The US market often rejects the hurdle return as the concept of risk in private equity is not easily compatible with cost-of-capital reasoning. The US view is that the investor simply puts money at risk and shares the returns on it with a qualified manager, and that is it. The European market more systematically uses the concept of a hurdle return and the associated cost-of-capital reasoning. The argument goes that as long as the fund manager has not covered the cost of capital for the investors, investors do not have a real profit; hence there is nothing to share with the management team. Alternatively, the hurdle return could be seen as the threshold above which the performance of a fund is perceived to be a success. Returning the capital may be a relatively good performance from some vintage years but does not necessarily meet the return objectives of an investor and hence should not be rewarded through carried interest.

Catch-up mechanism

Ultimately, the discussion will be a philosophical one rather than one of substance if the distribution cascade of profit splits between investors and fund managers foresees a catch-up on the preferred return distributed to the investors, once the full hurdle amount is paid. The catch-up mechanism typically foresees that, once the preferred return on a fund has been paid to investors, any subsequent distributions are allocated to the GP on a priority basis until the GP has received an amount equal to its profit share in the amount distributed to LPs as preferred return. Private equity funds have a return objective that is well beyond the normal levels of hurdle returns, which are typically in the range of 5 per cent to 10 per cent. Hence, if a fund delivers a private equity risk-like return, the difference for the fund manager is only a matter of timing in receiving its profit share of the preferred return through the catch-up mechanism.

Two concepts

There are two main concepts of structuring the preferred return, being either a percentage on capital drawn from investors (equal to a compound interest on net outstanding capital contributions or calculated as an IRR on all cash flows from and to investors), or as a fixed percentage on top of commitment or total drawdowns (for example, hurdle is a multiple of 1.2 of commitment or drawn capital to be returned to investors prior to paying carried interest to the GP). Both structures are found in the market and it is *a priori* difficult to assess which one has a greater benefit for either the manager or the investors. From an administrative point of view, a fixed multiple appears easier to handle but many investors favour the interest-based approach to add a time component to the level of preferred return.

Alignment of interest and the sharing of profits

Carried interest is the industry term for the participation of a management team in the performance of a fund. Private equity is high risk with equally high profit prospects. To take advantage of an investment opportunity, investors need to attract the most qualified people and ensure full alignment of interest. Therefore, they agree to reserve a substantial share of profits from their investment for a performance-related element in the management team's remuneration package. The share of carried interest varies from fund to fund but has settled at around 20 per cent of total profits made by the fund. Whilst industry players seem to agree on a performance-linked element in the fund manager's remuneration and the acceptable level, there is still discussion on what performance is actually used to measure any entitlement of carried interest for a management team.

Next to the divorce clauses allowing the management agreement between a fund and a GP to be terminated, as discussed in Chapter 9 in the section 'Removal clauses for cause and without cause', the clauses on carried interest are among the most discussed and fiercely negotiated in the closing of a private equity fund. The reasons for such a discussion are manifold and driven by the evolution of industry practice that greatly depends on the local market. Generally the US market is more GP-friendly than the European or Asian one. People sometimes refer to the United States as a manager market and Europe as an investor market, although best market practices are converging.

The important issue in discussions between the LPs and GPs is the definition of the performance that entitles a management team to carried interest. The US market had rather extreme mechanisms in the past where carried interest was even distributed on a deal-by-deal basis. The GPs were entitled to carried interest on profits realised on a specific deal no matter what the investment performance was on the remaining part of the portfolio. It is not difficult to anticipate that such carry structure can easily earn a GP carried interest while LPs are actually losing money on their investment.

As such scenarios increasingly materialised, the definition of performance became more relevant. Whilst there is still discussion on the concept and the justification of a preferred return for LPs (the hurdle return, discussed above), the consensus on the performance definition is now on the overall fund basis. LPs should receive back their entire capital prior to any carry entitlement of the GP. This is a straightforward definition with only one major disadvantage: the entire capital provided by LPs is, in the extreme case, only known at the end of a fund's lifetime, considering that most fund structures foresee the right for the GP to draw funds from LPs also in the divestment period of a fund for the purpose of follow-on financings and to cover the fund's operating cost.

As a result, the question of what should trigger the distribution of carried interest to the GP continues to have many answers. Again, it is the US market that has the most GP-friendly carry schemes which only in the aftermath of the collapse of the technology markets have seen some alignment with more LP-friendly trends in Europe.

The sections below describe the two dominant models of carried interest distribution, based on either repayment of full contributed capital or repayment of full committed capital (full-fund-back concept). They discuss their main advantages, from a GP and an LP perspective, as well as mitigating features that can be introduced for each of them.

Carry distribution based on repayment of full contributed capital

The concept based on repayment of full contributed capital foresees the GP receiving a share of profit once the LPs have been returned the entire amount of contributed capital as of the time of distribution. In funds where LPs are entitled to a preferred return, the threshold to be met by the GP prior to being entitled to carried interest also typically includes the full payment of any accrued hurdle return to LPs. Once this threshold of amounts distributed to the LPs is met, the GP participates in the profit split at the agreed percentage level, for example, 20 per cent. Obviously, in the case where the distribution cascade foresees a catch-up for the GP on any preferred return distributed to the LPs, the GP would receive such catch-up distribution on a priority basis prior to distribution of profits along the split agreed between the LPs and the GP.

Carry distribution and the J-curve of a fund

The above-described mechanism works fine as long as there is no abnormal pattern in the proceeds of a fund available for distribution. Under normal circumstances, the cash flow patterns of a fund follow a J-curve and show a negative balance of net cash flows for LPs well beyond the point where all commitments of LPs have been drawn. In which case there is not really an issue as the GP would return the entire drawn capital (which in such scenario coincides with the committed capital) prior to being entitled to carried interest distributions.

The situation becomes less clear when cash flow patterns of a fund deviate substantially from the typical J-curve profile. This may for instance be in the situation of an exceptionally profitable exit ('homerun') very early in the fund's life, or when substantial reserves are kept by the GP beyond the end of the investment period that are drawn very late in the fund's life or not drawn at all. In these situations, the GP may receive carried interest while LPs still have substantial amounts of their committed capital at risk. And, especially in the case of an early homerun, there may be a significant risk that the GP receives carried interest despite a negative overall performance of the fund. In the US market such cases happened in great numbers during the technology hype in the late 1990s. Similar cases have been observed in Europe, although to a lesser extent.

Protection for limited partners in the case of overdistributions

There are many mechanisms that try to cater for the risk of overdistributions to the GP, the most common ones being clawback obligations and escrow accounts.

Clawback mechanisms

Clawback obligations are an undertaking of the GP to return to the LPs, generally at liquidation of the fund, any amounts received in excess of the contractually agreed profit split (overdistribution). Whilst such undertaking serves the purpose of rebalancing the amounts distributed to the GP and LPs along the agreed profit split, it does not deal with the predominant concern of LPs with respect to overdistributions to the GP: the credit risk.

It is certainly desirable to have an undertaking of the GP to return any overdistributions to the LPs. But important questions remain.

- What is such undertaking worth in reality?
- Who can guarantee that the GP has not spent the amounts distributed as unearned carried interest?
- What comfort can be derived from a clawback undertaking given by a GP that, in most cases, is a special purpose vehicle with no meaningful financial resources?
- Will a GP that is removed for cause or without cause honour such undertaking?
- What if the GP does not?
- What sense does it make to win a case against a GP if the GP will most certainly file for bankruptcy before even a first instance ruling is obtained?

All these questions are rarely thought of at the launch of a fund, but may become very relevant if things do take a course other than that anticipated.

Again, the US market has been very creative in coming up with solutions to the concerns raised above: GPs have proposed partial bank guarantees for carry amounts paid out to them, and carried interest partners of the GP have offered personal security such as mortgage or pledge over securities. Historically, the enforceability of such security has been cumbersome, and the credit risk cover provided for LPs on overdistributions to the GP has been incomplete. The US market after the technology hype has even seen GPs that have waived their entitlement to the regular management fee to repay overdistributions to LPs. It can easily be imagined what impact such measure may have on the performance of a fund if the cash flows that were meant to cover the resource requirements for the day-to-day management of a fund are spent on repaying clawback obligations of the GP.

Escrow accounts

Another concept that has emerged to deal with the issue of credit risk on overdistributions is the mechanism of escrow accounts. It foresees that as long as LPs have part of their committed capital at risk the GP agrees to pay part or all of the carry distributions into an escrow account to guarantee the repayment of potential overdistributions. Any partial allocation of carry payments to an escrow account certainly mitigates some of the concerns raised above but does not solve them. It is up to the individual investors to judge what level of risk they are willing to take on this issue.

A full allocation of carry payments to an escrow account would provide solid comfort as to the credit risk that LPs are taking on carry overdistributions to the GP. But such allocation is inefficient for both the GP and the LP. The GP cannot access the capital in the escrow account, which means that the money parked in this account does not make any difference to the management team. On the other hand, money available for distribution that is not distributed to LPs, but kept in an escrow account, is like unused liquidity held by the fund partnership. It is money that is not put to work and ultimately has a negative impact on the fund's net IRR. In cases where LPs are entitled to a preferred return, escrow accounts may even destroy value for the GP since the preferred return accruing on capital drawn from LPs is typically significantly higher than the return achieved on amounts deposited in an escrow account. Thus, the ultimate merits of an escrow mechanism are doubtful, but it will be around for many more years as one of the tools to bridge the gap between the GP and the LP views on allocation of economic interest earned on a fund.

LPs agreeing to an escrow mechanism to cover credit risk on carry distributions to the GP should, however, look for adequate protection in the case of bankruptcy of the GP. There is no point in having carried interest parked in an escrow account to secure potential claims of LPs, if the GP eventually, and often on purpose, goes into liquidation and the escrow account suddenly is part of the bankrupt's estate. Mechanisms to ensure that escrow accounts are actually bankruptcy-remote include the pledge of the account to the partnership or holding of the account as a partnership asset. The form through which such protection is achieved depends on the jurisdiction governing the GP and the fund, and should be evaluated with the help of competent legal advice.

Carry distribution based on repayment of full committed capital (full-fund-back concept)

Concerns regarding overdistributions produced a different concept of carry distribution, especially in the European markets. It requires that not only is all drawn capital returned to

LPs prior to any carry distribution to the GP, but that an amount equivalent to the full committed capital (plus preferred return on drawn capital where applicable) has to be paid to LPs prior to any carry entitlement of the GP. This mechanism known as the full-fund-back concept has become a market standard in Europe since 2000, an evolution that was certainly reinforced by the difficult fundraising environment since the collapse of the technology markets. The advantage of this mechanism for LPs is obvious: there is no scenario of overdistributions of carried interest to the GP and hence there is no credit risk for LPs on the GP.

While the full-fund-back solves most of the questions discussed in the context of carry distribution based on repayment of drawn capital, it creates a series of other issues: if no overdistributions to the GP are possible under the full-fund-back concept, there may be scenarios of overdistributions to the LPs in the case where the GP does not draw down the full amount of committed capital over the life of the fund. So what then? Surprisingly, LPs in the first instance offered to the GPs what they had refused to accept as a measure to cope with overdistributions to the GP: a clawback mechanism on the LPs. They argued, and this reasoning certainly deserves some credit, that it is more affordable for GPs to accept credit risk on LPs, most of which are institutional investors with significant financial resources, than the other way round. LPs also offered the GP the possibility to rebalance the distributions along the agreed split at every distribution that is made by the partnership in order to reduce the likelihood of a clawback scenario on LPs.

Avoiding the clawback on LPs

Mechanisms of continuous rebalancing of distributions between LPs and the GP definitely help avoid clawback situations for the GP on its LPs. Nevertheless, there are scenarios where there remains a residual risk of overdistributions to the LPs. This gave rise to a more creative mechanism, which avoids clawback obligations and provides adequate protection to the GP in the case of overdistributions to LPs.

Considering that overdistributions to LPs can only occur in the case where not all the commitments of LPs to a fund are drawn and can only amount to a portion of the undrawn commitments, the GP may simply make an equalisation drawdown from the undrawn commitments to balance the distributions to the LPs and the GP according to the agreed profit split. This avoids any clawback obligation on either side. In addition, this practice gives the GP the comfort to draw from an existing commitment from the LPs which implies that a non-compliance with such equalisation drawdown would make such an LP immediately a defaulting LP with all the consequences defined for such a scenario. This is a much more powerful protection against credit risk than any clawback obligation can possibly offer, and more importantly, is immediately enforceable by virtue of the fund's legal documentation.

This chapter has discussed in detail the dominant concepts of carry distribution schemes with which LPs are typically confronted in the current market environment. The mechanism of carry distribution is typically one of the most intensively discussed topics in setting up a partnership. Some GPs argue that this mechanism is crucial for their motivation and that overly restrictive rules on the distribution of carry to the GP may make carry for the GP so remote that it actually disincentivises the GP. A heated discussion on this argument repeats itself over and over in the due diligence process, even with GP teams that claim to be the most successful in their market segment.

Many GPs are happy to start lively debate on the impact of distribution schemes and their effect on incentive structures. But most will keep rather silent when asked to present historical instances of where a distribution of carried interest on a full-fund-back basis would have made a difference to them. Most cannot because such funds are very rare, and those who can have to admit that such funds' cash flow pattern relied on one or two lucky winners rather than a systematic pattern of success. Some may turn the question back to the investor and ask why, if at the end of the day there are hardly any cases where it makes a difference, LPs have a preference for the full-fund-back concept? The answer is simple: the relevance of such a clause comes up if things between LPs and GP go wrong. Such clauses matter when LPs have to remove a GP, when GP teams fall apart or when fundraising for a successor fund fails. In these scenarios, the last thing a LP would like to deal with is the question of how to recover overpaid money from the GP.

Chapter 9

The legal documentation – how to protect your investment

The legal structure

Defining the legal structure for a private equity fund is among the most complex challenges investors and fund managers face when setting up a private equity fund. Tax constraints, legal constraints and regulatory requirements result in many aspects to consider in defining the optimal fund structure. The main challenge is that tax, legal and regulatory constraints may vary from investor to investor and defining the optimal structure of a fund concept may mean looking for a single solution in a multi-dimensional matrix. It is impossible to discuss all these issues within the scope of this book. Also, the regulatory framework, tax rules and legal aspects change frequently so that good advice today may be a recipe for disaster tomorrow. Hence, this book only touches briefly on the key aspects that drive the structuring of a private equity fund from the limited partners' (LPs') perspective, but does not go into the details of individual structures and their tax implications.

In terms of structuring a fund, a management team has several objectives in putting together an attractive fund structure for investors. Generally, the most important topics for a fund structure are limited liability for LPs, tax transparency, compliance with regulatory constraints and cost efficiency.

Limited liability for limited partners

Investors want limited liability up to the amount of their investment. This is crucial for investors to manage their own resources and to steer the exposure they take to private equity. The maximum exposure is vital for LPs' liquidity planning, asset allocation and portfolio management. Beyond that, LPs need to make sure that they are not exposed to unquantifiable risks.

In certain jurisdictions such as the United Kingdom or Delaware in the United States, the status of an LP is tied to a set of requirements and notably prevents the LP from influencing the day-to-day management of a fund. Non-compliance with such requirements would expose the LP to the risk of being qualified as a general partner (GP) and hence be liable with all its assets for the partnership's liabilities. Management teams acting as a GP for a fund face this same risk but limit it by introducing a limited liability company as intermediary holding for their GP's interest. For LPs, doing the same every time they invest in a fund would create an enormous administrative burden and additional costs. Hence, LPs need to look at a jurisdiction that gives them the necessary influence on a fund structure to adequately protect their investment without, however, jeopardising their limited liability status.

Tax transparency

The structure should also be tax-exempt or tax-transparent in order to avoid double taxation. Fund investors should not be worse off than if they had invested directly in the underlying portfolio companies. Taxes should not be levied at the level of the fund. The objective is to provide a structure where any profit generated at the level of the fund is only subject to taxation once it is allocated to an investor (tax transparency). Taxation at the level of the fund would unavoidably result in double taxation for investors and make a private equity investment pointless from a commercial return perspective. Defining tax-transparent structures is no trivial topic as various tax regimes with mutually exclusive tax effects on investors may make it impossible to gather all investors within the same investment vehicle.

Regulatory constraints

Regulatory constraints may also force investors to invest through special structures or only in vehicles that comply with certain standards. Some pension funds are, for instance, only allowed to invest in their own country; others may only invest in vehicles where they can hold transferable investment certificates. Others may need to opt out of certain investments that the fund may make in certain sectors, geographic areas or market segments. Sometimes the regulatory restrictions in the marketing of a specific structure may destroy the benefits identified at the level of investors' tax treatment. Under certain legislation, certain fund structures have specific requirements as to the qualification of investors. Investors may need to obtain approval from a financial markets supervisory body to be allowed to invest. This administrative and regulatory burden may cancel out the benefit of favourable tax treatment.

Cost efficiency

In all these cases, it may be necessary to create parallel structures where several vehicles suitable for certain investors co-exist and co-invest according to a parallel investment agreement. Such structures have some complexity as governance issues are normally tied to a specific investment vehicle. Hence, it requires additional legal structuring to create a governance structure that encompasses two or more investment vehicles. Setting up parallel structures also has significant administrative costs, not only in the set-up phase but also over the entire lifetime of a fund. Audit fees are incurred for each parallel vehicle, administration and accounting for each individual vehicle adds costs, and decision-making procedures at the level of LPs become more complex and expensive. All this may induce certain investors to decline to invest on the basis that a defined structure is more expensive than the economics of a fund can afford.

Creating an industry standard

The long-term solution is to reach global agreements where tax and legal regimes between several jurisdictions are mutually recognised. Unfortunately, little progress has been made to date on creating a platform that offers these characteristics to every type of investor on a global level. For US investors, adequate structures exist under Delaware law. The Delaware LP offers full tax transparency to US investors and has established itself as a suitable platform for dealing efficiently with the regulatory constraints of US-based institutional investors. Some offshore structures have replicated these features.

In a European context, the situation is less promising. Virtually every country has created its own investment vehicle with special tax treatment, but often only applicable to domestic investors or with substantial constraints with respect to the fund's operating activities. Offshore structures for Europe are offered from various places such as the Channel Islands, but some investors feel uncomfortable with their reputation of being a tax haven. Some countries have attempted to offer structures incorporating flexibility to accommodate individual investors' needs such as the UK LP or the Luxembourg SICAR, trying to replicate the possibilities Delaware structures offer for US-based investors. EVCA is also working on a project aiming at creating an EU-wide uniform investment vehicle but it will take some more years and additional efforts at the level of the European Commission until an EU-wide investment platform with a uniform tax treatment for investors across Europe will emerge.

Pending decisive progress on that front, European investors will continue to be exposed to a wide range of structures and have to find their way through the jungle of legal and tax implications such structures have on their own investment. This is definitely a domain where investors should seek competent legal advice. Unidentified tax or legal risk could eliminate a substantial portion of the return generated by their fund investment. Where needed, parallel investment vehicles for the same fund are a possible solution, and GPs, eager to collect money for their fund, proactively provide assistance to investors in identifying the optimal vehicle for their needs.

Protective clauses

Once the choice of a suitable legal structure is made, the challenge is to capture the commercial agreement between LPs and the GP in an unambiguous way, leaving as little room as possible for interpretation. The documentation of the partnership is in most cases drafted by the legal advisers of the GP. Hence, and despite the fact that investors ultimately pay the bill for the GP's lawyers through the set-up expense charged to the fund, LPs cannot be sure to get objective advice from the GP's advisers. LPs, therefore, should have the contractual agreements reviewed by their own legal advisers who preferably should have explicit experience in the private equity industry.

Next to the commercial terms of a partnership, it is of great importance that LPs also introduce adequate clauses in the agreements to protect their interest in situations where things get severely off track. These protective clauses are crucial for LPs to cut their downside risk. In many cases, these clauses reduce the degree of freedom to operate for the GP. This is why GPs normally will not proactively promote these protective clauses in the contractual agreements or will only do so for clauses that have become a commonly accepted market standard. But even for clauses that are part of generally accepted best market practice, GPs, with the help of their legal advisers, seek to reduce the impact of such clauses on their business to an extent that makes the individual clauses sometimes meaningless for the LPs.

The following sections discuss the main protective clauses that LPs should look for in the contractual agreements with a GP and comment on the main arguments of GPs and LPs in defending their point of view.

Key-man clauses

The experience and skills of the key individuals of a management team is the most important factor for success, or failure, that an LP can actively control. Ensuring the availability of adequate management resources is therefore a main concern for LPs. During due diligence LPs have identified those team members that are vital for successfully implementing the fund's investment strategy. However, life is not predictable and disagreement in the team, illness, accidents or simply changes in a team member's professional ambitions may lead to the unexpected departure of key individuals. In such situations, LPs need an appropriate mechanism for securing adequate and smooth replacement of lost competence in the management team. The key-man clauses in the legal documentation ensure that the key individuals are contractually tied to the fund, and their departure has direct consequences on its investment activity.

The key-man clause in the contract must capture the core team required to successfully manage the fund. Therefore, the LPs need to single out the individuals without whom they would not trust their investment to be adequately managed. This knowledge helps to structure a key-man clause that secures the minimum team to be in place. It is prudent to be rather restrictive in defining the key-man clause before the commitment is given. In any case, LPs can always soften their action upon occurrence of a key-man event when more elements are available to assess the situation. However, it is more difficult to tighten a clause when a team falls apart but the manager ignores the investors' concerns. Occurrence of a key-man event is a serious situation in a fund and should be followed by immediate action. Typically, the investment and divestment activity should be suspended with immediate effect, because the team's ability to successfully manage the fund is no longer a given. LPs should also avoid structures where the manager has six months or a year to cure a key-man event without any consequence on the investment activity of the fund: the money may be gone by the time they find a suitable replacement.

The contract should also contain measures for when the manager does not succeed in curing a key-man event within a reasonable time. The lack of a timely successful solution to the issue should trigger an escalation mechanism, which could lead to the liquidation of the fund. Otherwise, LPs run the risk of paying a management fee for a paralysed fund. However, the mechanism to cure a key-man event should not be structured in a way that gives investors an easy way out of their commitment. LPs must be aware that co-investors may try to use key-man events to reconsider their asset allocation. This cannot be the purpose of a key-man clause. Hence, the cure of a key-man event should be subject to the approval of investors but the required majorities should not allow individual investors to block a decision for reasons that might be totally unrelated to the key-man event.

Removal clauses for cause and without cause

Next to the mechanism for distributing carried interest, clauses governing the process of how a GP can be terminated are the most fiercely discussed items when defining the relationship between GPs and LPs, and there are solid reasons behind this. From the perspective of the GP, obviously as little discretion as possible should be given to the LPs to terminate the GP. GPs depend on their sole activity of managing funds and being removed from the management of a fund very likely deprives a private equity firm of vital financial resources and destroys a GP's future business prospects.

On the other hand, clauses to terminate a GP (removal clauses) are the most powerful tool LPs have to influence the development of their investments, which are of a very illiquid nature. Ultimately, removal clauses are the core element in the contractual relationship that allows LPs to cut losses on an investment if things irremediably get off track. Again, strong differences exist between US and EU market practices. The United States once again has a much more GP-friendly way of dealing with this issue, although convergence towards EU market practice is undeniable.

The following sections discuss the main aspects of removal clauses, the main reasons why they are so close to the heart of LPs, and the fears that GPs would name when looking at a potential abuse of such clauses.

Removal for cause

The removal for cause clause refers to the right of LPs to terminate the GP in the case the GP severely neglects fiduciary duties to the LP. A removal for cause, which typically requires a simple majority vote by the LPs, is always tied to clearly defined circumstances that describe misbehaviour of a GP against which the LPs are entitled to take action. Such GP misbehaviour normally includes gross negligence, fraud, wilful misconduct, material breach of contract or prosecution for an act of a criminal nature.

Whilst it may appear logical that LPs are entitled to take action against the GP in such circumstances, negotiations between GPs and LPs are, in reality, not that clear-cut. Some questions are fiercely discussed.

- When should a removal take effect?
- Who should decide what behaviour of the GP qualifies as a cause?
- Should a GP be given the possibility to cure such an event?
- What economic implications should it have in terms of termination payments, break-up cost and similar?

There may be a great deal of money tied to each of these questions, and the following elements may help the LP to understand why these questions are indeed very important issues to be dealt with.

Speed of action matters

There is no other situation in the life of a fund where the axiom 'time is money' is more relevant from the perspective of an LP than in the case where a GP needs to be removed for cause. Especially where criminal behaviour of a GP is involved, LPs cannot afford long procedures in taking action against a GP. This is why a central point of dispute is typically how a 'for cause' event is defined and by whom. GPs generally opt for a protection in the form of a court decision confirming their misbehaviour before LPs are allowed to take action. At first sight, this may seem logical and fair. However, such reasoning ignores the most important issue at stake for LPs: time. Getting a final court ruling in such circumstances may take substantial time, in certain jurisdictions even several years. By the time a decision is finally available, it may no longer be relevant, because the fund's lifetime has expired or the assets of the fund have been lost.

Arbitration on the definition of cause

Both the request of LPs for swift action and the GPs desire to have a neutral assessment of the 'for cause' event are understandable. But how can these two views be combined? To bridge the gap in the positions of GPs and LPs, lawyers have shown a great deal of creativity to come up with a compromise. They range from rather simplistic structures, such as diluting the requirement for a court ruling and substituting it with the decision of an arbitration body or a simple injunction obtained from a court, to more complex structures that seek to carefully evaluate the justified concerns on both sides and address them in specific contractual wording.

Some wordings adopted between GPs and LPs give LPs the possibility to remove the GP for cause even without specific court ruling but put them under the obligation to have their assessment of a 'for cause' event confirmed by a formal court decision. In the case where their assessment is rejected by the court, they would undertake to compensate the GP for any damage the GP may have suffered in being unjustifiably removed. Additional protection may be offered to GPs to assure them that action that may be taken against them is adequate and commensurate to the misbehaviour invoked by the LPs. This is a specific concern in the United States and other jurisdictions that are largely built on case law and where it appears easier to initiate court proceedings on alleged misbehaviour than may be the case in the code-based continental European jurisdictions.

Curing a 'for cause' event

In terms of the possibility to cure a 'for cause' event, there is room for compromise in some cases and less in others. If the GP committed systematic fraud, it is hard to see how such behaviour could be cured. On the other hand, if there has been a material breach of contract that can objectively be remedied, there will be no reason why a GP should not be given the opportunity to do so. Also, especially US GPs frequently come up with the argument that the GPs should not be held liable for misconduct of individual staff members of the GP or third parties acting on behalf of the GP. In most EU jurisdictions, this issue is addressed by prevailing laws, ruling that a party to a contract is responsible for delivering on its contractual obligations. This implies full responsibility for any act undertaken or omitted in fulfilling such contractual obligation even if the execution of such obligations is delegated to a third party. LPs are well advised to seek the same level of responsibility of a GP in their contractual agreements as any other formula erodes the protection of such clauses to an extent of making them meaningless.

Two basic principles

Whatever formula LPs and GPs eventually agree on, LPs should always keep in mind two principles.

1. Removal clauses should be negotiated upfront, that is, before a commitment is entered and not when the situation arises. Experience shows that it is virtually impossible to reach a sensible solution between the parties once the communication lines have been reduced to exchange of legal language between lawyers.
2. LPs should also make sure that agreed clauses are simple and quick in their application.

Economic implications for the GP

Once the definition of a 'for cause' event and the sequence of action in the case of a termination event are agreed, there remains the question of economic consequences for the GP.

Whilst the EU market has a fairly uniform view requiring that GPs who are terminated for cause are deprived of all their carry rights and do not get any compensation for termination, the US market has seen clauses granting GPs in the case of a termination event full carry rights and rather generous compensation for break-up cost, to an extent that the economic motivation for an LP to use such termination clauses becomes questionable. However, some

US-based GPs, especially those raising funds and investing also in Europe, have accepted the evolution in market practice in this area and now propose formulae more in line with European market standards.

Removal without cause

On the basis of the above discussion of removal for cause clauses, it is not surprising that views on the LPs' right to terminate the GP without cause are even more controversial. The removal without cause gives LPs, typically through a 75 per cent qualified majority vote, the right to terminate the GP, without having to specify any reason.

The rationale behind a removal without cause

The background of this meanwhile fairly established LP right is the fact that even a GP who formally does not misbehave, with respect to its fiduciary duties towards LPs, may still represent an unbearable risk for LPs. Such scenarios arise, for instance, if a GP does not make any investment during several years of the investment period, arguing that the deals available in the market are not of sufficient quality. Since a GP generally has no obligation to invest under the LP agreement (such obligation would be unhealthy since it would create investment pressure and potentially lead to investments in poor quality deals), a GP using such an argument could easily hide an inadequate access to reasonable deal flow. Another example is an extremely poor investment performance, maybe paired with supporting virtually dead investments through further injection of cash, possibly in order to keep the management fee at a higher level. Creativity shows no limits in finding similar scenarios, where the GP technically acts perfectly in line with the obligations under the contractual agreements and still destroys value for the LPs in a rather predictable way.

As such scenarios cannot all be defined *ex ante*, the right for LPs to remove the GP without cause exists. In fact, the term 'removal without cause' is in some ways misleading: it is actually not a right LPs would exercise without cause but rather a right for scenarios that cannot be described in a sufficiently precise and exhaustive manner. In other words, there is always a reason for LPs to trigger a removal without cause but this cause cannot be specified at the time when the contracts are signed.

Desire for protection versus risk of abuse

Naturally, there is ample room for argument. GPs may argue that this clause opens the door for LPs to remove the GP to get more favourable terms from a successor GP, to remove the GP to save carried interest and so on. Conceptually, these arguments are certainly justified, but they do neglect a series of aspects that actually makes it rather difficult for LPs to act in bad faith.

1. GPs should be aware that the worst-case scenario for an LP is to have to find a new GP for a running fund. There have been a series of private equity firms emerging in recent years that specialise in taking over portfolios from terminated GPs. However, those specialist teams are often workout teams trying to rescue residual value from a distressed portfolio or pro-forma GPs who step in to fill the requirement of having a fund manager but effectively only administer the liquidation of a portfolio.
2. A qualified majority of 75 per cent is very difficult to reach. Every LP who has ever tried to gather a 75 per cent majority of votes under LPs knows how hard this is and that it is only achievable with a very solid and uncontroversial case.

3. Unlike the removal for cause clause, the removal without cause scenario normally offers extensive protection for the economic interest of the terminated GP. Whilst the removal for cause scenarios typically lead to loss of carry rights and give no entitlement to compensation for termination, termination of a GP without cause grants the GP a portion of the carried interest (typically under a vesting scheme agreed in the LP agreement) and break-up cost, normally six to 18 months of management fee as a lump sum payment at termination.

Ultimately, the purpose of the removal without cause clause is to allow swift action without complication through legal procedures when things go seriously wrong. The fact that economic interest is retained by the terminated GP, in the form of a vested portion of the carried interest and adequate compensation for break-up cost, should ensure that LPs only use this clause to reduce their downside and not to enhance their upside.

Vesting schemes for the GP's carried interest

In a removal event without cause, the GP should have the right to retain a fair share of the carried interest from the fund. To determine the removed GP's share in the fund's profits, the concept of vesting of carried interest is vital. It aims to offer the terminated GP a fair compensation for its contribution to the fund performance while retaining sufficient carried interest as incentive for a successor GP. Vesting schemes for carried interest are manifold and there is no real standard in the market. Some examples show a vesting of carried interest that is linked to the time the GP has spent with a fund. This concept is simple and easy to apply but has the disadvantage of not recognising a GP's relative performance in creating value for the fund. In fact, such a concept may be overly favourable for the terminated GP, assuming that GPs, if removed, are normally removed for poor performance.

Another approach values the portfolio at the time of termination of the GP and sets this value in relation to the overall value created over the lifetime of a fund. Whilst this certainly better reflects the performance element contributed by the outgoing GP, it has some drawbacks in its practical application. Valuations in private equity, unless realised, are very arbitrary and the contribution of a successor GP in realising such value needs to be properly assessed and recognised.

Yet another approach grants carry to the terminated GP on the basis of the success of investments made at the time of termination. This concept is probably the weakest since it disincentivises the successor GP to look after the deals in the portfolio at the time of takeover. Further, it does not recognise the impact of operating expense on the performance of a fund and, finally, it may lead to an obligation of the LPs to pay carried interest to the terminated GP despite the fact that the fund may not have made any profit.

General principles the LPs should look for

The clause covering the LPs' right to terminate a GP for no cause will always be the subject of controversial discussions, and the final agreement reached may depend on many factors, the discussion of which would go beyond the scope of this book. However, there are a few useful tips that LPs should take to heart when looking at this type of clause.

- LPs should insist on a removal without cause clause. The clause may be very rarely used, but is one of the most powerful tools to protect an LP's interest in a fund, when needed.

- When negotiating such a clause, LPs should insist on a vesting profile applied to the GP's carried interest. No vesting profile means that the LPs will have to pay up to give an incentive to a successor GP.
- No matter what vesting profile LPs and GP agree on, LPs should make sure that the vesting covers the investment and divestment period. Building up a portfolio may be an achievement; harvesting value from it may be an even bigger one.
- LPs should go for a simple model of vesting. Such a simple model may not be perfect and lose out on a few scenarios, but there is no use in a vesting scheme that eventually exposes GPs and LPs to endless discussions, legal procedures, external evaluation and arbitration procedures, which may last longer than the underlying fund's residual lifetime.
- LPs should agree to compensate the GP for a termination but be reasonable in defining the amounts. They should also make compensation payments conditional on orderly handover of the partnership's accounting records and other vital business documentation.

This advice may not provide a ready-made solution but may help to avoid major pitfalls. The time spent on defining what happens when things go wrong may appear wasted time when everybody is enthusiastic about making a new deal. But the effort may save a great deal of money and time when it really comes to putting a contractual framework to the test.

Defaulting investors

Next to the performance of the GP, the willingness and ability of co-investors are the second biggest uncertainty that LPs face in a fund structure. A fund's investment strategy, diversification strategy and reserve policy, to name only a few, are all aspects that are defined with respect to the availability of a defined fund size. LPs not honouring their commitments directly jeopardise the basic assumptions of a fund's investment strategy. This must be a concern for LPs and GPs alike. There is no way to effectively protect a fund against a defaulting investor under all circumstances. If a substantial part of a fund's committed capital is no longer available, this may lead to the collapse of the fund's portfolio. Against this threat, no penalty for a defaulting LP can be severe enough.

With defaulting investor events increasing in number, measures to cater for this risk have become more draconian. Today, the consensus is that penalties should be as high as the jurisdiction under which the fund is incorporated allows. Typical penalties include the following.

- *Immediate cancellation of any voting rights*. This is of particular importance when taking action against a defaulting investor. If this is not ensured, there may be situations where a defaulting investor is even entitled to vote on the sanctions that the partnership may take against such investor. In the worst case, an investor with a sufficiently big commitment may even be in a situation to block such steps by its own vote.
- *Forfeiture of any interest in the fund*. This is a very useful tool, not only does it deprive a defaulting investor immediately of its voting rights, it also ensures that a defaulting investor does not get any economic interest from its fund investment. All the contributions of a defaulting investor prior to the event of default are instantly lost.
- *No compensation (or minimum compensation allowed under applicable law) for forfeited interest*. Attention is required for such measures under certain jurisdictions that do not

allow the forfeiture of partnership interests without compensation. Hence, on such clauses, the legal opinion of a local law firm is recommended.

- *Possibility to claim additional indemnification.* Any measures taken under the previous points should not prevent the partnership from introducing additional claims against a defaulting investor for damages suffered as a result of the default of an investor in excess of the amount implied by the default on a specific drawdown.

Given the consequences a default of an investor can have on a fund, LPs should ensure that there is no discretion of the GP in taking action against such an investor. This could be dangerous for LPs if specific ties between a GP and a defaulting LP exist which may prevent the GP from taking appropriate action against such a defaulting investor, to the detriment of the fund.

As some jurisdictions under the corporate law require minimum protection rights for ousted shareholders, LPs and GPs may make the scope of possible penalties for defaulting investors a selection criterion in choosing the jurisdiction for their fund.

Chapter 10

Avoiding or managing conflict of interest

Private equity investments suffer from information deficiency. It is very difficult for limited partners (LPs) to anticipate all possible ties and links that exist between a general partner (GP) and other parties having a direct or indirect interest in the activity of the fund. Hence, the contracts must clearly segregate the roles, rights and obligations of all parties involved in a fund structure, and ensure mechanisms to disclose any conflicts of interest to all LPs. Typical relationships that involve potential conflict of interest include conflicts between various activities of the GP (management of several funds, combination of investment activity and advisory activity) or in the relationship between the GP and certain LPs, such as a sponsor having a specific tie with the GP (captive funds). But also LPs may have a conflict of interest with respect to a fund's activity, be it through a direct economic interest in a portfolio company or an involvement in competing funds.

This chapter discusses specific situations of conflict of interest, resulting risks and suggestions on how such risks can be mitigated through adequate structuring of the fund's legal documentation.

Conflicts of interest within the scope of a general partner

In making private equity investments, investors seek to secure that the GPs focus their business efforts on the management of a fund's activities. This is not always obvious. GPs are usually involved at least in the management of previous funds which need to be divested while the GP is already investing with a new fund. These overlapping investment cycles secure an ongoing business for the GP.

However, overlapping activities across various funds, and also other activities that GPs may seek to pursue parallel to the investment management activity may be against the interest of LPs. For example, some GPs propose consulting their portfolio companies on a fee basis and argue that they enhance value creation through their service. What GPs forget is that they are asking to be paid twice for the same service: creating value in portfolio companies is what LPs ask GPs to do, and they compensate them with a management fee and a share in the fund's profits. If the GP seeks to sell the same service once more to the portfolio companies, a conflict of interest easily arises. Assuming the portfolio company is not doing well but provides plenty of consulting work for the GP, the GP may have an incentive to invest in such a business not because of the return potential for the fund and its LPs, but rather to keep the revenue stream from its consultancy business turned on.

But even within its own activity, a GP might have conflicting business objectives. Frequently GPs, especially in the early-stage segment, propose newly raised funds to be able to participate in follow-on financing rounds of portfolio companies from previous funds managed by the same GP. This situation can create disastrous scenarios of conflict of interest as a GP needs to make a trade-off between value creation in two different investment vehicles with very likely two different groups of LPs. In the fund that is already invested in a portfolio company, creating value means going for the highest achievable valuation, and in the fund that is about to make a new investment, value creation means achieving the lowest possible valuation. This dilemma will be difficult to solve for the GP especially if its own interest also plays a role in defining its approach: shifting value from one fund to the other may have an impact on the carried interest perspective of the GP in the previous fund or it simply may make the previous fund look better in the context of an ongoing fundraising.

Potential conflicts of interest are so manifold in the activity of a GP that it is virtually impossible to enumerate them all. But investors can follow a series of sound principles that make conflict of interest transparent, or mitigate or eliminate it by measures that remove the economic interest of the GP on one side of the equation. The following sections describe a series of measures that LPs can take to avoid or manage conflict of interest within a private equity fund structure.

Exclusivity clauses

An exclusivity clause should bind the GP to devote all business time to the investment management activity. Any carve-out from this obligation should be clearly defined up front, approved by the LPs and the time spent disclosed on a regular basis. There should be no raising of a new fund until the current fund has been nearly fully invested. The level is typically at 75 per cent of committed capital invested or committed to portfolio investments. Further, the LPs should insist on full fee offset for any income from portfolio companies. The GP may believe that charging such a fee to the portfolio companies stresses the value the GP brings to an investee, and may therefore be a useful educative measure for the management of the portfolio company. But the LPs should offset such fee income against the management fee they claim from a fund.

Overlapping investment activities

The LPs should ensure that the GP allocates sufficient time to each investment. Therefore, they must evaluate the workload for the GP on its overall investment activity and assess it against the resources of the GP. Generally, a rule of maximum five investments per senior investment professional appears sound. Anything beyond five becomes a challenge. This rule varies somewhat with the stage: for buyout deals the major value-added offered by a GP may be setting up the financial structure of the deal, while in venture capital-type investments value creation is spread over a long period of time from investment until exit. In this respect, a check is necessary on whether the expansion plans of the GP, in terms of additional staffing, are able to handle future activity. For small funds it may be useful to define milestones that need to be reached as investment activity expands. For example, these milestones could require the GP to maintain a certain maximum ratio of investments per senior investment professional, and to have new senior investment professionals approved by the LPs to ensure appropriate quality. Non-compliance would lead to a suspension of the investment activity of the fund and trigger a similar process as the occurrence of a key-man event.

Cross-over investments

A significant source of conflict of interest arises from two investments in the same portfolio company from two different funds, but managed by the same GP. These so-called cross-over investments should be avoided as much as possible. Typically, the LP agreement stipulates that the GP is not allowed to invest in any portfolio company that is already funded through another fund managed by the same GP. If this is not possible, and the LPs are happy to go along with such a potentially ambiguous investment strategy, mitigating measures should be agreed that make the valuation setting for an investment in such a company transparent.

Ideally, a substantial investment from a qualified and independent third-party investor, who has no other economic interest in the target company and sets the price, should accompany any cross-over investment. This is also the requirement of EVCA in its valuation guidelines to recognise a subsequent financing round as a basis for revaluing a portfolio company. However, LPs need to recognise that giving GPs the liberty to make cross-over investments may turn their fund into an annex fund of the previous fund managed by the GP. LPs who invested in both funds may not get exposure to a wider range of portfolio companies but may end up doubling their exposure to portfolio companies from previous funds.

Side or annex funds

Cross-over investments between funds managed by the same GP are a closely related topic to the issue of side funds or annex funds. They were a topic of great interest after the decline of the booming technology markets of the late 1990s, when exit prospects for portfolio companies were scarce. GPs needed to carry through their portfolio investments longer than initially expected and more importantly longer than anticipated in the reserve policy for the fund. As a result, GPs in individual funds experienced a real liquidity squeeze, which put them in a situation of allowing portfolio companies go into insolvency or asking their LPs to come up with further commitments to support the fund. LPs faced a real dilemma. They first needed to assess whether the GP had a real business case for preserving value in an existing portfolio company, or whether the GPs just looked to extend the oxygen for themselves in the absence of any hope of raising a follow-on fund or carrying on their current investment activity.

Even if the LPs can assume a commercial case for putting up more money, the question still remains of how to structure this process so as to avoid conflict of interest as much as possible. By far the easiest way, if technically feasible, is for the GP to recycle exit proceeds from portfolio companies and to reinvest them into other companies that need further funding. This option treats all investors equally, and maintains the incentive structure and economic interest of the GP within the original fund. However, recyclable amounts might not be sufficient or available, or no sufficient majority for this new strategy may exist among LPs. In this case, the creation of an annex fund or side fund may be the only option: investors in the original or main fund have to commit sufficient resources to eliminate the liquidity squeeze for the portfolio of the main fund.

Mitigating conflict of interest with side funds

The drawback of side funds is that conflict of interest will become unavoidable if not all investors of the main fund are able or willing to commit to the side fund. In that case, only mitigating measures, that may or may not prove to be sufficient in practice to manage conflict of interest, can be of help.

Structures mitigating conflict of interest will depend on a case-by-case assessment. However, a few general sound principles are as follows.

- LPs should make sure that the GP's interest stays with the main fund. No management fee should be earned on the side fund.
- Carried interest should be reduced for the side fund and linked to a performance trigger in the main fund. In no instance should carry in the side fund be paid before the main fund has returned its capital.
- If residual amounts are available for investment in the main fund, LPs should require a clear allocation of what is invested first. If GPs have the discretion to use funding from either the main fund or the side fund, they may be tempted to put the winners in the side fund (cherry picking) to create an impressive performance on the side fund rather than recovering losses made on the main fund. Generally, the main fund should be invested first before the side fund is used to keep the value in the main fund wherever possible.
- A body of investors for the main fund and the side fund should be in place to monitor the GP's approach to value setting for such investments and to render shifting of value between the main fund and the side fund more difficult.

Still, the need for a side fund always ends up as an unsatisfactory situation for some LPs. And even if deemed useful in some circumstances, the need for a side fund is still the result of sub-optimal investment management performance by the GP in the first place due to poor liquidity and reserve planning at a portfolio level.

Conflicts of interest involving limited partners

Conflict of interest situations are not limited to the GP's activities. LPs are often involved in conflict of interest situations themselves. This is particularly true in structures where LPs are substantially involved in the operational management of a fund. Some LPs sponsor a GP's fundraising. They allow their name to be used as a marketing instrument during fundraising, provide contacts to potential investors and often commit, up front, a sizeable amount to the fund to be raised. In return, sponsors often demand to be involved in the ownership structure of the GP (captive funds), in the decision-making process of the fund and also in the profit share allocated to the GP in the form of the carried interest. Sponsored and captive fund structures are complex for LPs as it is not always easy to differentiate the interest of the sponsor from the interest of the fund.

Depending on the structure, the independent assessment of investment opportunities by the GP may be at stake and the GP may be economically or formally dependent on the sponsor. Such a dependency may lead to situations where the interest of the sponsor comes first and the interest of the fund second. This is particularly the case where the core activity of the sponsor is overlapping with the fund's activities such as, for example, a banking institution or consultancy firm sponsoring the fund. It is unreasonable to assume that such a sponsor will stay neutral in the investment decision process on a portfolio company if the sponsor has a loan exposure on top of the equity exposure, or if its merger and acquisition division wants to land a mandate for a specific portfolio company, and so on.

Again, it is pointless to try to enumerate all possible cases of conflicts of interest that can emerge from such a link between a sponsor and the GP, but careful structuring of the corporate governance set-up of a fund may mitigate some of the risks involved.

Best market practice corporate governance

Generally, there is only one single tool that can mitigate such conflict of interest and this is best market practice in corporate governance. This implies a clear segregation of roles from all parties involved in a fund structure, and involves the following elements.

- Above all, it is vital to secure the independence of the management team both economically and in its operating activities while running the fund. If an LP makes a due diligence on an investment proposal, what matters are the individual people that run the fund, not the name of the sponsor.
- Hence, the management team should have control of the investment process and full liberty in deciding what to invest in, what services to purchase to create maximum value, when and to whom to sell investments and so on.
- The management fee paid by the fund should go to the team, and not to the sponsor. It should cover the operating expense of the fund, and not be a revenue source for the sponsor.
- The participation of a sponsor in the management company of the GP should not create any economic interest.
- The sponsor should not be able to decide on the recruitment and disposal of team members of the GP. This should be the privilege of the LPs.
- It may also be useful to assess the influence a sponsor can have with respect to questions pertinent to the relationship between LPs and the GP. For example, a sponsor, in the context of a decision to terminate the GP, may not have a fully unbiased view. Any economic interest the sponsor may have retained in the management company of the GP may as much influence the sponsor's decision as the reputational risk associated with the termination of a GP that has ties with the sponsor.

Limited partners' involvement in the management of the fund

What applies to possible influence the sponsor has and the detrimental effect this can have on a fund applies also to the influence of LPs in the investment decision process. In some markets there are still cases where funds have an investment committee with the major LPs participating in the investment decision process and voting. They thus decide on investments, exits and on investment policy issues of the fund. These practices are mostly seen in markets with a strong club behaviour of local investors who are perfectly fine with such structures as the personal and business ties between their institutions are sufficiently strong to control any negative effects from such a set-up. Examples of such structures can still be found, on a large scale, in the Scandinavian market, in the south European markets and small markets with almost exclusively domestic investors.

The level of comfort for international investors without ties to the local market may be significantly less. Ultimately, in order to get comfort such investors would not (only) have to make their due diligence on the management team of the GP but (also) on the institutions co-investing in the fund and their representatives on the investment committee. This is a rather unsatisfactory situation, because many things can happen to institutional investors over the lifetime of a fund: some enter private equity, others leave the asset class, mergers occur, asset allocation changes, ownership changes and economic difficulties may influence the ability to honour commitments. Accepting structures where LPs take part in the operational management of the fund implies accepting being exposed to all of these issues.

Limited partners' place in the corporate governance of a fund

To give investors a formal platform of dialogue with the GP, fund structures typically foresee an investors' committee or advisory board in which the largest investors of a fund have a seat and vote. This body should not influence the day-to-day operations of a fund[1] but should act as a kind of control body to the GP. Investors' committees or advisory boards typically review, on a regular basis, the fund's investment activity, the valuation methodologies used for portfolio companies, the investment strategy applied by the GP and also decide on conflict of interest issues the GP may be exposed to in certain situations. Obviously, an investors' committee can only take an independent view on such issues if its members are also independent from the GP.

Investing in private equity is risky enough. LPs are well advised to keep any risk packed on top of the intrinsic risk of the asset class to the lowest possible level. Insisting on sound corporate governance structures is a key aspect to this and time spent on getting this right may save a lot of money and time at a later stage. European markets can learn a great deal from the US market, which traditionally fiercely defends the independence of the management team in running a fund's operations. Despite the fact that US market standards in some instances appear to be overly favourable to the GP, this is an aspect where European players should take heart, and they have actually started to do so. Segregating the roles between GPs, sponsors and LPs has also become more important in Europe, partially because fundraising from local sources proved insufficient for a sustainable private equity market in any country. This enforces the internationalisation of the private equity industry which, in turn, results in convergence of market terms. From this convergence, all players in the industry will eventually benefit.

---

1 In some jurisdictions, such influence on the day-to-day activity of a fund could even be dangerous for an LP with respect to its limited liability status. Certain partnership laws consider that limited partners intervening in the operational management of the partnership are de facto GPs and are hence fully liable with all their assets for any liability of the partnership. In certain jurisdictions, influence of investors on the day-to-day management of a fund may also have an adverse impact on the tax status of the fund.

Chapter 11

Investment monitoring and crisis management

Warning signs in monitoring a fund investment

Monitoring of individual investments is not about enhancing the upside. This duty has been 'outsourced' to the general partners (GPs). It is the GP's skill-set to identify investment opportunities with superior return potential and to add value to its portfolio companies that is decisive for a fund to deliver a risk commensurate to return. There is very little limited partners (LPs) can do to help a GP in this task. But this does not mean that LPs should not follow their investments once they have made a commitment to the fund. While it may indeed be difficult for LPs to influence the upside of a fund investment's return, there is a lot LPs can do to enhance the overall performance of their investments by taking swift action to prevent losses if investments get off track. LPs' objective in monitoring investments is thus about detecting early warning signs for things going wrong.

Unfortunately, there is no checklist to help LPs in this process. Experience in dealing with problem cases in fund investments shows that each case has its own characteristics and requires its own solution. Being close to their investments is the only tool for LPs to form their own view. Exchanging views with other LPs, comparing the behaviour of different GPs in the market, and looking at industry reports are ways for LPs to stay informed on developments in the industry and to find reference points to benchmark the funds in which they have invested. Professional investors such as funds of funds benefit from a detailed view on a representative sample of the market through their own portfolio and exploiting the information at a portfolio level provides valuable reference points to assess individual investments.

No matter how big an investor's portfolio of fund investments, the tracking of specific parameters in a fund's investment activity is useful to detect early warning signs. Examples are outlined below.

Unusually slow or fast investment pace

The investment pace of a GP in building up a portfolio for a fund is an important although ambiguous parameter to watch. An exceptionally slow investment pace can be a sign of poor deal flow, unrealistic price expectations of the GP in bidding for portfolio companies, disagreement within the team on the investment strategy or individual investment proposals, or simply poor market conditions. On the other hand, a fast investment pace is not necessarily a sign of a successful team. Its reason may be a wealthy deal flow, but could as well indicate a lack of diligence in executing deals, overstated valuations when investing in portfolio companies, or investee-friendly terms and conditions at the expense of adequate downside protection for the fund.

Particular attention to a fast investment pace should be given when investing in the second fund of a team that has a promising but unrealised first fund. Often such teams are in a rush to invest their second fund to be able to raise funds again before the investment performance of their first fund becomes more tangible. This is a particular risk since failing to raise a third fund on the basis of their unrealised track record deprives them of the necessary resources to stay in the market. They will have to work on their unrealised portfolios for several years without being able to take on new investments and hence lose their deal-sourcing network over time. A team that over a longer period of time has no resources to invest is bound to disappear. Although there is no right or wrong investment pace, it is useful to watch the speed of deploying capital and challenge the GP on any unusual features of its investment pattern.

Quality of reporting

Another valuable source of information is the regular reporting of a GP, or more precisely the consistency in reporting. Elements that should give rise to concern are changes in the valuation methods, poor or contradicting information on the progress of portfolio companies and poor or little justification for follow-on financing provided to portfolio companies. Reporting in private equity has unfortunately a considerable time lag. Reports contain information that, depending on the reporting interval, is between two and eight months old. Hence, statements made in regular reports by the GP always need to be read in the light of subsequent events that have taken place since the reporting date. Professional GPs will introduce material events after the reporting date into their report, similar to the disclosure of significant post-closing date events in the financial statements of public companies.

General partner's transparency on valuation

A very useful tool to test the transparency of a GP, with respect to the state of a fund's portfolio, is to assess how conservative a GP is in valuing its portfolio. Professional LPs with a bigger portfolio of fund investments have a wider view and often can see the performance of individual companies through the eyes of several GPs. It is rather amazing to see how one and the same valuation guideline can sometimes be interpreted differently by various GPs. Generally, consistency in the valuation methodology matters more than the absolute value reported on a portfolio company.

There is no objective value for an investee company as there is no transparent market providing a fair market price, except possible third-party transactions. But the valuation reported by the GP can indicate how the portfolio company performs compared with the anticipated performance at the time of investment. Therefore, LPs should insist on this view being reflected in the GP's reporting rather than the GP's anticipated exit value. A clear reason for LPs to worry are cases where portfolio companies go into bankruptcy, but no warnings through value adjustments have been provided in the preceding reports to investors. There is nothing worse for an LP than to learn about required value adjustments on its investment out of newspapers. Apart from losing money on each investee that fails, LPs have to question what the real value of the remaining portfolio companies is or how many virtual bankruptcy cases are still hidden behind overstated valuations.

Lost investments

LPs should always investigate the reasons why portfolio companies were lost along the investment cycle of a fund. Just as during the due diligence process when the track record of a team is assessed, unsuccessful investments provide valuable information as to weaknesses within the skill-set of a team, systematic mistakes or flaws in an investment strategy.

Reserve policy in early-stage funds

In early-stage venture capital funds, one important element to watch is the reserve policy of a fund against the cash reach of the individual portfolio companies. Too little reserves to defend an early-stage portfolio in subsequent financing rounds can have a devastating effect on a venture capital fund, despite the fact that the portfolio companies all pursue brilliant business ideas. However, putting out seeds without having the money to pay for the harvest will not deliver tangible returns.

Stability of the management team

Other elements to watch are the fluctuations of investment professionals within the management team. The top layer of the team has been captured by the key-man clause but also the fluctuation of staff in the second layer of the team is a valuable source of information. A high fluctuation at this level should be investigated to learn about the reason for the departure of individuals. Have they left because they lost faith in the success of the fund? Have they been badly incentivised? If possible, LPs should try to get answers to these questions from both the senior partners and the people who left the team.

Decreasing commitment of co-investors

Danger for the investment of an LP does not only come from a potentially poor performance of the GP. The decreasing commitment from or defaulting LPs are also a great threat to the success of a fund. Penalties for defaulting investors have been discussed but they only deal with the consequences for the defaulting LP and cannot counter the effects of a defaulting investor on the fund's performance. Liquidity reserves or the portfolio diversification strategy are just two examples of adverse effects a fund can experience due to defaulting investors. It is therefore vital to detect decreasing commitment from other investors early on to take timely action. LPs should be aware that GPs are not always very proactive in communicating issues with individual LPs in a fund to the other investors, be it because they fear similar reactions from other LPs or because a defaulting investor has identified a major problem with the GP's performance and has decided that the cheapest way to get out of a potentially loss-making investment is to default on the future capital calls.

Again, there is little science behind detecting upcoming difficulties in a specific fund investment and the information to be explored does not always lead to clear-cut suggestions for action. LPs should be aware that even if there are no signs for worry this does not necessarily mean that there is no reason to worry. Being close to the investments, a solid network with other LPs and a sound level of mistrust in assessing the value of any information are useful principles in this industry. As an LP's portfolio grows, making optimal use of the wealth of information that can be derived from an aggregated view on all its investments can provide valuable insights for benchmarking the performance of GPs against each other. Part III describes measures that are useful to assess the development of individual funds.

What if everything goes wrong? – How to react in a crisis

Unfortunately, no LP can get it right all the time and fund investments go off track at times. Prevention prevails over treatment. Well set out clauses in the contracts and detecting early warning signs are crucial. That is why a substantial part of this book is dedicated not only to preventing mistakes in the first place, but also to the tools for when things go wrong. If warning signs become apparent, the LPs should always try to sort out the issues with the existing GP. Such a solution is nearly always the quickest, most efficient and cheapest solution. There may be empirical evidence that GPs withhold critical information from LPs if bad news is to be reported. However, once LPs are aware of a problem, GPs tend to be cooperative, even if only because of a lack of choice. In the long run, no GP can resist a majority of its LPs. Staying in business for a GP means winning and keeping the support of its LPs. However, at times, situations become incurable and go beyond the scope of what can be sorted out in an amicable solution. In such circumstances, systematic consultation among the LPs is required to take concerted action.

GPs under pressure have a natural instinct to protect their own interests. They are aware that their biggest advantage over the LPs is the lack of communication between LPs. GPs seek to engage LPs in bilateral discussions, pretend that they have agreement from all the other LPs, and that only the one LP's consent is missing. When the single LP has agreed, the GPs move on to the next, saying that this LP has just agreed and so on. An LP should define a desired line of action and try to find allies among the LPs to create critical mass. Once two or three LPs have teamed up, either a GP's attitude on the issue changes dramatically and readiness to cooperate on solution-finding improves drastically or the situation escalates to a hostile confrontation between the GP and LPs. In which case, it is even more important to have a commonly shared approach by the LPs. If an LP has a too small stake in a fund to launch action, the LP should contact the LPs represented at the advisory board or investors committee. They do have a fiduciary duty to represent all investors and not just their institutions, and typically listen to a smaller LP's concern.

If the situation escalates to the point that the GP needs to be removed, fast action is the best way to protect the LPs' interest. This is especially true if LPs feel that their assets are at risk. There are specialised firms dealing with removal scenarios providing interim management for distressed funds for as long as needed to agree among the LPs on the future of the fund. In defining the future activity of the fund, LPs should think about securing existing value first. This process usually requires the lead role of one major LP investor to gather other investors to secure required majorities for decisions to be taken. Then, the LPs need to find an interim manager. Pending the identification of a new team, investors have to decide what to do with the fund: continue investment activity, unwind, sell in a secondary or phase it out? The choice depends on the size of the portfolio at the time of removal of a manager and the intrinsic value of investments made.

Coming to the conclusion that a GP needs to be removed is among the most unpleasant experiences an LP can have in investing in private equity. However, at times it is unavoidable.

Unavoidable for protecting an LP's assets, and unavoidable also to keep the industry players aware of the fact that professional behaviour is at the core of this industry's foundations, which are needed to make this asset class viable as a whole and sustainable in the long term.

Part III

Managing a portfolio of private equity fund investments

Chapter 12

The challenges of portfolio and risk management in private equity

Goals and tasks of portfolio management in private equity

The portfolio manager's goals

The ultimate goal of portfolio management is to implement a long-term investment programme, that is, to stick to a chosen asset allocation and set of investment guidelines. By investing in private equity, the investor expects an additional return, but understands that this return comes at the price of higher risk. It is therefore the portfolio manager's duty to keep the portfolio within defined boundaries of risk. To do so portfolio management needs to monitor and forecast the portfolio and propose corrective measures to the investment policy over time.

However, in reality, these statements are far easier said than done. Even a public fund manager faces obstacles due to transaction costs, market jumps or investment constraints. The challenge to the private equity portfolio manager is even greater as a portfolio of private equity fund investments can easily diverge from the originally intended asset allocation, and the illiquidity hinders a quick and low-cost rebalancing. An unbalanced portfolio is therefore the norm rather than the exception. Nevertheless, the portfolio manager must keep as much as possible to implementing the long-term investment programme, which also means reducing diversifiable risks and managing undiversifiable risks. Moreover, fund investors face short-term challenges in liquidity planning as they need to meet drawdown calls with great uncertainty in their amount and timing, or reinvest distributions. This reduced predictability on the timing of capital calls by and distributions from funds add additional challenges to portfolio management.

Pragmatically speaking, the portfolio manager of a fund investor searches for answers to a number of questions.

- How to plan liquidity for a portfolio with commitments to several funds?
- How to assess the value of their unrealised investments?
- How to measure performance of a portfolio?
- How to project future returns?
- What conclusion to draw for future investments?
- How to diversify across stages, sectors and regions?

These questions cannot be answered by looking only at individual deals, and mostly involve quantitative risk management tools. The portfolio managers need an aggregated view across the entire portfolio, standardised and comparable data from individual investments, and industry-wide benchmarks. Thus, they take a global view on the portfolio of fund investments, as opposed to the local view of the investment manager who only handles a few fund investments and interacts directly with the fund management team. The portfolio manager typically knows less about a specific deal, but a lot about the overall portfolio. However, a global view on the past and current portfolio is not enough. Portfolio and risk management systems also need to improve forecasting, and try to identify systematic patterns that can serve to plan future investment activity. Based on the monitoring and forecasting, portfolio management allows for drawing conclusions on how best to steer the portfolio to attain a long-term return objective for a given risk level.

The portfolio manager's tasks

There is no unique list or classification of portfolio management tasks. Every private equity fund investor has different needs and capacity to implement the tasks. A pension fund that holds a private equity allocation as part of a bigger portfolio has a different focus than a specialist fund of funds. The most common tasks are as follows.

- *Information gathering*. The portfolio manager needs to decide which information to gather and how to place its own portfolio in a more global context by benchmarking the entire portfolio and sub-portfolios to trends and performance data obtained from external sources. Due to the opaque nature of private equity, this is an important task. Further, a well-structured database and interface should provide timely access to aggregated views and analysis of the portfolio, and is crucial for efficient portfolio management.
- *Market watch*. Portfolio managers should be aware of the current market developments, and how they could affect the portfolio. Following market trends is not always the best choice in private equity but in order for investors to position themselves with respect to market trends, they first need to know and understand them.
- *Portfolio monitoring*. The portfolio manager should be well informed about the past and current state of the portfolio, mostly using aggregated portfolio measures: total drawdowns, total net asset value (NAV), total exposure to sectors, stages, geographic areas and individual teams, average lifetime, performance on an overall and sub-portfolio basis, and diversification measures such as the exposure across different vintage years, regions or sectors.
- *Cash flow modelling*. Modelling future cash flows is crucial to portfolio forecasting, which inputs to portfolio steering. Portfolio managers need to evaluate and decide on the different possible modelling approaches. They need to understand a model's assumptions, reliability, that is, margin of model error, and validity, if possible.
- *Portfolio forecasting*. Forecasting the future portfolio is vital to understanding short-term and long-term uncertainties. Such uncertainties are reflected in risk numbers such as probability of missing a target, expected and unexpected loss, exposure, and more. Forecasting the future cash flows is also essential for: striking the balance between liquidity planning, that is, to have the appropriate amount of cash reserves to cover for liquidity squeezes, and overcommitment to maximise capital allocation in private equity activities (where future distributions cover future drawdowns); hedging currency risks; scenario analysis; and stress testing the cash flow models.
- *Portfolio steering*. Using the research, market information, and the outputs of portfolio monitoring and forecasting, the portfolio manager suggests how best to steer the portfolio: to manage the uncertainties of future events; to keep to a set allocation target; to achieve a better return, for example, exploiting market trends; to reduce unsystematic risk with

more diversification; and to reduce cash flow volatility. Active portfolio management is very difficult, and only secondary purchases, or choosing new suitable fund investments, can rebalance a portfolio, apart from costly secondary sales.

Identifying and reducing the risks of private equity fund investments

The concept of risk has several definitions. Here, risk is the uncertainty of future events, and not the possibility of a loss. Uncertainties in the short-term or long-term future can cause severe problems to the unwary investor, for example, under-allocation of capital resulting in an inefficient use of resources, over-allocation with the risk of facing a liquidity squeeze, or an unbalanced poorly diversified portfolio. A portfolio manager should therefore be aware of all types of risks that drive the uncertainty of future cash flows. Diversifiable risks need to be eliminated as much as possible by appropriate portfolio steering, and undiversifiable risks need to be quantified and precautionary action taken.

The uncertainty of the future fund cash flows mostly arises from the uncertain outcome of the 10 to 30 underlying direct company investments, that is, the uncertainty in the amount and the timing of the payment of the purchase cost and sales proceeds. There are many factors influencing these amounts and timings, and the unknown future behaviour of these factors creates the uncertainty. The uncertainties arising from some factors can cancel each other out because they affect the different direct investments in different ways, but others cannot such as liquidity or valuation risk, which are fundamental properties of the private equity market affecting all investments in the same way. The next section lists the most important drivers of risk.

Undiversifiable risks

Liquidity risk

Liquidity risk is an unavoidable risk, because low liquidity arises from fundamental properties of private equity such as long holding period, infrequent valuations and transfer restrictions. The low liquidity of the private equity market means that if unforeseen circumstances require fund investors to exit a fund before maturity, there are no guarantees that they will be able to do so quickly or at fair value. Such situations may, for instance, arise if investors are not able to comply with capital calls of a fund due to a liquidity squeeze, or if they are forced to sell the investment because of changes in legal or regulatory restrictions. The illiquid nature of private equity creates additional opportunity costs as investors need to hold liquidity reserves in low-return liquid assets in order to avoid being exposed to situations where they are forced to sell an investment.

Valuation risk

Valuation risk is an undiversifiable risk, because the difficulty in valuing an investment is a fundamental property of the private equity market. The future of an underlying company is fundamentally uncertain due to the many influencing external factors, such as the strength of the economy, new inventions or new market trends. Valuation risk is even amplified by the illiquidity of investments, because there are no market participants who constantly value the portfolio in the way that market participants agree on a market price in public markets.

Fund managers report the NAV of their own portfolio, which may expose them to a conflict of interest, as they might be tempted to keep valuations artificially high until they have completed their next fundraising.[1] The valuation of their portfolio companies depends also on the level of the stock market, because prices paid in the financing round of a portfolio company depend on the fund managers' perception of an exit price which, in turn, is influenced by the stock market. Thus, it is possible that the NAV of a portfolio is high due to a booming stock market, but this valuation is useless, because the companies may only be sold later when the prices have come down.

Diversifiable risks

Stage risk

Stage risk is the uncertainty of the future performance of the various stages of private equity. Every stage's performance is differently affected by factors such as interest rates or sector performance. Exhibit 12.1 shows that in the US market in the 1980s, buyout funds performed better, and in the 1990s venture capital funds performed better. Thus, US venture capital and buyout do not have similar performances for each vintage year. The performance of buyout funds is, for example, influenced more by changing interest rate levels, whereas the success of venture capital funds depends crucially on technology advances.

Manager risk

Manager risk is the uncertainty surrounding the quality of the fund manager and strategy, which affects the performance. The selection of a good team is the most important and controllable task fund investors have, but creates the uncertainty of whether they have made the right choice. Each manager has very specific risks. They have access to different deals, have non-overlapping portfolios, different skill-sets, act in different environments and according to different strategies. The bigger the portfolio of fund investments, the more managers and the more the uncertainty of their average quality reduces through diversification effects. Extreme cases of manager risk can be eliminated with thorough due diligence before investment by identifying and avoiding insufficiently skilled managers (see Part II).

Exhibit 12.1

Fund performance depends on stage: US early-stage venture capital versus buyout, 1983–98

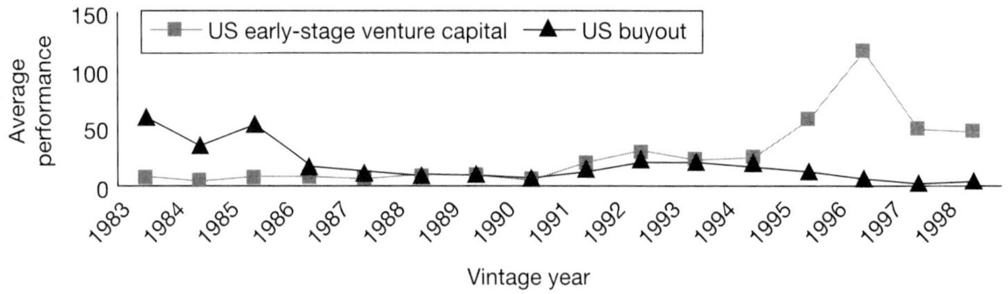

Source: VentureXpert data.

Industry sector risk

This is the uncertainty of the future performance of an industry sector. For example, in certain times the biotechnology sector might be booming, but the telecommunications sector stagnating. Two sectors rarely behave in synchrony. Sector risk reduces by investing in a generalist fund, that is, a fund that invests in different sectors, or by investing in several specialist funds of different sectors.

Geographic risk

The geographic (or region or country risk) is the uncertainty of the future evolution of the region-specific factors such as the local economic, tax or political environment. It also includes the risk of insufficient protection of private ownership under certain legislation, enforceability of protective rights for investors and issues of currency transfer and conversion. Exhibit 12.2 shows the average performance of US and European buyout funds for each vintage year. A portfolio with both US and European funds would be more stable as they do not move in total synchrony and many positive and negative events tend to balance out. For example, they have different performances in the mid-1980s and the mid- to late 1990s. Finally, an investor who invests in different regions might invest in funds working in different currencies, and has an exposure to currency risk.

Vintage year risk

Vintage year risk is the uncertainty of the future economic environment that funds face when starting in a given vintage year, that is, the first year of the fund's existence. The timing of a fund plays an important role, and is beyond the manager's influence. Theoretically, a fund manager should start investing during a deep recession when the entry prices are low and competitors are few and low on cash, and exit in a booming stock market with many trade buyers with cash. However, timing the market is very difficult to do, if not impossible. Exhibit 12.3 illustrates how the average performance varies with vintage year, with peaks around 1980 and the late 1990s. It is important to note that, even though investing in various vintage years reduces vintage year risk, cash flows from different vintage years occurring in the same year are affected by the general environment at the same time, for example, in a recession distributions from funds of all vintage years dry up but so will drawdowns.

Exhibit 12.2

Fund performance depends on the region: US versus European buyout, 1984–98

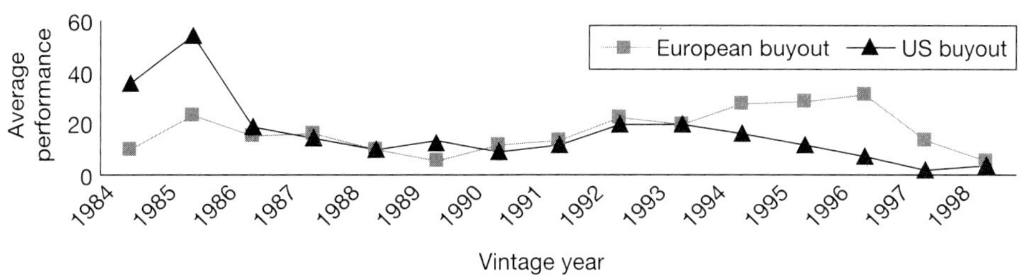

Source: VentureXpert data.

Exhibit 12.3

Different fund performance per vintage year for private equity worldwide, 1969–97

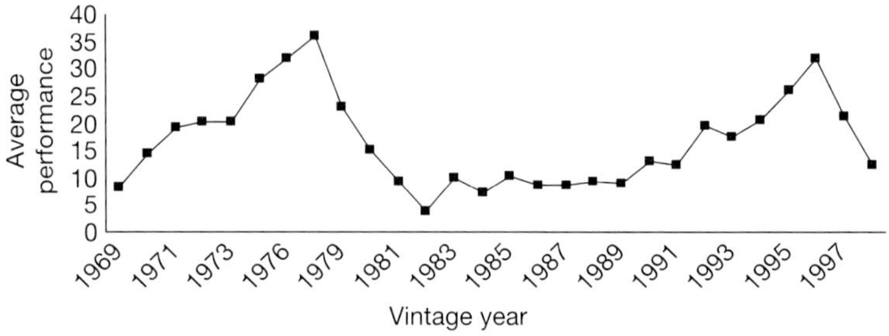

Source: VentureXpert data.

Reducing diversifiable risks

Funds are not 100 per cent correlated, that is, the performances of two funds are to some degree independent of each other. Thus, when one fund performs well, the other might perform badly and the average performance is mixed. Were they 100 per cent correlated, both funds would either perform well or badly and the average performance would be more extreme. The moderate correlation arises because funds have different teams with different skill-sets to manage them, have non-overlapping portfolios, act in different environments and according to different strategies. Therefore, the more funds a portfolio has, the more the extreme performances are balancing out. But this explanation is incomplete, because another diversification comes from the lower correlation between different vintage years, stages, sectors and regions, and the more funds there are in the portfolio the more likely they come from different vintage years, stages, sectors and regions.

Example of diversification by vintage year

Exhibit 12.4 shows the effect of having several vintage years in a portfolio of funds for a sample of European venture capital funds up to 2000.[2] In the simulation used, an algorithm generates thousands of portfolios containing the same number of historical funds across one, two, three, four or five consecutive years by randomly picking the funds from an historical dataset. For each of the five cases, the algorithm computes the average portfolio performance and the standard deviation of the sample of thousands of portfolios. The original risk is the standard deviation of generated portfolios of historical funds from one vintage year. In this specific example, the original risk decreases by 20 per cent for portfolios spread across five consecutive vintage years.[4]

Example of diversification by number of funds

Exhibit 12.5 shows the effect of an increasing number of funds in a portfolio, for a sample of European venture capital funds up to 2000.[3] Again, an algorithm generates thousands of portfolios containing a specified number of funds by randomly picking funds from an historical dataset. For all portfolios of a given number of funds, the algorithm computes the average portfolio performance and the standard deviation. The original risk is the stan-

Exhibit 12.4

Diversifying by vintage year decreases risk

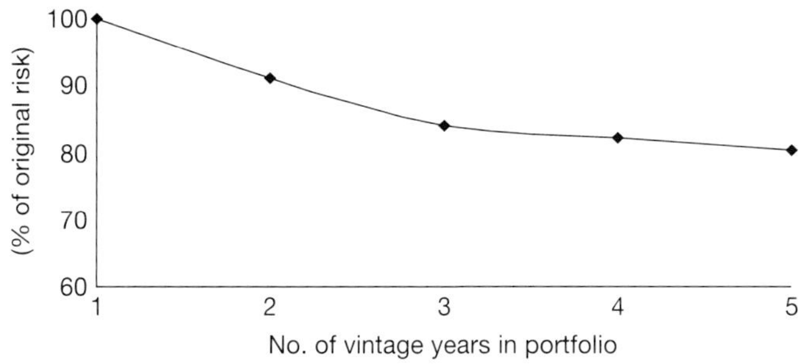

Source: Weidig using VentureXpert data from European venture capital funds up to 2000.

Exhibit 12.5

Decrease of risk with increasing number of funds

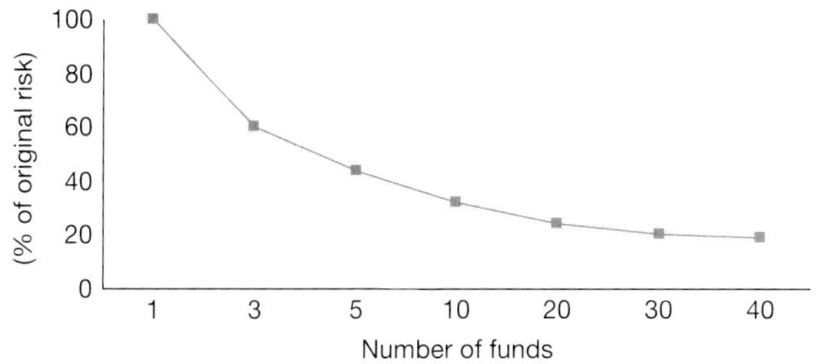

Source: Weidig using VentureXpert data from European venture capital funds up to 2000.

dard deviation of generated portfolios containing one historical fund. The original risk decreases by 80 per cent for a portfolio of 40 funds. In this specific example, the diversification effect is significant for the first 10 funds with a reduction of 70 per cent, and does not change noticeably after 30 funds.[4] It is important to remember that fees and costs are important and change the dynamics. For example, the costs per fund might decrease or increase more than linearly with the number of funds, and after a portfolio has reached a certain number of funds, the diversification effect does not compensate for higher costs.

Quantitative risk management in private equity

Reluctance towards the use of quantitative risk management practices

The different types of risk make an investor's life difficult. Quantitative risk management like cash flow modelling and portfolio optimisation management can make the investor's world more predictable and quantify the degree of unpredictability. Quantitative risk management provides recommendations on how to reduce diversifiable risks, and how to manage undiversifiable risks of a portfolio. It is an integral and well-established part of managing any portfolio of publicly traded products.[5] A generation of traders, academics and rocket scientists have taken up the challenge and developed quantitative frameworks to approach these issues in a consistent way without neglecting the importance of human input and judgement. Risk management is therefore both a science and an art.

In the past, the private equity industry has mostly focused on qualitative risk management in the sense of team selection and due diligence, as described in Part II. Investors thereby reduced their downside risk effectively. However, they seem reluctant to embrace the idea of quantitative risk management, including cash flow modelling. Quantitative risk - management is not easily adaptable to private equity, which is a people's business. There are no market prices, liquidity or reliable long-term data. All three aspects are core assumptions or inputs of standard risk management techniques. Further, private equity used to play only a very small or no part in many institutional investors' asset allocation. Thus, there was no need for a structured quantitative approach to portfolio management, and rules of thumb seemed to suffice. Fund investors were also not overly concerned about risks and liquidity issues, and looked for the highest possible return rather than the best risk-adjusted one. Finally, active portfolio management is costly and difficult to do. So what good is quantitative risk management?

Trend towards more quantitative risk management

The industry is changing its mind as more institutional investors invest more and demand the same high standards of risk management across their entire portfolio. Many investors have lived through the rough periods of the collapse of the internet boom, and were made painfully aware of the need to understand and manage the risks of private equity. This realisation is gaining momentum as the industry is issuing more complicated products such as bonds from a securitised portfolio, which requires accurate cash flow modelling to rate them. Thus on the one hand, the investors are incorporating quantitative risk management into their investment process, and on the other hand rating agencies and investment banks work on cash flow modelling for ratings.[6]

So why has quantitative risk management become necessary? It costs money to set up the infrastructure and recruit the professionals. To justify this cost, benefits from quantitative risk management need to be tangible. The reduction of cash flow volatility is one example of saving money, because less money goes into liquidity reserves in low-return liquid investments to cover for liquidity squeezes. The rules of thumb have not been working very well, and make it impossible to have an efficient over-commitment strategy, that is, to deploy the full amount allocated to private equity in investments.

For example, a rule of thumb says that an over-commitment of 150 per cent gives 100 per cent of capital invested in private equity. However, Frei and Studer (2004) simulate two portfolio set-ups with historical data using this rule and show that the one gives an under-allocation and the other one an over-allocation (see Chapter 16, 'Steering the portfolio'). They argue that their examples disprove the rule of thumb's usefulness, and warn that investors should not rely on it. They refer to quantitative models as the only way forward. Further, risk management is a 'nice thing to have' and can be an effective marketing tool, because it sends a positive and reassuring signal to the trustees of institutional investors.

Applying risk management techniques to private equity

Implementation challenges

Developing and implementing quantitative risk management is really pioneering work for a private equity investor. The private equity market is not an efficient market with market prices, high liquidity, and cheap and equal access to information. There is some literature and public discussion, but no established wisdom. The lack of transparency and free unbiased historical data is also a major impediment to academic research, which would be openly available. Thus, many investors are left on their own to develop and run portfolio management systems without reliance on established practices, many reality checks and easy access to information. They also face the need to recruit quantitatively minded people to undertake this challenge in a traditionally soft-skills environment.

Moreover, implementing quantitative risk management is not only about models and risk management tools, but also about changing the culture of debate.[7] Risk management also concerns the interaction between the different professionals within the investor's organisation, namely the investment managers, the portfolio managers and the senior managers. Implementing risk management means initiating change to provide a better framework for constructive debate that values the input from all parties involved. Combining the information obtained from individual investments with trends derived from a portfolio assessment enhances the quality of investment decisions and improves investment performance.

Challenges to modelling

In terms of modelling, private equity is challenging. First, there are no market prices for the direct investments in portfolio companies, that is, no market player guarantees to buy or sell the direct investment at a certain price and at a certain time. Second, the NAVs reported by the fund managers, which could act as a price, are often not a fair value of all underlying portfolio companies, especially for venture capital. The valuation rules are rather peculiar: the value is initially set at cost and only changes infrequently with a write-down by the fund manager or when a third-party transaction occurs. The observed volatility of valuation needed for the model is therefore artificially low. Correlations are even more problematic. Third, there is no easy access to historical data to estimate the input parameters. Another issue is the testability of the models. Funds are long-term investments and the market does not quickly punish modelling errors. The danger of ivory tower modelling arises.

Active portfolio management is difficult

Private equity also severely restricts active portfolio management, because it is not easy and sometimes impossible to sell a fund investment. Either the contracts do not allow it, or the fund investors have to sell at a high discount on the fair value of a portfolio, but not necessarily the NAV. This discount is the consequence of the low liquidity and lies at the heart of the difficulty-to-adapt standard risk management practices to private equity. The investor only has control by choosing the appropriate funds before the investment decision or by buying a limited partnership interest in a secondary transaction. Hence, the investors cannot sell if they expect the value of the fund to decline or if they face imminent drawdown calls from another fund. This fact also renders the widely used public market concept of value-at-risk and its input to capital allocation and risk budgeting useless, as this concept assumes a liquid market.

Private equity investors also face constraints that public equity investors do not face. For example, on the stock market every market participant sees all stocks and is able to invest in all of them. In private equity, the fund investor does not necessarily know of all the management teams in fundraising, and cannot freely decide in which fund to invest. The investor is also constrained in the sense that co-investors also need to invest alongside an investor to establish a fund. For example, an investor cannot invest in really bad teams, because no other investor would co-invest. Vice versa, the investor might have found the perfect fund manager, but no other investor shares this view.

---

1 See, for example, Kaneyuki (2003).

2 See also Weidig, Kemmerer and Born (2004) and Weidig and Mathonet (2004).

3 Ibid.

4 Please note that the figures may change considerably for a different investment or geographical focus.

5 See Dowd (1998) for an introduction to risk management.

6 The work by the rating agencies such as Fitch ratings and Standard & Poor's is freely available, but some is behind a proprietary wall. The literature on quantitative risk management practices is small: Frei and Studer (2004) and Atkins and Giannini (2004).

7 Dowd (1998) lists good risk management practice: see therein the annex to Chapter 12.

Chapter 13

Information for risk and portfolio management

The information deficiency in private equity

Sharing of information and the agency problem

In private equity, information is not equally shared between the market players unlike in public markets. In these markets there is cheap access to all historical market prices from a variety of data providers. Listed companies also need to disclose financial information, which is quickly absorbed in the market through analysts. This is simply not the case for private equity. There is a lack of information in this industry. It is impossible to collect data as easily as in public markets. Fund managers are not required to disclose their cash flows, and hence their performance, or any other information. Even their investors often only get condensed information in the form of quarterly reports. Fund managers reporting on business development or the cash flows of their fund feel almost as uncomfortable as a private person disclosing current and savings account transactions to anyone, even family members. Every fund manager claims to have a unique approach, which is its source of competitive advantage. Any additional information to a competitor on the valuation of their portfolio companies, their cash range, their performance versus the business plan could potentially expose the fund to loss of bargaining power or the risk of legal pursuit and destroy the return prospects for its investors.

Another issue to watch is the agency problem. Many market players face conflict of interest, and it is often not in their interest to reduce the gap and asynchrony of information. Information superiority is critical for success. Market leaders often prefer an opaque market with an air of mystery rather than a transparent market with a clear view on whether and how they make their money. Fund managers are often only really forthcoming in sharing information in times where they can derive a direct benefit for themselves such as during fundraising or when they are forced to retain support from fund investors.

Pressure to disclose

Fund investors have been under public and legal pressure from the media and some unions to disclose the performance of their fund investments. For example, pension funds regularly report the value and performance of their publicly quoted investments, but do not reveal the performance of the private equity funds or the underlying companies in which these funds have invested. The debate is about the right of the public and contributors to pension funds and endowments to know the performance of their investment versus the right of the pension funds' managers to keep investment information confidential for the sake of their business. The fund managers do not want to reveal the valuation of their portfolio and especially their valuations of each portfolio company as they are afraid that potential buyers could take advantage of this information in negotiations.

As a response to pressure, several pension and endowment funds such as CalPers, CalSTRS, Washington State, UTIMCO and the University of Michigan started to post interim performance data on their websites in 2002 and 2003.[1] Then, some of the biggest and most influential fund managers threatened to exclude these fund investors from their present funds and future fundraising. But as of 2004, CalPers, a Californian pension fund and one of the largest private equity investors, still regularly publishes on its website the investment data and performance of the private equity funds in which it invests. Disclosure of fund performance is debatable but company valuation is certainly too sensitive. Interestingly, the debate on disclosure has recently extended to the disclosure of management fees and carried interest.

Lack of information exchange standards

Sharing information is made difficult due to the lack of standards. There is no single commonly accepted global standard for information exchange and reporting in private equity. This lack of a common standard creates many obstacles for fund investors in getting information from their fund managers. Here are a few practical examples: some fund managers only send paper reports quarterly, and the information needs to be copied manually into an information storage system. Such a process is tedious. Other fund managers provide the financial information electronically in a spreadsheet, but spreadsheets are no perfect tool either, because every fund presents the information differently, and sometimes uses the same terminology to express different things.

From an investor's point of view, the attempt to impose its own reporting format is bound to fail. Each fund has several limited partners (LPs), some of which might ask for reporting with their standard. If a general partner (GP) gave in to each request, this might lead to excellence in reporting quality but not necessarily to satisfactory investment performance. Pending a better understanding among the large and leading fund investors on what information they require and in what form, there is little hope for an emergence of uniform reporting standards.

The demand for information exchange standards

Diem (2003) and Blaydon and Horvath (2002, 2003) at Tuck Business School researched the topic of information deficiency among industry players. Diem interviewed European industry players, and Tuck Business School conducted a survey of about 400 US players. The majority of LPs welcome the development of an industry-wide valuation and reporting standard, and cite improved LP reporting and greater transparency as the main benefits. Most LPs would also like to see direct electronic feeds from GP to LP to eliminate manual data entry.

The technology exists to make this flow possible, but the missing link is a set of standards for data content and format to make it work. However, less than half of the interviewed LPs are willing to participate in the process of developing valuation and reporting standards, and prefer the national associations to take a leading role. Moreover, they see challenges to developing a standard and have real differences of opinion about specific details of a standard. And, only half are aware of existing valuation and reporting proposals and standards (NVCA, BVCA or EVCA). Diem (2003) recommends the following actions: the national associations, especially the US NVCA, the European EVCA and the

British BVCA, should try to reconcile their differences. LPs should increase the cooperation with other LPs and derive common requirements. Diem's research shows the challenges ahead in defining common standards. Major improvements, if at all, are likely to be in the long term since they very much depend on intra-industry cooperation.

Developing reporting and valuation guidelines

So far, national associations have undertaken a series of initiatives to define reporting and valuation guidelines which are mostly followed by the fund managers. This is especially true for Europe. The European association (EVCA), British association (BVCA) and other European national associations were instrumental in establishing clear valuation guidelines.[2] Based on their recommendations, valuations should be prudent and applied consistently. A majority of funds follow these guidelines as many LPs, especially in Europe, request them. EVCA guidelines also require that fund managers clearly disclose methods, data and processes used for valuation.

The situation is less promising in the United States. The US association (NVCA) failed to come up with clear valuation standards in 1989, and has not tried since. This outcome still resonates in somewhat of a tip-toeing exercise around the issue, as illustrated in an extract from their website:

> The NVCA recommends that its members create, follow and communicate clearly the specific procedures and methodologies used for valuing their portfolios. These methodologies should be agreed to by the firm's investors (LPs), and conform when required to Generally Accepted Accounting Principles, recognizing that the ultimate responsibility for valuation remains with the general partner. When evaluating current valuation procedures or developing new approaches, the NVCA suggests its members include a review of the Private Equity Industry Guidelines Group (PEIGG) . . . We commend the fine efforts of PEIGG, an independent group which sought and reflected input from the NVCA and other industry stakeholders.

The PEIGG is a group of US fund investors that actively pursues a common standard. Still, the group took a considerable amount of time to come up with a consensus. Another driver of standards is CFA, formerly known as AIMR (Association of Investment Managers and Research), which issued guidelines under GIPS (Global Investment Performance Standards) that are often used in the private equity industry.

Another debate targets the review of International Accounting Standards (IAS) and their application to the private equity industry. Whilst the IAS Board seems to agree that for valuation purposes the fair value principle is a meaningful reporting standard, disagreement still appears to prevail as to the consolidation requirements for funds with respect to their portfolio companies. IAS argues that for funds holding controlling stakes in portfolio companies, the IAS consolidation requirements should apply.

Venture capital players and their associations argue that consolidated financial statements of a fund are meaningless information to all stakeholders in a private equity fund and should be avoided. EVCA demonstrated that over the lifetime of the fund the investments reported according to the consolidation mechanism required by the IAS do not reflect a true picture of the performance of the funds. On the valuation issues, industry efforts focus on refining the methods to establish an investment's fair market value. Various methods at the level of direct investments and fund investments are discussed. The outcome of these discussions will likely have some relevance for the treatment of private equity investments under New Basel Accord regulations, as the weighting applied to risk assets under the New Basel Accord criteria will be linked to the reliability of valuation methodologies used.

Overcoming the information deficiency

The importance of information management systems

A fund investor quickly loses sight of a large portfolio without a professional and structured information management system. Portfolio reviews and monitoring may take days to do. For example, assuming a portfolio of 50 funds, a fund investor every year needs to deal with 200 (50 times four quarters) quarterly NAVs, around 200 (50 times approximately four purchases/sales per year) cash flows, 500 (50 times 10) basic information items such as size and number of employees, 4,000 (50 times 20 companies times four company details) pieces of company information, and other information. This sum adds up to at least 5,000 data points! This information, plus any derived measures, need to be in a standardised electronic form, and easily available to end-users, or they cannot get a quick overview of the issue in which they are interested. For example, computing the average age of these 50 funds by going through each fund's documentation could take a day or two, but seconds or minutes if the vintage year of each fund is stored electronically.

Often, fund investors start out with a few funds, whose information is conveniently and quickly stored in spreadsheets. However, as the portfolio grows, the updating, following the data history and aggregating information becomes increasingly tedious. Even upgrades – from spreadsheets to off-the-shelf databases – only provide temporary relief, and eventually succumb to the avalanche of data. Small inconsistencies in data entry, format or storage quickly leads to enormous consistency or information synchronisation problems, analogous to a tiny leak that ultimately sinks a large ship. The complexity suddenly grows exponentially, which considerably slows down the portfolio manager's work resulting in a loss of control and overview of the portfolio. Professional databases are therefore indispensable, and need to be set up and managed by experienced IT professionals. The longer a fund investor waits, the more difficult its implementation becomes.

The quality of information

The data quality of raw and aggregated internal information, and external information should be as high as possible, or at the very least its quality should be known. It should be free of the following:

- systematic bias (eg, mistakenly only asking the best funds about their performance);
- statistical error (eg, sample size is too small to capture the whole population);
- mistakes (eg, someone enters the wrong data);
- conflict of interest (eg, the fund manager values its own portfolio);
- survival bias (eg, only successful funds raise a second fund, but would the less-successful team do as well the second time round?); and
- sales pitch (eg, during fundraising a fund only communicates positive information).

Finally, information needs to be aggregated to avoid information overload and gain oversight, but this process leads to a loss of information or quality.

Which information to trust?

Fund investors need information on many different issues such as: what fund managers are in the market, what is their absolute performance, what is their performance relative to their competitors, what are best market terms and conditions and so on. However, access to reliable information is difficult in this opaque market.

The first question is: which information can a potential investor trust? This question is not easy to answer, and relies on the judgement and experience of the professional. Investors may want to look at the conveyor of information, and ask whether that person or company has a conflict of interest. There are many possible instances of conflict of interest in private equity. For example, a fund management team does not explicitly remind the investor that their historical internal rate of return (IRR) performance in the memorandum is the gross rate, and not net of fees. Also, national associations, being a supporting network for general partners (GPs) in the first place, do not send a press release to the media and via their mailing list containing thousands of professionals telling them about research that shows underperformance of private equity, but they do when the statistics look good. Therefore, information in the market is often not reliable. Sometimes information could be plainly wrong, but very often the information is just misleading or incomplete. Investors should therefore be vigilant and combine various sources of information for a cross-check. The more independent the resources used, the higher the value of content. Sometimes the investor may have to use the raw material of information and re-compute the results from scratch. This may take time and effort but at least delivers reliable results.

Information from own funds

The investor's own funds provide a rich source of reliable information whose quality can be easily checked. The closer the fund managers are to a new fundraising round, the more eager they are to satisfy their current investors' needs and provide even more information! First, the cash flows of the funds are available, which include the amount and timing of investments, exits and fees. Second, the funds report their net asset values (NAVs) on a periodic basis, mostly quarterly, together with the valuation methodology. Third, the confidential contracts, profit split details, and basic fund information such as size, location, focus, stage and region are available. Fourth, the investment manager is in constant contact with the fund manager, and has considerable information on the track record of key team members. Fifth, the private placement memorandum (PPM) provides more qualitative description of the fund, which at the very least shows how the fund wants to market itself. Finally, the investment manager can provide the portfolio manager with vital information in personal interactions, defining and setting red flags, internal reports, rating a team based on set criteria, or operational issues.

Information from personal networks

Most valuable information comes from personal interaction. Thus, it is of utmost importance for a professional to build relationships with other professionals, and share information. A willingness on the part of a professional to share fully non-confidential information and expertise, will in the long term result in other professionals doing the same. Some might say that holding information gives a competitive advantage. This is certainly true for confidential information, but everyone understands that such information is not shared. Even for non-confidential information, this statement might be true in the short term in some situations, but the long-term benefits in sharing information outweigh this: an increased reputation, and a greater trust and eagerness of others to share information. This is especially true for LPs and their interaction with fellow LPs.

Information from private equity publications

Pre-print versions of many academic articles are freely available from the Social Science Research Network (SSRN) internet archive. The articles are published in the following academic and practitioner journals: *Journal of Private Equity*, *Journal of Alternative Investments*, *Journal of Portfolio Management* and *Journal of Finance*. Further, the bibliography of this book is a useful reference point for articles and books on various topics. There are also plenty of practitioner magazines, such as: *Red Herring*, *Tornado Insider*, *European Venture Capital Journal*, *Private Equity International*, *Buyout* and *Real Deals*.

Information from external sources

The portfolio manager should also keep up-to-date on the development of the private equity industry through various external sources. For example, the exit opportunities for private equity funds via IPO, or even trade sale, are significantly linked to the stock market. Small-cap and sector indices are good guides. Also, key industry figures, such as the number of funds raised and their investment focus, reflect the competitiveness of the market and hence investment opportunities. Information providers, such as Alt Assets, VC Experts and Thomson Venture Economics, play an important role in this opaque market, and they make their living by providing investors with quality and up-to-date information.

Some providers, such as Thomson Venture Economics, Cambridge Associates, Venture One and CMBOR database, have extensive private equity databases at a company level but also cash flow information at a fund level. These databases are the subject of the next section. The most important input for quantitative risk management is the historical and current performance and cash flow data. The historical cash flows are needed to do proper cash flow modelling. However, this kind of information is not easily available, and the own portfolio often provides a very limited sample of the total population. However, even the commercial data provider VentureXpert only reveals aggregated historical data to avoid disclosing the performance of individual funds. Nevertheless, this information can be useful for benchmarking (that is, in which quartile of its peer group is a given fund), as an index (that is, the change of the total NAVs of all funds from one period to another plus the interim cash flows) and to show historical fund performance (for example, the average IRR for all funds that ever existed).

Private equity databases

Can private equity databases overcome the information deficiency?

Private equity databases are useful to partially overcome the information deficiency problem in private equity. These data providers collect both basic and cash flow information on the funds in private equity using two approaches. Either, they ask GPs discreetly to fill out questionnaires on cash flows by promising absolute confidentiality and possibly cheaper access to their databases. Or, they take over the back office functionality of a fund investor for a discount, which allows them access to the full financial data. Of course, there are also large funds of funds that have invested in hundreds of funds and have the historical data. These methods of data collection raise significant issues such as conflict of interest, biased dataset and lack of independent verification. Another issue is that there are very few large data providers, and most investors or researchers need to rely on them without being able to verify the quality of their input data. This makes it harder to check the quality of research results and related statistics independently, and potential biases such as low coverage, systematic bias and statistical errors may remain undiscovered.

Despite these issues, the portfolio manager has absolutely no choice but to take these data with a pinch of salt. Nevertheless, it is extraordinary that virtually all analyses and academic research on private equity rely on two or three datasets, and very few researchers have actually done an extensive bias study on them. The following description of the databases is based on publicly available information. Exhibit 13.1 lists the different private equity databases.

VentureXpert (from Thomson Venture Economics)

VentureXpert is probably the largest database, with cash flows from about 2,500 funds (1,700 US funds and 800 European funds).[3] The database also includes basic information on many more funds, and underlying company investments. VentureXpert does not provide its customers access to the cash flows itself, but only aggregated cash flow measures such as average IRR or multiple. Virtually all analyst reports and academic research on funds work from this dataset, with some having direct access to the cash flows. Few reports on consistency and biases exist.[4]

First, Thomson Venture Economics collects the information mostly via questionnaire on a voluntary basis from both fund managers and fund investors, which raises some serious data collection issues. Second, VentureXpert has the cash flows of about 40 per cent of all funds where it has basic information. This creates the potential for a systematic bias, because the 60 per cent of remaining funds could have a different performance on average. There are some differences between these two groups of funds. For example, there are fewer small than mid-sized funds with cash flow data versus all funds. It is unclear

Exhibit 13.1

List of private equity databases

Name	*No. of funds (as of 2004)*	*Level*	*Access to data*
VentureXpert	2,500	Fund and company	Indirect and direct
Cambridge Associates	2,100	Fund and company	Direct
Venture One	–	Company	Indirect
Sand Hill Econometrics	–	Company	Indirect
CEPRES	264	Fund and company	Direct

Source: Authors' own.

whether this difference creates some bias, because smaller funds could have lower returns. However, funds with a low return are not less likely to report, because they agree to report before any return becomes apparent.[5]

A bias could occur when Thomson Venture Economics actively tries to complete the data retrospectively. A retrospective collection only collects data from the early funds of existing fund management firms. The bad firms are not part of the sample and therefore cannot report their bad first-time performance, because they no longer exist due to their bad performance. Third, the coverage of the whole industry is between 70 per cent and 80 per cent for recent vintage years, but the coverage is significantly lower before 1990. Fourth, the European dataset is probably less reliable and less free of bias than the US analogue. For example, 40 per cent of all European funds are from the United Kingdom, and German funds are significantly under-represented. Overall, the VentureXpert dataset is probably a reasonable representation of the private equity industry.

Cambridge Associates

The Cambridge Associates database is the second of the two largest private equity databases on funds. They have a total of 2,100[6] funds with cash flow data, and basic information on many more funds and underlying company investments. Cambridge Associates is a gatekeeper and not a professional data provider as such, and often takes over the back office functionality of fund investors, along with providing advice. This process ensures that the cash flow data is directly from financial data and not via questionnaires. On the other hand, they seem to be quite secretive, and no academic research has ever been published based on their dataset. They claim to cover about 80 per cent of all existing US funds. However, their European coverage is probably far less significant due to their late arrival to Europe.

Venture One

Venture One is a database on direct venture capital investments. Venture One has more than 17,000 financing rounds involving more than 8,000 companies, and claims to capture 98 per cent of financing rounds since 1992.[7] It records a financing round if 'it includes at least one venture capital firm with $20 million or more in assets under management.'[8] Kaplan, Sensoy and Stroemberg (2002) compared the Venture One data to a sample of 143 venture capital financings on which they had detailed information. They found that 15 per cent of rounds were omitted, and that post-money values of a financing round were more likely to be reported if the company subsequently went public. However, Gompers and Lerner (2003) claim that the missing valuations do not create a significant systematic bias.

Fund investors' portfolios

Large and well-established funds of funds have detailed cash flow information on their own fund investments, which does individually only represent a small share of the whole market. Most of these are not accessible to the public. Examples are: the CEPRES database from Venture Capital Management (VCM in Munich, Germany), with 264 funds and 6,000 financing rounds; the European Investment Fund (Luxembourg), with 200 funds from 1998 onwards; Sand Hill Econometrics (with Venture One and other sources); BVC sample collected by Hielscher and Beyer (2003), with 37 funds; and an anonymous sample used in Ljungqvist and Richardson (2003) with 73 liquidated funds.[9]

---

1 See, for example, Probitas (2003), Cumming and Walz (2004) and references in Cumming and Walz (2004).
2 See EVCA Guidelines (2001) and BVCA (2003).
3 As of 2004.
4 See Chen, Baierl and Kaplan (2002) and Weidig, Kemmerer and Born (2004).
5 Of course, some of these fund managers might stop reporting. In such cases, the fund needs to be excluded from the dataset ex post or measures need to be taken to cater for this now-known bias.
6 As of 2004.
7 Data sample from 1987 to 2000.
8 Cochrane (2005) and Peng (2001) use the dataset and look at biases.
9 This sample included funds from 1981 to 1993.

Chapter 14

Monitoring a portfolio

Portfolio measures

The importance and type of portfolio measures

The goal of portfolio monitoring is to provide a summary of the most important aspects of a portfolio. To avoid information overload, the portfolio manager needs to decide how to aggregate the portfolio information available into meaningful and useful portfolio measures. For example, the average age of the funds rather than a list of all fund ages or the total undrawn commitment instead of the list of undrawn commitment for each fund. Portfolio managers need to monitor these measures over time and get a sense of the direction in which the portfolio is going. Apart from portfolio forecasting, the judgement gained from monitoring these measures is essential for senior management to take informed decisions such as increasing liquidity reserves or not adding certain funds to a portfolio.

Three concepts are important when defining measures. First, there are three levels of aggregation possible: no aggregation, aggregation across investee companies and aggregation across fund investments. For example, the degree of country diversification could be computed using the nationality or the focus of the funds or using the country of domicile of the underlying companies. Second, information can be related to either the portfolio, the fund investment or the company investment. Each of them, that is, the portfolio, the fund investment and the company investment, can have an internal rate of return (IRR). Third, measures could be split into different types such as diversification measures, descriptive statistics of basic fund or company information, cash flow measures, valuations measures, performance measures or benchmark measures. These types focus on specific issues important to the portfolio manager such as diversification, valuation or performance. For example, the diversification measures show how diversified a portfolio is in terms of a risk factor such as geographic risk.

Measures at portfolio level

Descriptive statistics

Concerning descriptive statistics on basic fund information of the portfolio, the portfolio manager needs to ask the following questions.

- What is the number of funds in the portfolio?
- How much capital has been committed to all funds?
- In how many companies are the funds invested?
- What is the average age of the funds?
- What is the internal age of the portfolio and the average internal age?[1]

- What is the average commitment to a fund?
- What is the average share in a fund?

These statistics provide a quick and general overview of the size and maturity of the portfolio. Often, a fund investor has investment constraints such as total commitment maximum, or maximum in number of funds, and needs to check for any violation of these restrictions.

Cash flow measures

Concerning the analysis of past cash flows, the portfolio manager needs to know the following.

- How much money was paid to the funds?
- How much is it in percentage of committed capital?
- How much money could still be drawn down by funds, and how much is this in percentage of total committed capital?
- What is the current exposure of the portfolio, ie, how much money is invested in the funds?
- How much money has been paid back by the funds?

Diversification measures

Diversification measures are important to understand whether the portfolio is unbalanced and tilts towards a specific region, stage or sector. The portfolio manager should ask specific questions about the exposure to diversifiable risks.

- What is the number of funds in the portfolio?
- What is the weight of the different stages in the portfolio, at fund or company level?
- What is the weight of the different industry sectors?
- What is the weight of different vintage years?
- What is the weight of the different regions or countries?
- What is the age profile of the funds in the portfolio?
- What is the average number of companies per fund?

Valuation measures

Concerning valuation on the unrealised investments, the following questions are important.

- What is the total net asset value (NAV) of all funds?
- How does this value change if you account for valuation at cost and add a percentage such as 20 per cent to the young funds to adjust for underestimation?
- How many funds do not use standard valuation guidelines?
- How much of the total portfolio is valued at cost?

Performance measures

Finally, the portfolio manager should look at performance measures such as portfolio IRR,[2] average IRR, median IRR, capital-weighted IRR, portfolio multiple, average multiple, median multiple and capital-weighted multiple. Appropriate questions are as follows.

- What is the interim performance of the portfolio in terms of IRR and multiple?
- Do the IRR and the multiple tell a different story, ie, is one measure high and the other low? If so, why?

- What is the performance of the liquidated funds?
- What is the portfolio performance excluding younger funds that cannot provide reliable NAVs?

Measures at fund level

Similar questions to the portfolio level can be asked at a fund level. These questions concern the individual funds in a portfolio and are of utmost importance for investment managers monitoring the performance of individual funds but are also useful for the portfolio view.

- What is the size of commitment?
- What is the age of the fund?
- What is the internal age of the fund?
- How many companies have they invested in?
- Is it a specialist or generalist fund?
- Are there some red flags, eg, legal issues or key men leaving?

This information summarises key aspects of the fund investment. A portfolio manager sometimes needs this information to aggregate it for a specific analysis of the portfolio, and therefore it needs to be available in a quantitative form. Concerning cash flows and NAV, the same questions as for the portfolio apply. Concerning the performance, the manager should compute the IRR and the multiple. As described in Part II, a comparison of the difference between gross and net IRR is useful, and the implication of a large difference is explained.

Measures at company level

Holding complete and up-to-date information on underlying companies is a challenge. The most relevant and useful information then is valuation, purchase and possibly sales price, share in the company, type of the investment instrument (such as equity, restricted equity, subordinated loan), cash burn rate and cash reserves. Interesting questions to ask are: which funds have investments in the same companies? Do their valuations match? If not, why? This gives valuable insight into the trustworthiness of information received from specific funds.

Monitoring diversification

How can the portfolio manager check the degree of portfolio diversity? There are two ways to monitor diversification. First, the portfolio manager plots a graph that shows the distribution within a risk class. For example, Exhibit 14.1 shows an example of an age profile, that is, the number of funds per vintage year of a portfolio of fund investments. A visual inspection quickly reveals an unbalanced portfolio with few funds in year 2001 and 2002. This could also be done for capital invested rather than number of funds. Another example would be a pie chart of the weight of each sector, region or stage. Exhibit 14.2 shows a portfolio where later-stage and buyout is under-represented. However, this method is not quantitative, that is, it cannot be used as an input, for example, to a model, and is not totally objective as different people come to different conclusions. Therefore, for more automatic portfolio management, diversification measures are essential. The next paragraph illustrates such a measure.

Exhibit 14.1

Distribution of funds across vintage years, 1998–2004

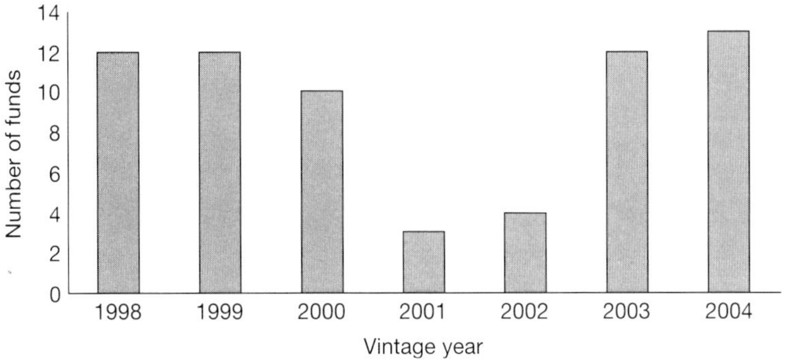

Source: Weidig.

Exhibit 14.2

Stage diversity

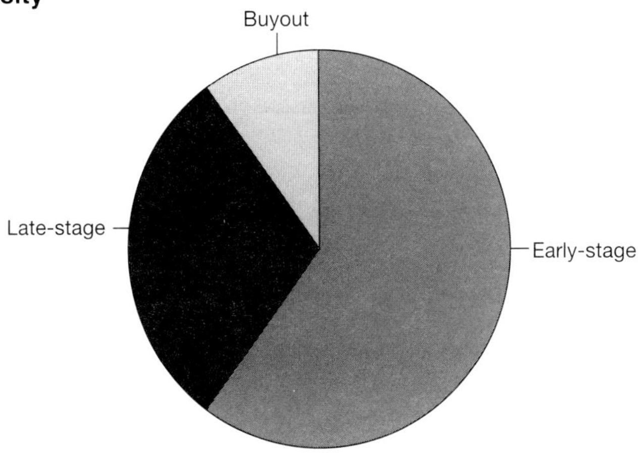

Source: Weidig.

For example for vintage year diversification, the following formula could measure diversity:

$$1 - \frac{T}{2 \cdot (T-1) \cdot N} \sum_{i=1}^{i=T} \left| \frac{N}{T} - N_i \right|$$

where T = the length of the investment period (in years)
N = the total number of funds
N_i = the number of funds in the i-th vintage year

The sum in the formula measures the difference of number of funds per year N_i from its ideal of equal number of funds per year N/T. This measure goes from 0 per cent to 100 per cent. For example, for a perfectly balanced portfolio in terms of vintage year risk, every vintage year has the same amount of funds, that is, $N_i = N/T$. The second expression is zero and the diversity score is 100 per cent. For a maximally unbalanced portfolio, all funds are in a single vintage year, that is, all N_i are zero except one. The second expression simplifies to 1, and the diversity score is 0 per cent. For Exhibit 14.1, the number of funds N_i are 12, 12, 10, 3, 4, 12 and 13 for the respective vintage years, the number of years T is 7 and the total number of funds are 66. These numbers are then plugged into the formula of the diversification measure, which leads to a diversity score of about 21 per cent.

Monitoring the value of the portfolio

The importance of valuation in private equity

Apart from monitoring risks, the most important monitoring aspect is the valuation of each fund's unrealised portfolio of direct company investments. The investor would like to know what the investment is worth. So how trustworthy is the NAV reported by the fund managers? What are the fundamental issues in valuation? As investments are long term, the value of a portfolio of companies is an estimate of the total amount of money for which the fund managers can sell the portfolio at a certain moment during the fund's lifetime. Fund investors in turn should know how much their total portfolio of funds is worth. The people giving money to the fund investors such as pension fund contributors have a right to know how much their investment is worth. The portfolio value is also an indicator of the future level of distributions. Further, the valuation, especially for mature funds, contains useful information for most cash flow models, as discussed in Chapter 17, 'Advanced cash flow modelling', and they themselves are the input to portfolio forecasting including liquidity planning. The first step to understanding the valuation issue is to look at the standard valuation approaches.

Valuation methods for companies

The valuation of companies is important for the fund investor as such valuations determine the value of a fund's portfolio companies and hence of a portfolio of fund investments. So how are companies typically valued? Valuing a company is very important for both the potential seller and buyer, because they want to have a fair value in mind as a basis for negotiations. Many different methods exist. The methods are typically designed for publicly traded companies with established products and historical cash flow history. The two methods most relevant to privately held companies are discounted cash flows and market comparables ratios.

Discounted cash flows

For the discounted cash flows, the net present value (NPV) of all projected future cash flows of the company is calculated using a discount rate that reflects the cost of capital of the company, which increases with higher intrinsic business risk. There are different discount rates for different types of companies. This method only has a chance to work if cash flows can be reliably forecasted.

Comparable ratios

Finding ratios on the basis of market comparables is another method. For each company that has a quoted price or recent trade sale price and revenue history, performance ratios of its activity such as price/earnings (P/E) ratios exist. An approximation of the price of a to-be-valued company could be the product of the average P/E of the same type of company and the earnings of the company to be valued.

Difficult to use in private equity

The two methods only really work for mature companies with stable and predictable cash flows. Seed and early-stage companies with little or no revenues would cause a problem. Notably, during the internet boom, only revenue-based ratios were used, which proved to be highly unreliable. Most would agree that these two examples of valuation methods are not perfect and only roughly indicate the fair value. It is very difficult to reliably predict cash flows and put in a meaningful discount rate factor, and even if the method does come up with the fair value, it is not necessarily possible to sell it for the fair value price in an illiquid market with few buyers.

Special considerations when valuing portfolio companies in private equity

Venture capital companies are young companies and start-ups with no established product, little historical cash flow data or accounting records. They typically are in a cash-burning phase, and do not have profits. Virtually all valuation methods in this segment are suspicious. Venture-backed companies often do not have reliable and meaningful ratios or predictable cash flows. The value of the company is really in the hope of selling a product the market potential of which is still untested. The outcome of such projects is highly uncertain, and depends internally on the abilities of the entrepreneur and externally on factors such as competition, technology advances and financing environment.

Exhibit 14.3 shows the return distribution of US venture capital direct investments by giving a probability for a certain multiple to happen. The curve illustrates the extreme spread or uncertainty in returns from investing directly in venture capital companies. Every third investment results in a total loss, but also more than 10 per cent of investments return more than a multiple of 10. Fund managers therefore face the impossible task of accurately valuing their portfolio companies as there is such a wide outcome and a small misjudgement leads to a vastly different end-value. Thus, they face an equally difficult task to provide an accurate fair value for their portfolio companies to their limited partners (LPs).

Exhibit 14.3

Distribution of returns on US venture capital direct investments

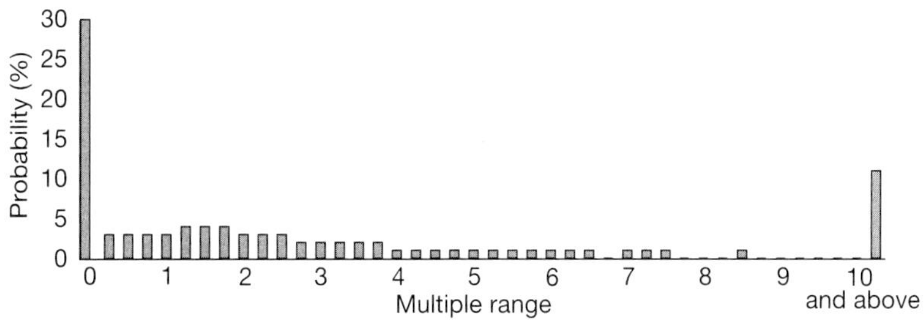

Source: Cochrane data (2005).

However, the fund managers investing in mid-market companies or for large buyout deals have a much easier task in terms of valuation. The companies are established and the purchase and sales price lie within a certain boundary, fixed by valuation methods. As they have a cash flow history and an established product or service, mid-market or large buyout funds use standard valuation methods such as ratios or discounted cash flows.

How fund managers compute the NAV

To provide guidance in valuation for private equity investments, national associations have set up valuation standards, which are mostly followed by the private equity fund managers.[3] The valuation standards are not legally binding and members do not have to apply them, but many fund investors require them from the fund managers. The guidelines require that the methodology is disclosed and consistently applied over the fund's life, and a review conducted by outsiders at least twice a year.

The valuation method distinguishes between quoted and non-quoted companies. Quoted companies in the portfolio are valued at the stock price minus a discount for illiquidity (up to 20 per cent) and lock-up period (not less than 25 per cent). For non-quoted companies, a conservative and a fair market value approach are possible. For the conservative approach, all unquoted investments should be at cost unless there has been a new financing round, a partial sale or a write-down. A new financing round or partial sale should be 'a material investment/ sale by or to an independent third party at arm's length', where a material share is typically more than 5 per cent of the shares. Write-downs are in multiples of 25 per cent for material events.

For the fair market value, it is the price an independent buyer can be expected to pay on the day of the transaction. Such value can be determined by comparing similar companies or using a valuation methodology. EVCA suggests several methods. The fund investor should make sure that the guidelines are rigorously followed and should question valuations reported, for example, by cross-checking them against the valuation by other general partners (GPs) that the fund investor has access to and that have invested in the same company.

How useful are these guidelines to the fund investor in practice? Kaneyuki (2003) gives an uncompromising view on many potential conflicts on valuation. For example, two fund managers know each other well and have different funds. They both have a troubled portfolio, and desperately need to look good, because both are soon starting new fundraisings. Each of them could buy a small stake in one of each others' worthless companies for too high a price. As the two purchases are third-party transactions, the two fund managers can revalue the company using the third-party transaction price, and their NAV moves up for both.

The nature of the private equity NAV

The private equity NAV falls between the accounting and fair value approach. At the beginning of a fund, the valuation of a fund's portfolio is accounting-wise at cost. Hence the NAV contains no really distinctive information and is only a reflection of the accounting practice. It is very similar for all funds, and is not a useful input to a cash flow model or for monitoring purposes. The fund NAV in most cases leads to an underestimation of the performance, because, in the early days, a fund's operational expense and set-up costs have an over-proportionally high impact on the NAV of the fund.

Exhibit 14.4

J-curve of interim IRR

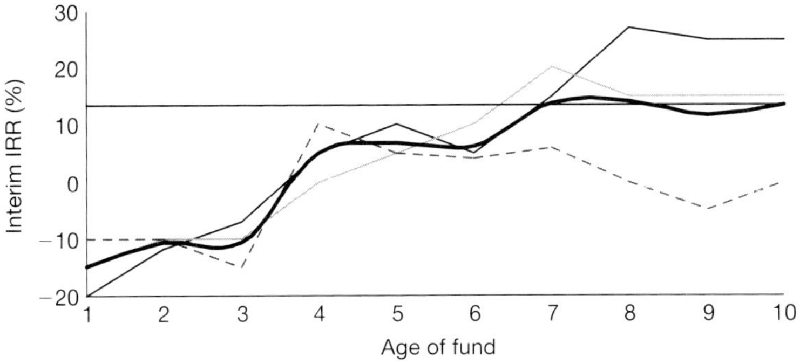

Source: Weidig.

For example, a fund starts its activity, draws down set-up costs of 2, wants to invest 100 in a company, drawdowns 100, and then values the investment at cost 100. The fund's NAV is now 100, which results in a loss for the investor of −2, that is, the NAV of 100 minus the total drawdowns of 102. This phenomenon also causes the J-curve effect of the interim IRR,[4] with a systematic underestimation of the final performance in the early years. Exhibit 14.4 shows the evolution of the interim IRR of three different funds across the age of the funds. All funds start with a negative interim IRR, which becomes less negative or positive as the fund gets older, the NAV represents a more realistic value and the interim IRR is closer to the final IRR. The thick curve represents the average of all three curves. Over the years and typically after the investment period, the NAV is slowly changing to a fair valuation as new information from financing rounds, partial or full exits or write-downs on portfolio companies improves the predictability of a fund's final performance. For mature companies, valuation methods such as discounted cash flows or ratios add further towards fair value, but often they do not provide more insight as they are easily manipulated and at the fund manager's discretion.

Monitoring performance using a benchmark

Benchmarking the fund management team to its peer group

Part of portfolio monitoring is to gauge how well the management team does in comparison with its peer group, that is, benchmarking. This is a very difficult issue, because the contribution of the team to the overall fund's performance needs to be untangled. Apart from the team factor, many other important external factors such as vintage year, industry focus and regional difference influence the success of a fund. For example, the biotech industry might boom but the high-tech industry does not. Is it the team's fault to miss out on a boom that will happen five to 10 years down the line? A team might effectively and professionally pursue a strategy, but were unlucky not to make an impact due to external factors such as a downturn in the economy, a new tax law or regulation.

Despite the many issues that make monitoring a team's performance against a benchmark difficult, the industry wants and needs to compare the fund manager with its peer group. Also,

Exhibit 14.5

Average performance per quartile, 1988–98

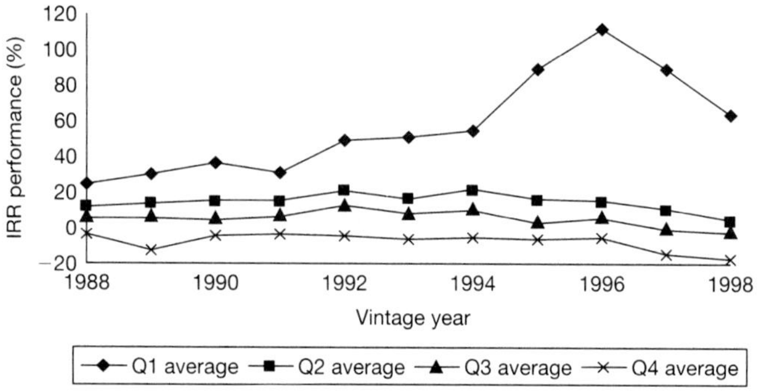

Source: VentureXpert data.

most investors require such monitoring. The most common benchmark is in terms of quartile performance. A commonly asked question is: is the fund in the top quartile, that is, is the fund in the top 25 per cent of its peer group in terms of IRR performance? The peer group can be defined as all funds in the same vintage year, and possibly the same market and stage. This notion is widespread, also due to such practice in the Venture Economics' benchmark report (see Thomson Venture Economics), which gives the quartile boundaries for each vintage year for a given market, stage and sector.

To illustrate the industry's focus on top quartile funds, Exhibit 14.5 shows the average performance for each quartile in a vintage year for private equity funds worldwide. This empirical data shows what many emphasise, namely that the top quartile has disproportionally high returns; the difference in IRR and multiple between the top quartile and second quartile being several times larger than between the second and third quartile, or between the third and fourth quartile! This disproportionally high return might be an effect of some extreme winners in their portfolio.

Do too many teams claim to be top quartile?

However, investors need to be extra careful about benchmarking numbers, and not solely rely on them for their investment decision. The quartile benchmark is of utmost importance to the fund manager who wants to raise a new fund, and this fact gives rise to some remarkable effects. For example, 50 per cent of all funds claim to be top quartile, that is, in the top 25 per cent. This observation is mathematically incorrect, because only 25 per cent can be in the first quartile by definition. So how can more than 25 per cent claim to be in the first quartile?

First, they might only use a different peer group, and look for a group where they are top quartile. If it is not Europe-wide, it will be for German venture capital biotech funds, for example. Second, there might be a survival bias. The performance data of the worst performers in a peer group such as 4Q becomes invisible to the general market as the funds do not exist anymore, or do not raise a new fund, or do not talk about their bad performance. Also, only the 1Q and 2Q funds publicise their good past performance in memoranda. Therefore, a data collection of funds making quartile statements has less 3Q and 4Q funds. Third, a comparison to a benchmark only starts to become reliable in the late life of a fund.

As mentioned above, the interim IRR or multiple only becomes reliable in the last years of the fund, but often fund managers are fundraising before the liquidation of the fund and so they use the interim quartiles. Some claim[5] that only 14 per cent of the final 1Q funds were in the interim 1Q of year one, and only 50 per cent of the final 1Q funds were in the interim 1Q of year five. These figures are amazing. So most funds will at some point in their life be in the interim 1Q even though they might not be 1Q at the end! The fund manager will of course only quote the period where they are top quartile. To summarise, fund managers are doing nothing wrong as long as they quote the source and method accurately, but of course their behaviour is misleading. Therefore, the investor should be careful about claims of top quartile performance.

Is past performance a good indicator of future performance?

Several studies and analyst reports claim performance persistence, while others claim the contrary.[6] VentureXpert has information on each fund as to whether the fund is a first-time fund or not. The difference between first-time and non-first-time funds is quite small, only a few per cent of IRR, and well within statistical error. Actually, an analysis is tricky because it is not possible to know what would happen to a second-time team that did badly the first time, because they are unlikely to raise a second fund. Such teams might also have a better performance with a second fund, because they learned from their mistakes, or just have a bit more luck with one or two key investments. Another issue is that successful first-time and second-time funds might suffer from personnel and structural change, as discussed in Part II. Unexpected things diffuse the picture. To conclude, a team should mostly be valued by its current state and not past glorious performances.

---

1 The internal age measures how close a fund is to its full liquidation, ie, to what degree a fund has drawn down its commitment and sold off its portfolio companies. See Weidig and Meyer (2003) for a description of the internal age concept.
2 The portfolio IRR is the IRR when all the funds' cash flows are pooled together to compute the IRR.
3 See EVCA Guidelines (2001) and BVCA (2003) for Europe. The US association has relied more on industry groups such as PEIGG and AIMR.
4 Please see Part I, Chapter 5 for an introduction to the IRR concept.
5 Frei and Studer (2004).
6 See, for example, Frei and Studer (2004).

Chapter 15

Forecasting the future portfolio

Forecasting the distribution of future cash flows

The need for cash flow modelling

The portfolio manager not only needs to monitor the current portfolio, but must also forecast its future. Forecasting the future portfolio is about predicting the future cash flows, that is, drawdown calls and distributions. Projecting the portfolio into the future is a very important aspect of risk management, which allows an estimation of the final performance and risk measures of the portfolio. The portfolio manager can compute any such measure using the future cash flow distribution, and use this information for liquidity planning, performance forecasting, keeping reserves and others.

For example, the distribution of future cash flows leads directly to the distribution of the final internal rate of return (IRR), or multiple, for the portfolio or for each fund. The final IRR distribution of the portfolio allows the determination of the average final portfolio IRR and its standard deviation (or fluctuation) from the average. The future cash flow distribution also allows for the computing of risk measures such as the probability of getting back the original capital or of reaching a given target of final IRR or multiple.

The following numerical example illustrates this process. First, a fund has past cash flows. For example, a fund has drawn down 20 in every year of the first five years. Second, the cash flows over the next five years are modelled, that is, a cash flow model generates future cash flow scenarios. For example, to keep it simple there are three cash flow scenarios:

- 10 for every year over the next five years with a probability of 50 per cent;
- 20 for every year over the next five years with a probability of 40 per cent; and
- 40 for every year over the next five years with a probability of 10 per cent.

Third, these cash flow scenarios allow us to compute many different measures that answer different questions. Here are some examples.

- What is the final multiple of the fund? It is computed from the past fund cash flows and the future cash flow scenarios. Thus, there are three possible outcomes for the final multiple. The final multiple is 0.5 with a probability of 50 per cent, 1 with a probability of 40 per cent and 2 with a probability of 10 per cent.
- What is the expected final multiple of the fund? It is the probability weighted average of all possible outcomes for final multiple. Thus, the expected final multiple would be $0.5*50\% + 1*40\% + 2*10\% = 0.25 + 0.4 + 0.2 = 0.85$.
- What is the probability of not getting back the original capital? A multiple below 1 means that less than the original invested capital has been returned. There is only one outcome of final multiple that is less than 1, namely a final multiple of 0.5 with a probability of 50 per cent. Thus, the probability of not getting back the capital is 50 per cent.

This simple example shows how the future cash flow scenarios are essential for forecasting critical measures.

Important issues on the use of cash flow models for forecasting

The portfolio manager needs to keep in mind two concepts crucial to forecasting cash flows: the difference between expected future cash flow and future cash flow scenarios where each scenario has an associated probability, and the difference between predicting an individual fund's cash flow and a portfolio cash flow. In its simple form, a cash flow model would give the expected future cash flow, for example: a fund has a net asset value (NAV) of 100 and two more years to go, thus an estimate for the future cash flows for the two next years could be 50 for each. This prediction gives the portfolio manager more certainty about the future, but does not help with liquidity planning because the prediction does not associate probabilities with a cash flow scenario. Thus, an investor cannot safely allocate 50 to a new fund for next year, because the prediction does not say by how much the future cash flows could deviate from the expected future cash flow. For example, what is the probability to fall short of receiving 50 back? Therefore ideally, a cash flow model needs to assign a probability to each cash flow scenario. Furthermore, even if the portfolio manager has the cash flow distribution for each fund, the forecast will not help the portfolio manager to plan the liquidity needs of its portfolio. The reason is that the cash flow scenarios for the individual funds do not move completely independently, that is, they are correlated to some degree. For example, in a recession the cash distributions from many funds are all taking longer to be realised and probably at a lower level. Thus ideally, a cash flow model gives the probability with which each portfolio cash flow scenario will occur.

Forecasting the portfolio of young funds is less reliable. Young funds have no useful information available on the underlying portfolio companies, which are either valued at cost or are not yet in the portfolio. As the funds mature, the valuation of the portfolio companies gets closer to a fair value, which gives some indication of the future distributions. An analogy would be the life expectancy of a person judged at birth and again at the age of 30 with extra information on lifestyle, past illnesses and social environment available.

Monitoring risk numbers

Risk numbers are very important to portfolio managers, as they indicate a risk or uncertainty in an important aspect of the portfolio. As mentioned above, a cash flow model should deliver portfolio cash flow scenarios. The simplest risk numbers are easily formulated in questions such as those below.

- What is the probability of obtaining a target portfolio IRR of, say, 10 per cent?
- What is the probability of getting at least the capital invested back?
- What is the probability that the liquidity reserves are not sufficient next year?
- What is the maximum the portfolio will lose in 95 per cent of the scenarios?

Portfolio managers are interested in these questions because the answers quantify the degree of uncertainty the portfolio of fund investments face. For each question, a risk number can be defined, and computed from a distribution of future cash flows as shown above in the section entitled 'The need for cash flow modelling'.

Other useful tools for portfolio and risk management are scenario analysis and stress testing. Scenario analysis looks at how the portfolio reacts to certain extreme macroeconomic scenarios. For example, a portfolio manager might simulate the behaviour of the portfolio using historical data from a boom followed by a recession period, for example, starting in the late 1990s. Such an analysis affects the risk numbers and is very useful to see whether the portfolio and the liquidity reserves can withstand such extreme scenarios. Stress testing, on the other hand, analyses how sensitive the portfolio outcomes are to extreme changes in parameter input. For example, the portfolio manager might drastically increase the correlation assumption between individual funds or countries, and look at how much the risk numbers change.

Forecasting the performance of the portfolio

Using the interim IRR

Forecasting the performance is straightforward with a future cash flow distribution. Each portfolio cash flow scenario is used to compute an IRR or a multiple, and leads to a distribution of final portfolio IRR or multiple. The fund investor, being an institutional investor, needs to report back the status of its portfolio and therefore would like to know the expected final performance. The difficulty lies in getting the cash flow model right. The portfolio manager of some fund investors might not have the resources or time to go through this difficult process. They can also do a quick and rough portfolio projection without relying on more sophisticated cash flow models.

Two measures are often used: the interim IRR and the interim multiple. The interim IRR is the IRR using the past cash flows of a fund, and its NAV is taken as a cash flow at the last valuation time. The interim multiple is just the sum of the NAV and the distributions divided by the total drawdown. The measures are not a reliable estimate of future performance at the start of a fund's life. Actually, at the beginning of a fund's life, the interim IRR is often negative and the multiple less than one, because the operating expense has an overly important impact on a fund's NAV and the portfolio is often valued at cost in the absence of external revaluation events. However, after some years and especially after the investment period, valuation is approaching a fair value, and is no longer an on-average systematic underestimation and can become a simple but useful estimate for final performance.

Improving the forecasting power of the interim IRR

This approach can be made somewhat more sophisticated by adjusting for the J-curve effect of the interim IRR as shown in Chapter 14, Exhibit 14.4 and adding a qualitative judgement for the valuation. For example, in Exhibit 14.4, the resulting systematic underestimation could be measured and used to calibrate the interim IRR upwards to get a better and unbiased estimate for the final IRR.

For example, if on average the interim IRR in year two underestimates the final IRR by say 5 per cent, all interim IRRs of funds in their second year could be corrected by adding

5 per cent. The adjustment is derived from historical data, and decreases with age. Another option is to multiply the NAV of funds with a quality factor. Investment managers of the fund investor often have their own judgement on how reliable the reported NAV is, and often come up with their own NAV upon checking all documentation on the underlying companies. Depending on whether these investment managers of the fund investor sense an under- or overestimation, they could add or deduct say 25 per cent to or from the NAV. Or, they could propose their own estimate of the NAV. This new corrected NAV can then be used as an input to the computation of the interim IRR.

Chapter 16

Steering the portfolio

General issues

Steering a portfolio of private equity fund investments is difficult because the portfolio manager cannot use the same tools as portfolio managers of publicly traded assets. There is not a lot the portfolio manager can do once the contracts are signed, but to prepare for the worst-case scenarios. Rigorously implementing a private equity investment programme with a strictly defined portfolio allocation is a very difficult, if not an impossible, task. A deviation from the targeted asset allocation is the norm, and not easily rectifiable.

A re-balancing is difficult due to the high costs of selling fund investments. Therefore, the investor must concentrate on carefully selecting appropriate funds or buying them second-hand in order to rebalance the portfolio. Moreover, often there are no appropriate funds available, and the investor must make compromises. In addition to the maintenance of long-term goals, portfolio steering also needs to account for short-term uncertainties. These short-term issues (for example, liquidity planning) are very important to ensure a stable and smooth investment programme. Therefore, the portfolio manager must prepare for these uncertainties by allocating capital to liquidity reserves while at the same time maximising the resources allocated to private equity through overcommitment.

Liquidity reserves

The goal of liquidity planning is to minimise the liquidity reserves and reach the desired allocation to private equity while avoiding liquidity shortfall that would result in the investor's inability to follow a capital call. Thus, the portfolio manager faces a contradictory challenge: on the one hand, the more money goes to the liquidity reserves, that is, liquid assets that can be converted into cash at short notice, the safer the portfolio is against short-term liquidity squeezes, but on the other hand, the more money is invested into private equity the better the return expectations on the portfolio.

A complicating factor is that, unlike a portfolio consisting only of bonds and stocks, the allocation to private equity funds only reaches its target exposure after a few years of drawdowns by the fund managers. Thus, a private equity portfolio manager cannot just once buy stocks and keep a reserve in liquid low-risk bonds, and then infrequently rebalance due to a valuation change in bonds or stocks. The portfolio manager faces a situation similar to holding futures contracts or underwriting options, implying margin calls that need to be honoured right away. The equivalent of margin calls in private equity are the drawdown calls from the fund manager. Thus, liquidity reserves are very important. A model forecasting the distribution of future portfolio cash flows can help to handle this problem. For example, during a scenario analysis, the portfolio manager can ask: what is the probability that the current liquidity reserves are sufficient? Or, how much should the liquidity reserve be to withstand 95 per cent or 99 per cent of all scenarios? Is the liquidity reserve sufficient in certain scenarios? The portfolio manager should then allocate capital to the liquidity reserves according to the level of safety needed. For extreme scenarios, standby credit facilities may be a solution.

Overcommitment

Overcommitment is specific to private equity, and arises because the fund investors cannot directly invest all the capital into a fund from the outset. Fund managers typically draw down commitments over several years and some distributions may occur before the last drawdowns for a fund are made. This results in a situation where an investor only ever has an effective exposure of 50 per cent to 70 per cent of the total commitments made. This is very different to the asset allocation of portfolios of publicly traded assets, where fund managers can immediately gain exposure to the asset class for the amount they seek to invest.

In private equity, a commitment of 100 could well mean an asset allocation to private equity of 50 to 70 maximally, and the remaining capital waits in low-return and low-risk liquid investments.[1] Therefore, a portfolio manager might want to overcommit, that is, 100 are allocated to private equity, but 150 are committed to funds. In this way, the portfolio might reach an exposure closer to the 100 allocated and not just 50 to 70.

On the other hand, overcommitment could lead to a default on a capital call if an over-allocation leads to liquidity problems, that is, the fund investor does not have the money to honour the capital call. Or it may result in a breach of investment regulation, for example, if a pension fund's policy forbids more than 10 per cent allocation to private equity. According to Frei and Studer (2004), many investors use a rule of thumb and commit 150 per cent of the desired asset allocation. However, they claim that this strategy does not always work well and could lead to significant over- or undercommitment (see Exhibit 16.1).

Exhibit 16.1

Historical analysis of the quarterly investment level development for a globally diversified private equity programme

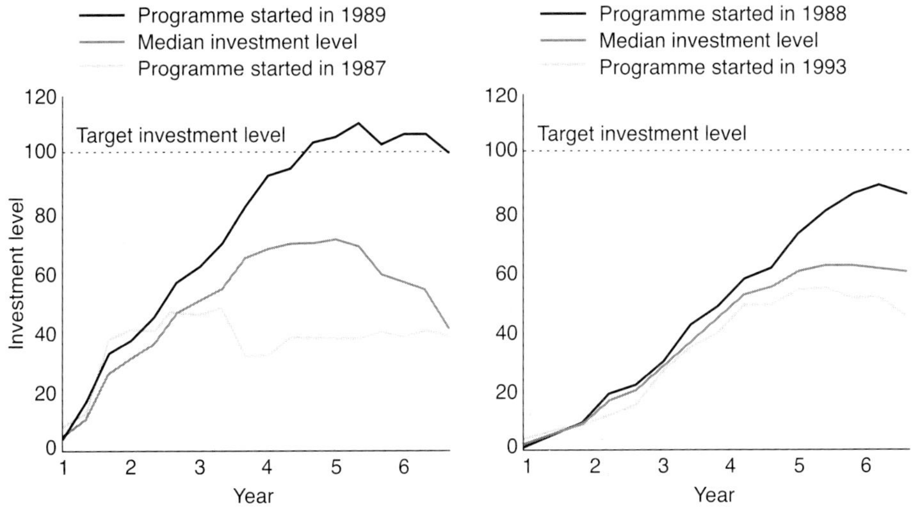

Source: Partners Group analysis based on Thomson Venture Economics data.

Overcommitment is effectively liquidity planning that needs input from a cash flow model. Thus, running an overcommitment strategy requires sophisticated cash flow models and skilled quantitative portfolio managers.[2]

Diversification

Apart from taking action against liquidity squeezes and an inefficient capital allocation to private equity, a portfolio manager should also focus on eliminating diversifiable risk of the portfolio as much as possible. The more diversified the portfolio, the less uncertain the future outcomes and the easier the planning of liquidity reserves and overcommitment. The investors can influence the diversity of an existing portfolio with their choice of new funds, and sometimes by selling or buying active funds in secondary transactions.

In practice, implementing a diversification strategy, that is, balancing a portfolio across region, sector, vintage year, stage and manager is tricky due to the constraints imposed by the opaque and illiquid market. For example, there might just not be enough good funds of a certain type to rigorously follow a diversification scheme. Nevertheless, the portfolio managers should monitor the portfolio of fund investments via diversity measures and aim to diversify as much as possible. The portfolio manager should look at the impact on these measures as an input to the decision on a new fund investment. This cannot be done by some mathematical algorithm, but there may be situations where an investor decides against one out of two equally qualified fund managers due to diversification reasons, or the investor might decide to stop investing into funds from certain regions or sectors due to an overexposure. Finally, diversification can be improved by adding more funds to the portfolio. However, the additional diversification benefit for a portfolio of more than 20 funds is quite small.

---

1 See discussion by Frei and Studer (2004).

2 Frei and Studer (2004) and McIntire, Conner and Nevins (2004) discuss overcommitment.

Chapter 17

Advanced cash flow modelling

Cash flow modelling

The importance to fund investors

Cash flow modelling is very important to the portfolio manager for several risk management tasks such as liquidity planning, liquidity reserves, overcommitment and portfolio projection. The amount and timing of cash flows are uncertain but have constraints specific to the fund structure. Understanding these dynamics and degrees of uncertainty means being able to do proper quantitative risk management. The emergence of quantitative risk management and securitisation products in private equity has forced investors to develop better cash flow models. Put simply, the better the cash flow models the more money investors make and the less risks they face.

Some fund investors have developed models internally. However, it is difficult to know the exact number and the degree of sophistication as they tend to keep the models secret. On the other hand, rating agencies are traditionally more open about their models. The recent wave of securitisation forced rating agencies to develop cash flow models, because cash flows are essential to compute the probability of meeting interest and capital payments. Standard & Poor's and Fitch Ratings have modelling papers out, but Moody's has not published a methodology.[1] Further, some academics or researchers have also looked at modelling. All the models are described in the following sections, listed in Exhibit 17.3 and referenced in the bibliography under the topic of cash flow modelling.

Public disclosure

Many fund investors are reluctant to make their cash flow model public,[2] but publication and open discussion of models is important and even beneficial to the fund investor. It is difficult to judge the quality of a secret proprietary model. There might be some short-term advantages, such as marketing and better (than the competitors) liquidity planning, for a model to be proprietary. But, a proprietary model would also not face public scrutiny which could possibly reveal embarrassing weaknesses or flaws. Often a highly acclaimed proprietary model is just the standard straightforward model that everyone knows about from the cash flow modelling literature.

The long-term benefits of public disclosure should outweigh the advantages of it being proprietary. First, it is far better to be told from the industry that one's model is wrong than to enter into a situation where the faulty model suggests a wrong overcommitment strategy, which leads to severe liquidity problems. Second, the fact that others copy one's model is not really a problem. It is a sign that the model becomes the market standard, and is reliable in the eyes of others. In fact, even if another investor uses the same model, the strength of a model does not come from the mathematical formulae, but from the quality of the inputs and its implementation environment such as the IT system. Thus, a fund investor with excellent investment and risk management professionals actually gains from making their model public!

Such a situation exists in public products modelling. For example, in derivative modelling, the Black-Scholes framework is well known to everyone, and is the backbone of a framework within which traders price options. The competitive advantage is not from the model itself, but from a better estimation or prediction of inputs such as understanding and fine-tuning the model, and the overall infrastructure such as middle office, risk management, quant support and efficient IT infrastructure. Thus, a common framework for pricing is what counts. For example, such a common framework in private equity would make securitisation cheaper for the seller of the portfolio as the rating agencies would feel more comfortable and refrain from using an ultraconservative rating approach to these bonds. The same applies to the costs of insuring a portfolio against capital loss. Without a common framework, everyone is worse off, including those investors with proprietary models.

The challenges

Modelling cash flows for private equity funds and portfolios of funds is no easy task due to the specific features of private equity detailed below.

- First, a fund's cash flows follow a specific pattern. Cash flows are constrained, and modelling needs to include these constraints. The cash flows are constrained in three ways: drawdown typically up to commitment; the bulk of drawdowns until end of investment period with drawdowns for follow-on investments also in the divestment period; and divestment until end of fund life.
- Second, the value of the portfolio is never judged by a market, but by the fund manager who has a potential conflict of interest.
- Third, unlike in public markets, performance data is hard to get. Only very few data providers sell access to aggregated cash flow data such as historical performances. Access to the historical cash flows is not possible. Venture Economics gives access to cash flow data to some researchers, but rarely for institutional investors. Getting the right historical data is crucial for modelling.
- Fourth, a fund investor has more direct influence on the fund manager, whereas a mutual fund investor does not have this influence.
- Fifth, fund investors cannot hedge themselves against private equity risk. For example, a public market fund could buy a future or an option on the index to reduce its exposure to stocks. In private equity, this is not possible yet.
- Sixth, the past historical data might not be a useful input to a model as the private equity market is still structurally evolving.

High model risk

Good cash flow modelling can help make money for the fund investor, but bad modelling can have disastrous consequences such as liquidity problems. Thus, cash flow modelling leads to model risk, that is, uncertainty on the quality of the model for the fund investor. Due to the number of models, lack of literature and the opaqueness of the market, it is difficult to choose the right model. However, even with a sensible model, the fund investor needs

Useful guidelines for portfolio managers

- Never forget that models only approximate reality.
- Remember that a model is only as good as its inputs. This is especially true for private equity, where data is private and possibly biased.
- Make sure the model is checked by an independent person.
- Do not let semi-experts develop models. This is a recipe for disaster.
- Be aware that testing models in private equity is very difficult.
- It is always better to have a simple model that everyone understands, than a sophisticated model that only one person understands.
- Go for the simple approach. At least you know that it has weaknesses.
- Do not use a model that you do not understand fully.

access to reliable historical data in private equity. The difficulty of testing a model also adds to model risk. As funds are long-term investments, it is difficult to change an overcommitment strategy once the contracts have been signed. It is hard also to untangle the input error from model error. Moreover, a simple model might not capture all features, but at least it is easy to implement, is understandable to most, and its weaknesses are known.

Cash flow patterns as a guide to fund investors

The pattern of fund cash flows

The first step in modelling cash flows is to look at the pattern of historical cash flows. Cash flows underlie constraints arising from the fund structure. Exhibit 17.1 shows the typical cash flows of a private equity fund from the perspective of the fund investor. The curve shows the sum of all past cash flows versus fund age and follows a J-curve. First, there are negative cash flows and then positive cash flows. The fund manager draws down money to invest, and distributes the proceeds from the sales later, which are hopefully greater than the total drawdowns. The drawdowns are far more predictable than the distributions.

The total amount of drawdowns cannot exceed the total commitment, and their timing is limited to the investment period, apart from drawdowns for management fees or follow-up

Exhibit 17.1

J-curve effect of cumulative cash flows

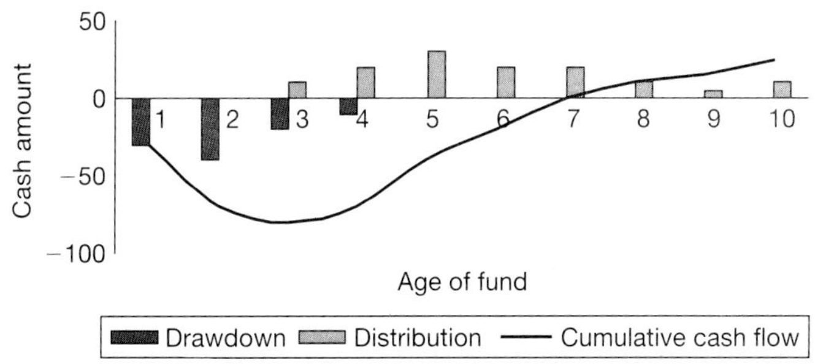

Source: Weidig.

financing. The timing of the drawdowns depends considerably on the availability of good deals. The availability of candidate companies also depends on the state of the general economy. The size of drawdowns also depends on the price paid for individual companies which, in turn, depends on the competitive environment, and the state of public stock markets. During boom periods, investors have a lot of money to give to fund managers, and this could lead to the syndrome of 'too much money chasing too few deals'. Fees are also drawdowns and include set-up costs at the beginning of the fund, operating expense to the fund and typically yearly management fees for the general partner (GP), which often vary over time.

The distributions are less constrained and less predictable. The timing is limited to the lifetime of the fund with a typical eight to 10 years plus one or two years of optional extension. The amount and timing of the distribution significantly depends on the quality of the portfolio companies and the exit environment, that is, availability of trade buyers or the possibility of an IPO in a booming market. The first distributions come in with the first sales and the last one can be in year 12 or 13 if the exit market has been bad and the fund managers waited for a better price. Thus, the distributions are very difficult to estimate, because no one knows the state of the market in five to 10 years' time. Therefore, for a new fund, most fund investors focus on the management team, the contracts and the fund structure, as these aspects are the only factors they can control and that influence cash flows.

Studies on historical patterns

The fund cash flows are nothing else than the collection of cash flows from investing into and exiting 10 to 30 direct company investments. The fund managers determine the timing, based on market conditions. The average expected return certainly depends on the general environment, but it is interesting to study the return distribution on direct company investments. It is extremely widely dispersed. Exhibit 14.3 in Chapter 14 shows the return distribution of US venture capital direct investments.[3] Around 30 per cent of all US venture capital direct investments result in a total loss of capital, but others return a multiple of a hundred or thousand times its capital invested. This large spread of direct investment returns significantly increases the cash flow uncertainty, and creates discontinuous jumps every time an extreme profit happens. Thus, fund cash flows are often not smooth due to high or extreme winners in its portfolio, that is, the fund investor does not receive a continuous cash flow stream of similar amounts but sometimes a high amount followed by a period with no cash flows. These jumps are less severe for buyout transactions as the underlying companies are mature with more reliable valuations which reduces the possibility of extreme winners.

What you need to know about cash flows

- Required capital as percentage of total commitments needed to meet drawdowns: between 50 per cent and 70 per cent.
- Average drawdown within a year: around 25 per cent.
- Average drawdown within three years: around 60 per cent.
- Average 50 per cent of commitment back: around year 3.
- Average 100 per cent of capital back: around year 7.
- No dependence on size of fund.
- Average time to 100 per cent capital back varies with vintage year.
- Cash flow pattern of a fund portfolio is not smooth but has jumps.

Exhibit 17.2

Illustration of the volatility of net cash flows of private equity funds

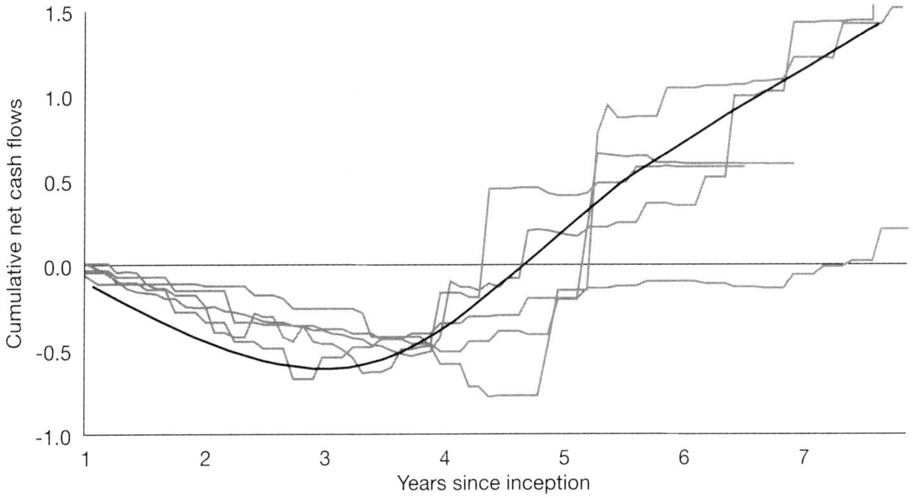

Source: Partners Group.

The box on the previous page summarises the most important findings of several studies.[4] Standard & Poor's notes that even a portfolio of funds does not have a smooth cash flow but contains undiversifiable short-term cash flow fluctuations. This fact fits well with the above-discussed distribution of direct investment returns. The short-term fluctuations or jumps are positive distributions from extreme winners. Exhibit 17.2 shows four different sums of cash flows versus the age of the fund, and the sum is not smooth but in steps. Several studies have looked at the numerical features of cash flows.[5]

Different types of cash flow models

There are different ways to model cash flows. The simple models only estimate the average cash flow for a future period, but not the uncertainty or typical fluctuation around the expected average cash flow. Thus, liquidity planning is not possible in terms of giving a probability that the cash flow will be above a certain level. Sophisticated models, however, estimate a cash flow distribution, that is, various cash flow scenarios are given a probability of them happening.[6] In the next sections, the publicly known cash flow models will be discussed, but some general conclusions can already be drawn.

First, cash flow modelling could be done at the fund level or it could treat a fund as a portfolio of portfolio companies. The next section discusses cash flow modelling at company level, but these approaches are useful only for investors who have direct access to company information and whose portfolio of companies is not too big – for example, fund managers themselves or investors who hold direct co-investments. Thus, most cash flow modelling is clearly at the fund level, that is, the fund is modelled as a black box with few characteristics. A black box means that the content of the box is ignored, and described with a few external parameters such as the shape or weight of the box. For example, a stock is also often treated as a black box for portfolio optimisation or option pricing, but, of course, an analyst or auditor would do a fundamental analysis of a company in great detail. To conclude, approaches at company level might appear to be more accurate. However, the errors associated with the estimation of the input parameters, the complication of aggregating them at the fund level, and access to and management of a very significant amount of data outweigh any added benefits.

Second, both data and parameter-driven approaches are possible. A parameter-driven model describes a system with a few input parameters, that is, it models the structure, and factors influencing its behaviour need to be well understood. Such models need to be tested on three issues: the assumption about structure, parameter estimation and past versus future relationship. Model risk is high, because the input parameters and the model approximate a system. For a data-driven approach (or bootstrapping), structure and factors do not need to be well understood and historical data such as historical cash flows sets the direction of future data.

Unlike a parameter-driven approach, model risk is low, because the description only reflects the past behaviour of comparable funds. Testing is easier as mainly the past versus future relationship is tested. For example, for a new fund a data-driven model in terms of using historical cash flows from similar past funds is far easier and probably better than designing a model that simulates the cash flows with a few inputs such as quality of manager, economic condition and so on. On the other hand, for a mature fund a parameter-driven model, for example, using the NAV as an input parameter might be better.

Third, it is difficult to see how to properly model cash flows without information from the underlying direct investments. For example, a close-to-zero NAV of a fund means absence of future cash flows, and a high NAV means high probability of significant future cash flows. Modelling the cash flows without this information would lead to significantly wrong forecasting. However, this error is less severe for a portfolio of fund investments, because under- and over-estimation might balance out to some degree. However, during the early years, the NAV is of little use and the underlying portfolio is typically valued at cost. The NAV does therefore contain no information on future distributions, and probably the only option is to expect an analogy with historical cash flows for comparable funds to happen, possibly with the inclusion of a judgement call by the investment manager on the quality of a fund investment. However, the closer a fund is to liquidation, the more relevant and more available the knowledge of the fund's portfolio of companies becomes to estimate the future cash flows. This valuation is of course only a rough estimate, because it is not easy to guess the timing of sales, and the valuation of the fund manager might not reflect the buyer's bid. The story might be slightly different for a large, mature and well-balanced evergreen portfolio of funds, where the effects described cancel out and the portfolio behaves in a similar way to the private equity market as a whole.

Models of a fund as a portfolio of direct investments

Model based on manager cash flow estimates

There are at least two approaches to model a fund as a portfolio of direct investments in portfolio companies. They are especially useful for fund managers, but only for some fund investors, namely those with direct access to portfolio companies. The first approach is entirely based on the input of a private equity fund manager investing into or exiting a company. For each direct investment, the manager gives estimates for time and amount of investment or exit for each company. For example, each estimate could involve an expected amount with a minimum and maximum exit price plus a probability associated to the expected amount. Collecting all the estimates from all managers, a simulation randomly generates scenarios, which leads to a distribution of future cash flows.

Unfortunately, such a model needs a lot of information and manual input, and requires well-paid and qualified analysts. Fund investors rarely have access to detailed information on the portfolio company, and need to deal with many companies. A simple computation shows, for example, that a fund investor with a portfolio of 100 funds, which are invested in 2,000 companies, would need to deal with at least 10,000 estimates per quarter. Further, the correlation between companies is impossible to model and hard to estimate. But the correlation is important, because companies move independently only to some degree and are influenced by the same factors such as the economic environment and the stock market situation. Another source of correlation might be the private equity fund manager who holds a direct participation in the companies, has insider information and exercises direct control. The decisions, quality or constraints of the fund management and the added value of the fund manager, have an impact on the performance of all investee companies. Moreover, it is also difficult to impose reporting standards that would reduce the workload of information collection. And, a fund investor would need to ask indirectly, via the fund management, for information on the underlying companies.

Model based on company grading

The second approach relies on both historical and fund manager's input. The companies are described as correlated random variables with a probability of purchase and exit as a function of time. The input parameters are the average correlation, volatility and mean return for the companies, and an exit probability function, and are estimated from historical data. A simulation generates different future cash flow scenarios for the fund by generating the companies' cash flows and adding them up. In fact, it would be possible to give a grading to each underlying company and assign a different mean return to each grading class. This model would work for new funds or existing funds. This would be a convenient way to include a judgement on a company into a model.

However, this approach requires direct access to the companies, and is therefore only suitable for fund managers or fund investors who co-invest in and have direct access to all of the companies. First, the correlation estimation problem arises again. Second, the estimation of the input parameters introduces considerable uncertainty into the model. At the very least, the model needs 13 input parameters for the use of the same mean return, volatility, correlation and one exit probability for each year of a lifetime of 10 years. To summarise, this approach is more realistic for a fund investor, but still difficult to implement without direct access to the underlying companies, for example, as a co-investor.

Non-probabilistic models at fund level

Simple approach

The simplest models are not necessary bad models. They are easy to implement, and everyone understands them and is aware of their limitations. Often, they turn out to be as effective as the more sophisticated ones. Here is the simplest cash flow model for a fund in the investment period: the drawdown per year is simply the undrawn commitment divided by the number of investment years. The distribution per year starts after the investment period and is an annual amount A for the remaining years after the investment period. This amount A could be such that the internal rate of return (IRR) of the cash flows equals the average historical IRR of the same type of fund. For example, if investors want to model a US venture capital fund, they could get the historical average IRR, then adjust A until the IRR of the modelled cash flows is equal to the historical average. For a mature fund, that is, in the divestment period, the distribution per year is the NAV divided by the number of remaining years. The NAV can be multiplied by a factor to incorporate a judgement. Another simple model for a new fund is to take the historical cash flows of all similar past funds. This gives a distribution of future cash flow scenarios. However, this model is not accurate for more mature active funds, as their NAV does not generally coincide with the NAV of a comparable historical fund.

Takahashi and Alexander's model

Takahashi and Alexander (2002) propose a simple cash flow model for illiquid alternative assets. It is a simple payment and distribution scheme, where the fund works effectively like a savings account. Money goes into the account (fund) according to an investment schedule, grows at a certain rate G, is recorded on the account's balance (the fund's NAV) and flows out according to a disinvestment schedule. According to Weidig (2003), the proposed model by Takahashi and Alexander (2002) uses one specific distribution function, but others are possible as well. This function has one parameter called the bow factor, and the smaller the bow factor, the earlier the NAV is paid out. The economic interpretation is that a smaller bow factor indicates good divestment conditions and vice versa.

Their model is simple and easy to understand. The structure of the model restricts the cash flows of the fund to a few input parameters and allows for running through various scenarios by adjusting the parameters. However, the model does not assign a probability to each scenario and cannot possibly capture all structural aspects due to its simplicity. The ambiguous estimation and the number of parameters also reduce the usefulness of the model.

Weidig's interim IRR model

Weidig (2002) uses the fund's interim IRR to compute the future cash flows. The interim IRR is simply the IRR of the past cash flows of a fund plus the NAV of the unrealised investments as an extra cash flow at its reporting date. As the share of unrealised investments or NAV decrease over time in the portfolio, the interim IRR converges to the final IRR. Investors often look at the interim IRR as an indicator of the final IRR. But, the interim IRR on average underestimates the final IRR, especially in the first years due to at cost valuation. The estimate can be improved by allowing the investment manager to adjust the NAV upwards to reflect a better fair value. The key point of Weidig's approach is that, once the interim IRR is said to estimate the final IRR, it is not possible anymore to independently model cash flows because the modelled cash flows give a different estimation of the final IRR. This happens because the NAV used to compute the interim IRR is effectively an aggregation of the future cash flows. Weidig shows that consistency is restored if the cash flows are modelled using the Takahashi and Alexander (2002) approach with the input for the growth rate being the interim IRR. Thus, the growth rate is fixed by consistency and the distribution factor scheme is the only free parameter.

To summarise, this approach works, but is tricky and delicate in the sense that the IRR should ideally not be used as an input to a model. The cash flows should be modelled first and then the expected final IRR computed from the cash flows. The model does not assign a probability to each scenario.

Probabilistic models at fund level

Fitch Ratings model

Fitch Ratings wants to compute the probability that the distributions from a portfolio of funds is insufficient to serve interest and capital repayment of a bond for which the portfolio of funds serves as collateral in a securitisation. It explicitly describes its methodology in Fitch Ratings (2002) and Romer, Moise and Hrvatin (2004). To get a probability of default, Fitch needs to generate future cash flow distributions, but does not have access to historical cash flows. Thus, it decided to generate the fund cash flows using information available from the Thomson VentureXpert database, which are aggregated historical IRRs, historical yearly drawdown and distribution. Fitch also adds a random component to the cash flow pattern by using a probability distribution with the mean being the historical yearly drawdown and distribution. This random component produces a distribution of generated future cash flows of a fund. However, it still has two problems to overcome. First, it proposes an algorithm to adjust for constraints that occur when modelling the future cash flows of active funds as opposed to new funds with no past cash flows. Second, it proposes two ways to produce the cash flow distribution of a portfolio of funds: either via a bottom-up approach by aggregating the individual funds' cash flow, or via a top-down approach using a distribution of portfolio IRRs as input to generate cash flows.

To summarise, Fitch's approach is only useful if no access to historical cash flows is possible, but, as it says itself, its work on mature funds and a portfolio of funds' view is ongoing.

Standard & Poor's model

Standard & Poor's faces the same issues as Fitch Ratings, and describes its methodology in Cheung, Kapoor and Howley (2003a) and (2003b). They found that the private equity cash flows underlie short-term fluctuations, and this supports the view that real cash flows are needed for modelling. They use historical cash flow patterns by calibrating them to be no better than a public index. Standard & Poor's says that the public market equivalent (PME) of the private equity cash flows should not outperform a public index, because there is a lack of a wide and unbiased dataset of cash flows. The PME is the performance of the private equity cash flows invested into a public index, that is, drawdowns (long index) and distributions (short index). To avoid an outperformance, they scale all private equity cash flow distributions to be no better than the public index. Finally, they introduce volatility to the public index return, which directly translates into volatility in cash flow scenarios via the PME scaling.

Their approach is based on real cash flows and is methodologically sound. However, they are extremely conservative with their assumption that the PME of private equity cannot outperform the public market.

Weidig internal age model

In Weidig and Meyer (2003), Weidig proposes a method to use historical cash flows based on the internal age concept. He defines the concept of internal age as the measure of how far advanced the fund is at a given time in the investment and disinvestment of its companies. As the extent of divestment depends on the level of the NAV, it also allows the inclusion of an expert opinion or expert NAV. His approach addresses the problem that historical cash flows are tricky to use with active funds. For new funds, the use of historical cash flows from other funds to model future cash flow scenarios is reasonable. However, the older a fund is the more past history it has including the value of its portfolio. Thus, the active fund is generally in a different internal state than the historical funds at the same age. Weidig now assumes that a fund is a black box that is described with a single parameter measuring its state, the internal age. It has to be estimated for active funds and expert opinion is included implicitly. The active fund then has an internal age and Weidig assumes that the historical cash flows from comparable funds starting from the same internal age, and not the calendar age, are continuing the past cash flow of the fund.

His approach is a good compromise between the non-probabilistic models and the technically very sophisticated models such as Malherbe's. It is conceptually and technically easy to understand, and its assumptions and approximations look reasonable, although certainly need further independent scrutiny.

Partners Group model

Frei and Studer (2004) describe the Partners Group's approach as follows:

> The methodology employs statistical fitting (which can be systematically fine-tuned to precisely mimic historic patterns) and specific adjustments (because future cash flows can and will differ from the past). Based on concepts from insurance mathematics, this approach ensures that the model forecasts are constantly adapted to the actual development and the future outlook of the portfolio being modelled. The approach combines top-down portfolio overview with a qualitative bottom-up assessment of the underlying investments targeting forecasts as accurate as possible.

Further:

> We update our models each quarter to reflect actual cash flows and NAV development, as well as qualitative assessments of specific funds and market conditions.

The details of the model are not public, but we assume that they are using historical cash flows and modifying them in two ways: selecting only cash flows from funds that survived a similar macroeconomic environment, and adjusting the cash flows with the NAV or evaluations of their own managers. They also mention that historical data must be enriched with forward-looking assessments of industry and market trends. Thus, they possibly fine-tune the timing of distributions with an appropriate measure. As The Partners Group's is a proprietary model the details are not public, however the model has been extensively used in a real environment including where rating agencies and investment banks were involved.

Malherbe model

Malherbe (2004) proposes by far the most sophisticated model in terms of use of mathematical methods. He models the drawdown and repayment behaviour as exogenous squared Bessel processes expressed as a stochastic differential equation. He goes on to find the solution to this stochastic differential equation. The parameters of his model need to be estimated from historical data, which are neither tradable nor observable on a market. This is in contrast to option pricing models, where the input to the option model is the volatility, which is observable as volatility implied by market prices of options of different strike and time to expiry. He also mentions that products linked to fund performance such as securitisation notes are difficult to hedge. Further, he states that his model is useful to have confidence bounds around a fair trade price.

No doubt Malherbe knows a lot about financial modelling, but his approach is very technical and he might underestimate some private equity-specific issues. For example, he models the NAV as a random unbiased variable, even though the NAV is a systematic underestimation of the fair value in the first years. Nevertheless, his approach is interesting, and deserves attention.

Kaserer and Diller model proposal

Kaserer and Diller (2004) have studied cash flows and have also generated the distribution of the time at which the capital is fully returned to the investor. They find an average of about 90 months. They also show a transition table of the drawdown per paid in capital, where they calculate the probabilities to end up in a given quartile based on the total distribution per total drawdown for a given year. Based on this study, they suggest that this information could be used for cash flow forecasting as they can estimate the probability of a new fund returning the money after a given time. However, this is fine as long as it is a new fund. But, as seen in the Weidig model using the internal age, mature funds differ significantly from the historical fund's portfolio. The internal state is different and cannot be directly compared with the historical cash flows. Thus, they would need to use the NAV or some other input to calibrate.

Exhibit 17.3

Cash flow models

Reference	*Technical difficulty*	*Level*	*Description of cash flow model*	*Comments*
Malherbe (2004)	Very high	Fund	Model for drawdown, distribution and NAV derived from stochastic differential equation approach	Promising but theoretical with little discussion on private equity specifics and practical issues

Exhibit 17.3 (Continued)

Cash flow models

Reference	*Technical difficulty*	*Level*	*Description of cash flow model*	*Comments*
Partners Group (Frei and Studer (2004)	Unknown	Fund	Combines historical cash flows analysis and current portfolio data and amends for market conditions (top-down) and judgement on the funds (bottom-up). Risk management through Monte-Carlo simulations and tailor-made scenarios.	Used to steer programs in excess of US$3bn. Details not publicly available, but disclosed to involved deal parties such as investment banks and rating agencies.
Weidig in Weidig and Meyer (2003)	Medium	Fund	Using historical cash flows that start at the same internal age as the fund whose future cash flows are modelled	Simple approach if cash flows are available, but assumptions and approximations untested
Standard & Poor's (Cheung, Kapoor and Howley (2003a) and (2003b)	High	Fund	Using historical cash flows calibrated so that their PME does not outperform a public index	Assumes that private equity cannot outperform public index. OK for rating agency to be conservative, but does not help with accurate modelling. How do they deal with mature funds?
Fitch Ratings (2002) and Romer, Moise, and Hrvatin (2004)	High	Fund	Using historical IRR distribution and generating cash flows by using historical data on average drawdown and distribution for each year, and add a random component	Uses IRR which is a bit problematic but an option if no cash flows are available
Kaserer and Diller (2004)	Medium	Fund	Gets probability for a cash flow to happen in future year of a new fund from a matrix computed from historical cash flows	Still in development it seems and they do not say how to handle mature funds
Takahashi and Alexander (2002)	Medium	Fund	Cash flow modelled as savings account, ie, money is paid in, grows at a certain rate, and is paid out at a certain schedule	Simple but does not give probabilities
Weidig (2002)	Medium	Fund	Cash flow is modelled using the Takahashi and Alexander model with the growth rate being the (corrected) interim IRR	Uses IRR which is a bit problematic and not probabilistic

Exhibit 17.3 (Continued)

Cash flow models

Reference	*Technical difficulty*	*Level*	*Description of cash flow model*	*Comments*
Simple approach	Low	Fund	Drawdowns are undrawn commitments divided by remaining investment years, and distributions are the NAV divided by remaining years, and more	Very simple but not probabilistic
Cash flow model based on manager estimates	Medium	Company	Cash flows come from a Monte Carlo simulation that uses the estimates of the manager for future timing and amount of all investments and exits	Very data and labour intensive but feasible for a dedicated fund manager
Grading-based model	Medium	Company	Cash flows come from a Monte Carlo simulation that uses the grading of a company by a manager together with historical data on average returns for a given grading plus volatilities plus correlations plus investment and exit schedules	Easier to do in terms of data and labour than previous model. Feasible for a fund manager or fund investor that co-invests

Source: Quantexperts.

1 As far as the authors are aware.
2 For example, Frei and Studer (2004) write that: 'The model is a proprietary quantitative private equity risk management tool. Hence, the authors cannot publicly disclose more details'.
3 Based on Cochrane (2005).
4 See, for example, Cheung, Kapoor and Howley (2003a) and (2003b), Kaserer and Diller (2004) and Ljungqvist and Richardson (2003).
5 EVAC (2004b) and Ljungqvist and Richardson (2003).
6 As a side note, the IRR should not be estimated with a model or used as an input parameter, but only estimated using modelled cash flows. The IRR is non-linear and ill-defined, which causes some problems.

Part IV

Alternative private equity investment vehicles

Chapter 18

Helping institutional investors to access private equity

The role of the alternative investments

The most popular alternative to fund investments is an investment in a fund of funds. Exhibit 18.1 shows the proportion of capital committed to funds by funds of funds in Europe, with a similar story for the United States. In 1990, less than 1 per cent of the capital to funds came from funds of funds, but the share has increased to almost 17 per cent, with about US$5 billion in 2003 in Europe (see Exhibit 18.1).

The funds of funds are now among the largest group of private equity investors alongside pension funds, insurance companies and banks. Apart from funds of funds, other alternative ways to gain exposure to private equity have emerged, but are marginal in terms of their total impact on private equity markets. Finally, secondary markets now provide an additional way for investors to get into private equity by buying exposure to private equity funds either directly or through secondary funds of funds. The secondary market is now worth several billion dollars worldwide, and up to 5 per cent of investors use it to exit from private equity fund investments.

Alternative private equity investment vehicles mitigate some of the most stringent constraints of private equity investments by offering enhanced liquidity, easy investing and lower overall risk or tailor-made risk profiles. Such features are increasingly in demand, and truly bridge the gap between the entrepreneur and the non-expert capital market investor.

Exhibit 18.1

Contributors to funds

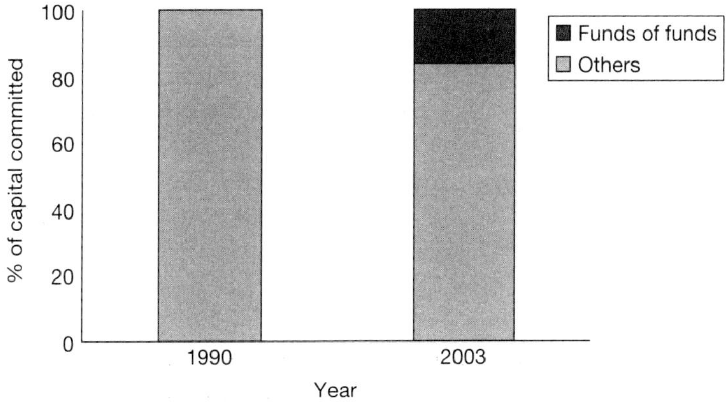

Source: EVCA/PwC.

In the past, only skilled institutional investors could invest into private equity, either directly into a privately held company or into private equity funds. Nowadays, any wealthy generalist investor can gain private equity exposure, without the need for real expertise.

Outsourcing

Outsourcing the tasks involved in being a limited partner (LP) is a safer way to get into private equity for a generalist investor. Private equity is an opaque market, where superior information and skills are of paramount importance, as explained in Parts I and II. There are many opportunities for superior returns, but as many pitfalls. The discussions in Part II show the great number of such pitfalls and lists the checks that a serious LP needs to go through. This requires a specific infrastructure in terms of human resources, information systems and monitoring tools. Portfolio management creates extra challenges, as described in Part III. These challenges are quite scary for a new inexperienced investor: if not for its management, certainly for the trustees or the board of directors who supervise the investor. Professional fund of funds management teams offer an alternative and have a wide range of experience and skills. They know the best market practice terms and conditions of the industry, have better bargaining power, privileged access to the best fund managers, and more. True, there are disadvantages, such as an additional layer of fees, but new investors do not need to spend money on own resources and get peace of mind.

Exiting private equity

Flexibility is another major issue for some investors. This is especially true when it comes to liquidity and exiting opportunities: investors cannot easily, quickly and cheaply exit private equity if they choose to. There are many possible reasons why an investor might seek to exit its private equity investment: a change in strategy, severe liquidity problems, a rebalancing of the portfolio, change in asset allocation and more. Also, investors who might not have a strict long-term investment horizon are keen on public market characteristics. Enhanced liquidity is one of them, even if the secondary market price often includes a discount to the fair value. Nevertheless, it is still a tradable asset. Equally, having a guaranteed floor value on an investment, as is the case for certain structured instruments guaranteeing a minimum return or a portion of the investor's capital, makes private equity accessible to more risk-averse investors. This is especially true for investors who pursue an absolute return strategy. They are ready to give away some of the upside potential of their investment in exchange for increased visibility on the downside risk.

Providing liquidity for private equity investments was always perceived as one of the biggest challenges of the asset class in attracting a broad investor base. This aspect was amplified by the events of the late 1990s and thereafter when some investors got severely burned during the burst of the technology bubble. This not only induced certain investors to seek to exit their private equity investments as a matter of choice; many were actually forced to liquidate their investments in order to be freed from commitments they had taken on and were unable to serve. While the US market has known a relatively developed secondary market for some time, the liquidity squeeze experienced by many investors in Europe in the period of the technology crash kick-started the secondary market in Europe. However, an exit comes at a price, especially in situations where the seller is in distress. Heavy discounts were applied by buyers in secondary transactions, bargaining on the seller's lack of options. Fund investors should carefully consider their investment horizon beforehand, their requirements to be able to divest at a certain time and the cost they are ready to pay for such divestment possibility. Thus, exit options should be a selection criterion in their choice of the investment instrument.

The most common exit channel is a secondary sale. There are specialised firms that buy limited partnership holdings, or even direct investments. However, the sale of a partnership interest often comes at a high price. The sale price is often at a discount to the reported net asset value (NAV), even though the NAV is in most cases an underestimation of the future fund distributions, especially during the first years of a fund. Another exit channel is to invest in a listed private equity fund or fund of funds. They are traded at the stock exchange and investors can exit at any time. Still, quoted private equity vehicles usually trade at a discount to their NAV as well. However, the industry has been quite creative, and offers further liquidity options such as periodic exit opportunities at a guaranteed NAV.[1] Finally, a recent exit option is securitisation notes. However, this exit channel is only suitable for investors with a large and well-diversified portfolio and transaction costs are high. Small investors should seek an arranger who can originate collateral from other sources to create a critical mass for a transaction. The effect of securitisation notes is more that of a capital relief rather than a full exit as such investors are only able to sell off the high-rated bonds and often need to keep the equity element and low-rated bonds themselves.

---

1 Frei and Studer (2004) quote as an example 'the closed-ended private equity fund CSA Private Equity offered to pension funds in Switzerland, which provides the possibility of exiting their investment on a quarterly basis at 99 per cent of the fund's reported net asset value'.

Chapter 19

Funds of funds

In its structure a fund of funds is similar to a fund investment. The fund of funds investors are limited partners (LPs) in the funds of funds, and commit capital to the funds of funds. A management company owns the general partner (GP), and its team invests the money into limited partnerships. Thus, instead of investing into several funds themselves, investors give the capital allocated for private equity to a fund of funds who invests on their behalf in several funds.

Advantages

Why do some investors prefer to invest in a fund of funds? As seen previously, holding limited partnership agreements in several funds poses significant challenges to the investor. A fund of funds is an ideal investment vehicle for new and smaller investors to avoid these challenges.

Outsourcing

The fund of funds investor does not need to build up the necessary resources internally. Required resources include professionals who have the expertise and skills to select and manage fund investments both on a fund-to-fund level and on a portfolio level. Further, on an organisational level, a back office, an IT system and a database are essential. Building the necessary resources requires considerable dedication on the part of investors, and a strong belief that their organisation can do it well. Outsourcing may be a powerful alternative.

Larger networks

The opaqueness of the private equity market is especially frightening for new investors, but also for more experienced investors who are aware that continuous careful information gathering is essential. A large and dedicated fund of funds management team has a better insight into the market, especially in comparison to new investors. It is clear that the economy of scale benefits the fund of funds concept, because a fund of funds management team is bigger compared with the team a small or medium-sized investor would have built up. And new investors need to build up their networks, or hire professionals with networks at a cost.

Accessibility

Smaller investors cannot enter private equity via private equity funds, because they do not have enough money available. Considering that more than 10 fund investments are necessary to achieve diversification, investors need at least US$50 million to be a meaningful investor in their fund investments. A smaller investor might not have such an amount of money. However, an investor in a fund of funds needs no more than US$1 million, or in some instances less to invest, and can benefit from exposure to the same number of funds or more.

Increased diversification

A fund of funds spreads investors' money over a significantly broader area of the market than they could have done by themselves. Thus, investors get more diversification for the same amount of money invested. As seen in the last argument, an investor can invest US$1 million and have an exposure to 10 or more funds. Investors might even want to invest in several funds of funds, perhaps one in Europe, in the United States and in Asia, and possibly in venture capital and buyout. Most investors would find it hard to get the same degree of diversification if they had to build up their own portfolio.

Deal flow availability

A fund of funds typically benefits from a wider pool of deal flow, including access to the most successful teams. Many fund of funds management companies have been around for quite some time, and know many fund management teams, have worked with them in the past, and the fund managers know them well. For the most successful funds having the opportunity to invest is not a matter of choice but a matter of invitation by the GP. Fund of funds managers have the weight in the market to establish this kind of relationship. Often this relationship has grown over many years and dates back to times when a then-novice GP raised its first fund.

Greater bargaining power

Its sheer size also gives a fund of funds more bargaining power. The size of the cheque they can bring to the table gives them a different weight, for example, in the negotiation on terms and conditions.

To summarise, funds of funds allow investors to outsource the tasks of holding a portfolio of fund investments, and are especially beneficial for new investors and small and medium-sized investors. The funds of funds provide an antidote against the opaqueness of private equity, more diversification for the same amount invested, and no administration or extra resources burden against a predictable management fee.

Disadvantages

Additional layer of fees

Investing into a fund of funds is not a free lunch and comes at the price of an additional layer of fees for the investor. Funds of funds charge a management fee on top of the fee to fund managers in their portfolio. A fund of funds manager receives an annual management fee, which is typically between 0.5 per cent and 1 per cent. The fees cover the running costs, including the remuneration of the staff. Typically, the fund of funds managers also receive a carried interest to create an incentive. The percentage may be up to 10 per cent of the overall profits. This reduces the average return for investors.

Less control

A fund of funds investment is a blind pool investment. The investors typically give up any right to participate in the governance of a fund of funds losing the ability to influence the development of their investment.

Illiquidity

Fund of funds investments are illiquid and long term. As investors are LPs, it is not possible to quickly and easily exit. Also, the investment period is even longer than for a fund. For example, a fund of funds might invest into funds over a period of five years, and thus the last cash flows will be more than 15 years after the first drawdowns for the first fund.

Hard to find perfect match

A fund of funds does not have a tailor-made investment focus for one investor, as the views of all LPs and the area of expertise of the GP are also considered. For example, investors having an overexposure to some countries or industry sectors might find it difficult to find a fund of funds whose investment focus precisely matches the areas of their underexposure. If investors build up their own portfolio, they will be able to have their preferred investment exposure.

Overcrowded market

The share of funds of funds contributing to private equity has grown considerably. In boom periods, as in the internet hype period, there is the danger that there are too many and too large funds of funds, and too much money might be chasing too few investment opportunities in good funds. This may lead to investment pressure at the level of fund of funds and deteriorate the quality of their portfolio.

Selecting a fund of funds management team

Like the fund investor, the potential fund of funds investors need to select their manager carefully. Many issues concerning the fund investors are also relevant for the fund of funds investor, such as the quality of the management team or a successful track record based on a disciplined implementation of investment strategies. Therefore, the discussions in Part II are not only useful for fund investors. However, there are also questions specific to funds of funds.

- How do they access funds?
- How do they select funds?
- How high are the fees and carried interest?

Ability to access the best fund management teams

The ability to access the best fund management teams is a critical criterion in the selection of a fund of funds manager. Investors need to convince themselves that the manager can either access the best-performing fund managers or pick promising first-time funds. Therefore, they need to look at the specific strategy of a fund of funds. Several different intermixing philosophies of strategy exist, and the investor should look at whether the managers have the right experience and skills to implement a strategy, and how much such a strategy costs in terms of higher management fees.

Targeting promising or innovative teams

The first approach is for a fund of funds to target unexplored opportunities, which could be investing into first-time teams. Investors might also choose a specialist fund of funds that invests in an emerging market or a new industry sector such as nanotechnology. An investor should be aware that such a strategy is more risky than a generalist fund of funds. On the other hand, such a fund of funds may face less competition for access to funds and have more bargaining power.

Research-focused selection

Second, the fund of funds managers could entirely rely on researching the entire market for funds, and select the best ones based on their reputation and track record, and try to be accepted as an LP. Investment banks often sponsor funds of funds that employ such a strategy. However, investors should be aware that such a strategy costs a lot of money, and the best brains in investment banking are not necessarily competitive compared with fund of funds managers with 20 plus years of experience combined with a powerful network, the trust of the industry and insider information. The latter may be able to apply a third approach to deal-sourcing, namely building on long-term relationships.

Relationship-focused selection

Such fund of funds managers do have access to the best-performing funds, either because they invested in their first funds or due to their reputation. Their wide network allows them to be first to know about new promising fund management teams, and to be first to commit capital to their fund. As private equity is an opaque market and a people's business, investors might prefer such a fund of funds with a relationship-based access strategy. However, as mentioned above, established managers might charge higher fees and carried interest, and past investment success does not guarantee future investment performance. Generation change and key individuals that are too well off to remain motivated for new challenges are only two examples that can change the dynamics of a successful team.

Investment strategies as differentiating factor

Another separating factor between funds of funds is their overall investment strategy: is it a top-down or a bottom-up approach? Do they have the right skills for such a strategy?

Top-down approach

In a top-down approach, the fund of funds managers first decide the allocation to the different countries, stages and sectors for the best possible diversification, and then select the best possible teams within the sub-segment. A top-down approach is either forward-looking qualitative by analysing factors such as political developments, availability of exit opportunities, economic factors, new legislation and more, or historical and quantitative by adopting an asset allocation à la Markowitz using historical returns, risks and correlations between the sub-segments. Investors should be especially mindful of the value of such quantitative schemes, as the past does not necessarily reflect a good prediction of the future, and the nature of private equity makes their implementation very tricky, as explained in Parts I and III.

Bottom-up approach

In a bottom-up approach, the managers scan all fund management teams that raise funds, and select the best ones. A bottom-up approach should not be dismissed from the outset for its possibly low diversification. There is nothing wrong with a specialised fund of funds that only invests in one sector, but therefore has an excellent team of sector experts and a wide-ranging network. Investors could always achieve diversification by investing in several specialist funds of funds of different sub-segments. Thus, fund of funds investors should check whether they want such exposure, that is, whether it fits in their overall portfolio, and make sure that the managers have the right skills.

Most strategies lie somewhere in between these two extremes, and balance the desire for diversification with the necessity to invest in the best teams on the market.

Other selection criteria

Finally, three more distinguishing features between fund of funds managers help the potential investors to make up their mind.

Co-investment strategy

First, some funds of funds have a strategy of co-investing in the portfolio companies of their fund investments, that is, when the GP invests in a company, the LP co-invests a certain percentage. These co-investing LPs would argue in favour of such co-investments because they are free of management fees and carried interest. However, co-investments often result in a conflict of interest with fellow LPs, and also GPs are not inclined to grant this 'free lunch' to individual LPs unless they absolutely need to do so to complete their fundraising. As a consequence, this feature is not very common anymore. Instead of co-investment rights alongside the fund, GPs tend to offer co-investment opportunities to LPs when the deal size exceeds the investment capacity of their fund.

Size of stakes

Second, funds of funds may increase their relative stake in funds when deal flow is scarce. During a recession, big funds of funds often face the dilemma that they find a good fund manager, which is however unable to get to the fundraising target due to a lack of investors. On the other hand, the fund of funds managers sit on their money, and are unable to invest. Thus, some funds of funds decide to take bigger stakes per fund to place their capital. In doing so, a fund of funds ends up with exposure to fewer funds and therefore with more risk.

Portfolio and risk management practices

Finally, portfolio and risk management practices of funds of funds should be a selection criterion for investors in a fund of funds. These issues are also discussed in Part III. The fund of funds investor should make sure that the fund of funds managers have state-of-the-art information systems and quantitative risk management tools and monitoring processes to implement a long-term investment programme and deal with short-term liquidity squeezes.

They are vital for dealing with risks inherent in a fund of funds' investment activity. Their absence increases the risk for fund of funds investors without providing additional return.

The risk profile of a fund of funds

Potential fund of funds investors should understand the risk–return profile of funds of funds. However, this is not an easy task. For example, Thomson Venture Economics has performance data on more than 1,000 funds, but very few on funds of funds. Weidig, Kemmerer and Born (2004) have discussed the risk–return of funds of funds. Using conceptual arguments and a method to construct artificial historical funds of funds, they show that funds of funds are not very risky investments, in general.

First of all, portfolio diversification is working. Ten investments of US$10 million have the same average return as one fund investment of US$100 million, but are much less risky. As there is a minimum requirement to becoming an LP in a fund, a small private equity investor who has, for example, US$5 million should not invest it in a fund, but in a fund of funds which invests in 20 or more funds. In this way, the private equity investor indirectly invests in 400 or more companies via the 20 or 30 funds and should achieve a broad diversification. To summarise, the fund of funds investors get a diversified portfolio, that is, lower risk, but have to pay fees and carried interest to their manager, which results in a lower return.

The story is different for a private equity investor with US$100 million or more. Such an investor can decide to invest directly, for example, US$5 million per fund and in 20 funds, and build up the resources to execute and monitor its investment programme, or to outsource the investment activity to a fund of funds, and pay a management fee and carried interest.

Coming back to the risk–return study, Weidig, Kemmerer and Born (2004) have shown how to construct historical funds of funds artificially using historical funds to study the historical returns of funds of funds. The method is straightforward. Investors have a tool to estimate the historical distribution of historically feasible funds of funds, and can decide for themselves whether the risk–return profile is appropriate for their purposes. The key is to construct artificial portfolios of funds of the same number and type of funds in line with the fund of funds the investor might want to invest in.

For example, a future fund of funds wants to invest in 10 US venture capital funds over two years. Thus, the analyst chooses all venture capital funds, for example, from a period starting in 1990 until 2000. Then, the computer algorithm starts in year 1990, simulates an investment programme by randomly selecting five funds from year 1990 and 1991, computes up the return of the portfolio with deduction of fund of funds fees and carried interest, and repeats this procedure many more times and for every vintage year. In such a way, the user ends up with a distribution of historically feasible funds of funds, which gives investors a rough idea of the risk and return faced by a fund of funds structure. If investors possess cash flows and not only total returns from historical funds, they can follow the same procedure and then look at the variability and patterns of the future fund of funds drawdowns and distributions.[1]

---

1 Details of the algorithm are given in Weidig, Kemmerer and Born (2004).

Chapter 20

Secondary transactions

Private equity is illiquid and a secondary market is not very extensive as it is not easy to sell and buy a limited partnership. There is no open market, and the spread between bid and offer can be considerable. The secondary market typically increases in times of crises such as the aftermath of the technology bubble. Even though statistics are difficult to compile, the secondary market has generally grown bigger and more efficient, and the industry is benefiting from greater liquidity at a lower discount. In the past, many deals were done on a proprietary basis, but auctions have become more popular. Especially larger fund investors can rely on auctions to sell for a reasonable price, and clear off their whole portfolio in one go. Typically, up to 5 per cent of all investors are in some way or another involved in secondary transactions.

Secondary transactions deal with securities that are bought and sold following their initial sale while investors in the primary market purchase their investment instruments directly from the issuer. Secondary transactions can be executed at the level of direct investments where a fund acquires equity holdings in portfolio companies from other private equity funds, or at the level of fund investments through secondary funds of funds. Secondary funds of funds are funds that acquire an interest in existing private equity funds.

This chapter deals with secondary transactions as a mechanism for private equity fund investors to acquire or sell interests in private equity funds, giving them some liquidity for their private equity investments.

Motivation and considerations on the sell-side

Reasons to sell

There are many reasons why an investor might seek to divest its interest in a fund despite the long-term commitment taken in the first place.

- Investors may have overcommitted or overestimated the backflow from their earlier investments, and now need to create liquidity.
- An investor's asset allocation may have changed.
- Changes in regulations may lead to new investment restrictions or make existing investments in private equity more expensive investments, in terms of capital charges. Thus, banks might want to reduce their regulatory capital charges, and free capital from the balance sheet, for example, for other investment areas that they consider more lucrative.[1]
- A large fund of funds may want to rebalance its portfolio for diversification reasons or reduce its exposure to a specific country or sector.

To summarise, private equity investors will face the real risk of having to sell even if they are very committed to a long-term holding period at the start. Many things can go wrong over the years. Therefore, investors should carefully analyse how to safeguard themselves against such events, and think about exit options before investing.

Disadvantages to selling

The main disadvantage is often a considerable discount to the reported net asset value (NAV) or fair value. Especially in times of crisis, secondary buyers have considerable bargaining power. The prospective seller wants or needs to get out as fast as possible, and there might be few buyers in the market. However, in good times the opposite might be true. The specialist secondary buyers such as secondary funds may have raised too much money, and need to find sellers. Fund investors who only sell a few limited partnerships might well have to do a proprietary transaction and cannot rely on an auction as the deal sizes they propose will be of no interest to the large players in the secondary market. Moreover, the selling fund investor might encounter opposition from the general partner (GP) and limited partner (LP) who often have to consent to the transfer of a limited partnership share from one investor to another.

LPs in a private equity fund often have a right of first refusal in the case of the sale of the interest of a co-investor in the partnership. GPs often have the right to refuse the admission of a new LP to the fund. This is to prevent the entry of LPs that have insufficient standing to honour their obligations towards the fund. This is of particular relevance if a fund interest is sold at a time when the GP still has the right to draw commitments from the LPs of the fund. In such a case, if a new investor is unable to comply with the capital calls of the GP, this can jeopardise the investment strategy, reserve policy and value creation prospects of a fund. Hence, the transfer of partnership interest is typically restricted or tied to compliance with specific conditions. These conditions are vital protections for investors and fund managers in a private equity fund but make secondary transactions sometimes more cumbersome.

Motivation and considerations on the buy-side

Secondary transactions in private equity are not only an exit channel for investors, but also present an interesting investment opportunity with possibly anti-cyclic returns. Secondaries provide investors with an opportunity to quickly build up a mature and diversified portfolio of fund investments and can be a useful tool to proactively change the allocation structure with respect to stage, geographic or sector risk within an existing portfolio. Many investors are contemplating investing in secondary deals with the objective of accessing second-hand limited partnership stakes, if possible at a steep discount.

The secondary market for fund investments is becoming increasingly liquid. There is interest on both the buy- and sell-side. And the more players there are the lower the spread between bid and offer due to increased competition.

Advantages

Buying at a discount

In secondary transactions investors may be able to buy the limited partnership interests at a discount to fair value. The more bargaining power the buyer has, the higher this discount which is typically in times of crises or in a situation where the seller has pressure of any kind to divest.

Anti-cyclic performance

Secondaries have anti-cyclic behaviour. In times of a down cycle in the private equity industry, the primary funds may be performing badly. Buying limited partnership interests at that moment may give investors the opportunity to buy entire portfolios at low valuations and to benefit from attractive returns as the market improves. In a poor general investment climate, secondary investors may be able to pick up participations in limited partnerships from distressed investors, enjoy greater bargaining power and buy at higher discounts.

More visibility than primary investor

The buyer in a secondary decides on an existing portfolio of companies and has thus superior visibility on a fund's return potential than a primary fund investor. Also, the management team in which a secondary buyer invests has a few more years of track record, and the buyer has a better base to judge whether the team is stable, experienced and skilled. Generally, there is much less uncertainty about future results and the secondary investor consequently faces less risk.

Picking the right investments

The secondary fund investor can often cherry pick from many different limited partnerships across a range of vintage years and fund types. This choice is very useful to rebalance a portfolio by adding secondary limited partnerships. The buyer has an active choice, and effectively avoids the blind pool investing of the original LP.

Diversification effects

Secondary investments offer interesting diversification effects. Especially for the diversification of vintage year risk, secondaries appear useful, as for poor-performing vintage years secondaries typically lower the overall cost of a fund investor's investments in a given vintage year through the acquisition of limited partnership stakes at a discount.

Access to good fund management teams

A buyer may gain access to new funds by buying the limited partnership interest. This is useful for building a relationship with the fund managers, and possibly invest in a future fund. Thus, buyers might gain access to successful fund management teams.

No J-curve

The buyer is not faced with the J-curve effect, that is, honouring drawdown calls for several years and getting the money back only many years later. In a secondary transaction, the limited partnerships are already a few years old, and the buyer can expect mostly distributions and very few drawdown calls. Thus, the money invested is not tied up for a decade but just for a few years. Also, the buyer faces little complexity in planning its liquidity needs for capital calls, and mostly only faces the uncertainty of unknown distributions.

Disadvantages

Low bargaining power in good times

Despite the apparent advantages, buyers in a secondary deal need to wrestle with several issues. In good times, there might be too many buyers with too much money and too few investors willing to sell. This situation considerably reduces the bargaining power, and discounts might be very low or non-existent. The popularity of auctions further cuts into the discount, and so does a more efficient market.

Execution difficulties

Also, in secondary transactions, speed of execution often matters. There may be a trade-off between getting access to a deal and due diligence work that can be done to gain comfort with the valuation. Often, secondary buyers can only access a limited amount of information on the assets they buy. Thus, they might miss out on some skeletons in the cupboard. Skills, resources and experience of secondary fund investors are crucial elements to address this issue. Secondary fund investors should know that investing in secondary deals requires potentially more resources than making a primary investment because, next to the skill-set to evaluate the management team of a fund, investors need to assess the intrinsic value of the portfolio – effectively requiring direct investment skills.

Outsourcing the investment into secondary transactions

A way to bridge this potential gap of resources is to invest in secondary funds of funds. They operate like normal funds of funds except that their speciality is to pick up limited partnership interests from investors who seek to partially or fully divest their private equity fund exposure. They typically have specialised investment professionals combining the knowledge of a fund investor with the skills to evaluate the return potential of individual companies in the underlying portfolio. Funds of funds in secondaries can add an interesting dimension to the diversification of a portfolio, especially with respect to vintage year risk. For reasons of improved visibility on the return potential of the underlying asset as exposed above, secondary funds of funds carry less risk than primary funds of funds or fund investments.

---

1 In this respect, the New Basel Accord might also play its role as the new capital charges are expected to be considerably higher and rules require the same charges for a direct investment or a fund of funds investment, despite its significant difference in risk. Discussions between national associations and the Basel Committee are ongoing to find a viable compromise for the classification of risk assets and the impact this has on banks as a funding source for the private equity industry. This issue is more important to Europe because a quarter of the capital invested in European private equity comes from banks as opposed to 5 per cent in the United States.

Chapter 21

Securitisation and structured instruments in private equity

With the increasing sophistication of the private equity industry, novel products satisfying specific investors' needs emerge. The most paramount examples are certainly attempts to use private equity portfolios in securitisation deals and structured hedge fund-like transactions that allow the risk profile to be modified according to investors' preferences.

Securitisation of private equity funds

Securitisation of a private equity fund portfolio or collateralised fund obligations (CFOs) is a recent phenomenon in the United States and Europe, with a handful of completed deals in recent years such as PEPS I from Aon's fund portfolio, Silver Leaf from Deutsche Bank and Pine Street 1 from AIG. CFOs are in the process of establishing themselves as an alternative to secondary sales as they allow the capital allocation to private equity to be reduced by converting the private equity risk of a portfolio into bonds with quantifiable default risk and selling it off to fixed-income products investors. Exhibit 21.1 illustrates the mechanism of a securitisation of a private equity fund portfolio. In a securitisation, an existing portfolio of assets with future cash flows is repackaged and sold as rated bonds and unrated notes with the income stream of the portfolio as collateral. Specifically, the arranger sets up a special purpose vehicle and this vehicle then issues rated bonds and unrated notes. The bonds are rated by a rating agency based on stringent criteria such as for diversification, legal requirements, existence of liquidity reserves, quality of collateral and more. The sale proceeds of the bonds and notes are then used to buy the existing portfolio of private equity funds.

Private equity securitisation truly bridges the gap between unruly private equity and the capital markets. It provides a new exit channel for private equity. Exiting investors can securitise their portfolio of funds and sell off some parts if they have a sufficiently large and diversified portfolio or find an arranger who embeds their portfolio in a bigger transaction with other assets.

Benefits

CFOs conveniently package the unruly nature of private equity into well-known bond characteristics with interest payments, measurable probability of default with associated ratings by Standard & Poor's, Moody's or Fitch, and a well-defined maturity. These features also make them attractive to institutional investors who can sell the bonds at any time, and also improve their return and asset diversification by investing in these innovative products. Due to the innovative nature of the collateral used in CFOs, rating agencies apply a conservative modelling approach, which means that the rating assigned to the private equity-backed bond

Exhibit 21.1
Securitisation

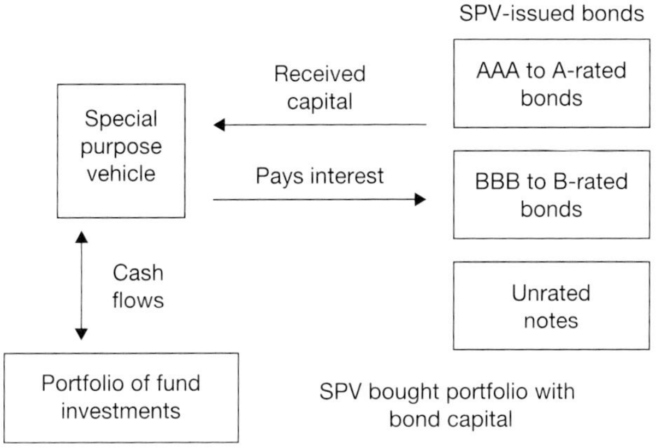

Source: Authors' own.

might in reality reflect a lower probability of default than for the same rating of a standard bond. Thus, the bond investor gets more return for the same risk taking. In addition, the private equity bond's default is at best moderately correlated to the default of standard bonds, and a portfolio of private equity-backed bonds and standard bonds has therefore a lower joint default probability.

On the sell-side, securitisation is a useful tool for an investor to reduce the exposure to private equity. Arrangers and originators of securitisation deals typically collect funds of comparable structures but with a well-diversified exposure in terms of stage risk, geographic coverage and industrial sectors and use it as collateral for a synthetic or true securitisation deal. An investor who wants to free capital or liquidity for other operations, to reduce regulatory charges, or exit private equity but wants to keep the upside can ask an arranger to sell part of its exposure in a structured deal. This exit channel is especially useful in recession times, when secondary sales are unattractive due to the high discounts.

Disadvantages

However, there are also disadvantages to securitisation schemes. The most important one is certainly the high cost for everyone involved, whether on the sell- or buy-side. On top of the cost structure of the underlying assets, the transaction and rating costs are around 1 per cent of the deal amount, with a minimum cost of around US$500,000 plus rating maintenance cost, plus extra management time. Moreover, there are the costs for additional security arrangements for investors in the deal, such as a liquidity facility to bridge any mismatch between cash flows from the underlying private equity portfolio used as collateral and interest payments due to bondholders in the transaction. Ultimately, these costs need to be priced into the structure or have to be borne by the selling investor. This is why securitisation deals require a critical mass in the structuring to be affordable. Specialist arrangers have emerged globally who collect private equity exposure in all forms to use for securitisation. Some also try to combine it with other assets to compensate for lack of volume of underlying assets or to enhance the diversification of assets used for collateral, thereby improving the rating of the various risk tranches.

Another aspect to watch carefully is the immature nature of these instruments. The transactions so far have been few and recent, and no bond is even close to its maturity. Many aspects, especially with respect to the legal structure, remain untested, especially in troubled waters. Further, rating agencies do provide the investor with a rating based on a probability of default, but how reliable is their analysis? The default crucially depends on the modelling of the future cash flows of the portfolio, and as seen in Part III, cash flow models are not well established and are untested. Moody's has not published its model, but Standard & Poor's and Fitch have published their models, which seem reasonable but may be too simple and too conservative. Rating agencies pride themselves on conservative ratings, but this may mean a higher implicit discount for the seller of the collateral.

Prospects

The future evolution of private equity securitisation is uncertain. Generally, securitisation involving private equity assets has only happened a few times. The market for CFOs is still, to a large extent, supply-driven. Securitisation deals still mainly serve the purpose of investors to partially exit their exposure. On the demand-side, interest in CFOs has been limited and in several cases they could only be placed with the help of monoline insurers taking the default risk on various bond tranches.

There is still a lack of understanding on the buy-side of the risk associated with private equity serving as collateral, hence sellers of private equity portfolios in CFO deals are typically required to retain the first-loss piece in the transaction. With increasing liquidity and transparency of the market this highest risk layer of a securitisation deal in private equity may also be placed with specialised investors and may even become tradable on a regulated market. This will eventually lead to higher transaction volumes both in number and size. Higher volumes in number lead to increasing standardisation of the deal structures which in turn reduces the upfront structuring cost and running cost of a deal. Lower transaction cost in turn attracts additional volume of underlying assets for collateral. Some see securitisation as a true alternative to secondaries, while others argue that there is room for both in the wide spectrum of financial instruments, more pessimistic market players argue that securitisation will not break through due to the inability to model private equity risk for the purpose of transforming it into a fixed-income product. Market response will decide.

Structured instruments and hedge funds

Another class of instruments that has emerged over time is the use of hedge fund-type structures for private equity. The objective is to tailor the risk profile of the instrument according to the risk appetite of specific investor groups. By combining various financial instruments including debt instruments, equity instruments and derivatives, the issuer of structured products can create almost any cash flow pattern with an associated risk profile for the investor.

Most of the products launched so far have had a zero-bond structure or capital insurance as a basis to guarantee capital repayment to investors at maturity. In a zero-bond structure, part of the capital subscribed by the investors in the hedge fund would be invested in zero bonds.

The amount invested would be such that the accrued interest at the maturity of the bond, which coincides with the maturity of the hedge fund, is sufficient to repay the guaranteed capital amount to investors. The remainder of the capital subscribed by investors, less the structuring cost and ongoing management fee for the hedge fund, would be invested in a private equity portfolio, either in primary or secondary assets. This allows investors to gain exposure to the return potential of private equity without being exposed to the risk of losing their capital.

Many structures of this nature have come to the market. One of the first attempts was probably Princess and Pearl issued by Partners Group, a Swiss-based fund of funds manager. In 1999, it sold capital guaranteed convertible notes worth US$700 million, which can be converted to shares in the private equity vehicle Princess. The bonds were rated by Fitch and insured by Swiss Re against capital (or principal) loss. A similar deal, but with a 2 per cent coupon, called Pearl was issued in 2000 for €660 million. Whilst this transaction was aimed at fund of funds investors, structures with capital guarantee for investors have also been launched by general partners to diversify the risk profiles they can offer to potential investors in their funds. They had a good response from investors willing to take less than pure private equity risk. The concept of a floor value at maturity makes these investments particularly interesting for investors with an absolute return strategy. However, at the level of a private equity fund, having different risk profiles within the same investment vehicle also poses significant challenges. Full-risk-taker investors might dislike the fact that low-risk-takers decide with them on questions such as investment strategy or, even more extreme, on action to be taken against the manager in the case of poor performance. In such situations different risk profiles of investors may lead to diverging interests and consequently make it more difficult to find a sufficient majority for actions to be taken by limited partners.

Nevertheless, the outlook for hedge fund-type structures is positive, as there is a demand from both sides of the spectrum. Fund managers both at the level of funds and funds of funds are eager to see new products arriving on the market to target new investor groups and to attract more capital to their asset class.

On the investor side, hedge fund-type products have appeal as they provide a soft entry to the high-risk asset class private equity. With structured transactions, virtually any risk profile can be built and proposed to investors who then can gradually learn the features of this asset segment and increase their exposure to risk as they gain confidence in their ability to manage those risks.

The result will be very positive for the private equity industry as a whole. A greater diversity of investors, more liquidity in the market, higher-skilled investors, more market transparency and a higher degree of standardisation are all features that will bring the private equity segment more in line with public equity market characteristics and hence make it more accessible for a wider public of investors and make it an even more powerful funding source for the private equity industry.

Other products: publicly traded private equity

Listed private equity structures are an attempt by the private equity industry to attract new and small investors by bridging the gap between private equity and the capital markets. Investors can push their outsourcing even further than being an LP in a fund of funds by just buying shares on the stock markets which they can sell at any time. Funds of funds and fund managers have been quite creative in offering tailor-made structures.

Publicly traded private equity can be grouped into three categories:[1] listed companies whose core business is private equity (for example, 3i), quoted investment funds (for example, Schroeder Ventures Trust) and specially structured investment vehicles (for example, Castle Private Equity). Despite the ease of access to private equity and the promise to provide more liquidity to the investor, investors should be aware that such products are often traded at a price below the reported NAV or the fair value of the underlying portfolio.

A subtle but important difference between such structures and limited partnerships in funds or a fund of funds is that many listed structures are linked to evergreen funds of funds or funds that reinvest their investment proceeds on a continuous basis as opposed to self-liquidating structures that distribute investment proceeds to their investors until full liquidation. Thus, the proceeds are reinvested until an agreed liquidation date. The investor has to wait until liquidation, which might be years away, or sell the shares at a sizeable discount. Therefore, investors cannot expect a much better exit deal than on a secondary market, but the identification of a buyer may be easier than in a secondary deal. As there are many different structures that cater for various types of investors, the investors should look around for the most appropriate structure fitting their profile.

Bauer and Zimmermann researched the risk–return relationship of publicly traded investment vehicles for private equity.[2] They found nearly 300 such products, of which about 100 have a sufficient capitalisation, trading history, trading volume and trading frequency for further investigation. They claim to have found a higher Sharpe ratio for publicly traded private equity, that is, a high risk-adjusted return, but caution is needed as the data mostly represents the boom period of the 1990s. In the follow-up paper,[3] they use a sample over a wider time period, and create different indices with their sample of listed products. After correcting for biases, they find a high risk-adjusted performance before 2000, and very different results when the time period extends to 2003. These results should show to the investor that return can vary considerably over time and that a diversification over vintage year is recommended.

---

1 See Bauer and Zimmermann (2001).
2 See Bauer and Zimmermann (2001).
3 See Zimmermann, Bilo, Christophers and Degosciu (2004).

Chapter 22

Conclusion

Private equity has come a long way to establish itself as a core part of alternative investment strategies used by institutional investors to maximise the risk-adjusted return of their portfolio. Every year, institutional and private investors commit more than US$100 billion globally. With the increased amounts invested, the markets have gained in sophistication: fund structures catering for specific investors' needs have emerged, instruments with risk profiles tailored to the risk appetite of individual investors are offered in a lively and competitive market, and finally, fund managers, fund investors and industry organisations work together in creating fair and transparent industry standards. These developments have made private equity a maturing industry.

Despite considerable progress over a relatively short period of time, a lot of things remain to be done. Today, despite all the efforts undertaken, private equity is still an expert industry, with little regulation and protection for the unskilled investor. Nevertheless, a growing private equity industry depends on a growing number of skilled investors, who can understand and manage risks associated with private equity investments and deliberately take such risks as investors committed for the long term.

Providing a guide to fund investments for sophisticated investors seeking exposure to private equity was the main goal of this book. It aimed to give not only institutional and private investors, but also private equity lawyers and academics a comprehensive insight into the dynamics of this industry, allowing them to separate the myths from reality and facts from fiction. The book also offered a close look behind the scenes of the main industry players, shedding light on the relationship between fund managers and investors. This industry should not be about competition between general partners and limited partners, but about the mutual benefit from pursuing a common interest. Understanding each other's needs and constraints is essential and this book wanted to contribute to this dialogue. Moreover, this book set out the concepts on which investors could build by developing tools to increase predictability of their portfolio prospects and decrease randomness of their returns when investing in private equity funds. This is vital to gauge the risk investors can take and allows them to seek the instrument that is appropriate for their specific needs. A discussion of the main types of instruments offered in private equity has been provided in this book.

Private equity is a vast and ever-evolving industry. Nevertheless, this book strived to be a complete and unbiased guide to private equity fund investments. Trends of today that have been discussed in this book will fade, and new trends will emerge, pushing the limits of this industry.

Without doubt, new standards in valuation and reporting will develop and increase transparency for investors. Portfolio management techniques and quantitative risk management tools that are currently developed secretly by a few sophisticated investors will become public knowledge and subject to open discussion. Further, improved statistical data will allow forecasting models to be tested more efficiently and make them more reliable. Harmonisation in taxation will drive standardisation of fund structures, and an increasingly educated interaction between general partners and limited partners will lead to standardisation of terms and conditions governing the relationship between the fund investors and fund managers. New instruments will emerge catering for new investors' needs, and existing instruments will become more tradable. These developments will remove some of the biggest current constraints of private equity investments. Many other developments that today are not even thought of will be common market practice in a few years' time.

The private equity industry has transformed itself from a niche investment area to a maturing industry, and its exciting journey is far from over. Hopefully, this book has conveyed the state-of-the-art of today's industry, and provided readers with a comprehensive guide for their daily professional life to push the industry further.

Glossary

This glossary is kindly provided by the European Venture Capital Association (EVCA), with additional terminology defined by the authors.

Added value	A private equity management team's exceptional experience, know-how or valuable business contacts, which constitute a vital input for the growth of investee companies.
Allocation	The number of securities assigned to an investor, broker or underwriter in an offering.
Angel financing	Capital contributed by independently wealthy private investors. *See* business angel.
Anti-dilution (full ratchet)	Anti-dilution provisions in which the price at which the anti-dilution instruments are converted is the lowest price at which ordinary shares have been sold. For example: in a prior round of financing that raised capital at €2.00 per share, investors received full ratchet anti-dilution protection. A subsequent round of financing was consummated at €1.00 per share, and the early-round investors therefore had the right to convert their anti-dilution instruments at the lowest (ie, €1.00) price. *See* anti-dilution provisions, anti-dilution (weighted average).
Anti-dilution (weighted average)	Anti-dilution provisions in which the price at which the anti-dilution instruments are converted is calculated by a weighted average formula. For example: in a prior round of financing that raised €1 million of capital at €2.00 per share, investors received weighted average anti-dilution protection. A subsequent round of financing was consummated for another €1 million at €1.00 per share, and the early-round investors therefore had the right to convert their anti-dilution instruments at a weighted average-adjusted price of €1.50 per share. *See* anti-dilution provisions, anti-dilution (full ratchet).
Anti-dilution provisions	Provisions in a company's charter and by-laws designed to discourage undesired takeover bids. These take the form of options or institutional equity instruments (eg, convertible preference shares), which can be converted to ordinary shares on any issue of new stock in a subsequent round of investment financing or in a takeover bid. The price at which this conversion

	takes place is determined by the type of anti-dilution provision. *See* anti-dilution (full ratchet), anti-dilution (weighted average).
Arm's-length	The relationship between persons (whether companies or not) who deal on purely commercial terms, without the influence of other factors such as: common ownership; a parent / subsidiary relationship between companies; existing family or business relationships between individuals.
Asset allocation	A fund manager's allocation of his investment portfolio into various asset classes (eg, stocks, bonds, private equity).
Asset class	A category of investment, which is defined by the main characteristics of risk, liquidity and return.
Average IRR	The arithmetic mean of the internal rates of return (IRRs). *See* internal rate of return (IRR).
Bad leaver	An employee who leaves the company within a short time or who is dismissed for cause, or under other circumstances where the employee is not permitted to retain the benefit of profit-sharing arrangements such as increased value of shares or carried interest.
Balanced fund	Venture capital funds focused on both early-stage and development with no particular concentration on either.
Basis point	One hundredth of a per cent (0.01 per cent). Used to measure changes in or differences between yields or interest rates.
Benchmark	A previously agreed-upon point of reference or milestone at which venture capital investors will determine whether or not to contribute additional funds to an investee company.
Beta	A statistical measure of a security's volatility, compared with the overall market. A beta of less than 1 indicates lower volatility than the general market; a beta of 1 or more indicates higher volatility than the general market. *See* volatility.
BIMBO (Buy in-management -buyout)	A combination of a management buy in (MBI) and a management buyout (MBO). In a BIMBO, an entrepreneurial manager or group of external managers financed by venture capitalists buys into a company and teams up with members of the target management team to run it as an independent business.
Black-Scholes formula	A model developed by Fischer Black and Myron Scholes for pricing financial options.

Bridge financing — Financing made available to a company in the period of transition from being privately owned to being publicly quoted.

Burn rate — The rate at which an investee company consumes investment capital.

Business angel — A private investor who provides both finance and business expertise to an investee company.

Buy-and-build strategy — Active, organic growth of portfolio companies through add-on acquisitions.

Buyback — A corporation's repurchase of its own stock or bonds.

Buyout — A transaction in which a business, business unit or company is acquired from the current shareholders (the vendor).
See management buyout (MBO), management buy in (MBI), leveraged buyout (LBO).

Buyout fund — Fund whose strategy is to acquire other businesses; this may also include mezzanine debt funds which provide (generally subordinated) debt to facilitate financing buyouts, frequently alongside a right to some of the equity upside.

Capital gains — If an asset is sold at a higher price than that at which it was bought, there is a capital gain.

Capital under management — This is the total amount of funds available to fund managers for future investments plus the amount of funds already invested (at cost) and not yet divested.

Capital-weighted average IRR — The average IRR weighted by fund size.

Captive fund — A fund in which the main shareholder of the management company contributes most of the capital, that is, where the parent organisation allocates money to a captive fund from its own internal sources and reinvests realised capital gains into the fund.
See semi-captive fund, independent fund.

Carried interest — A bonus entitlement accruing to an investment fund's management company or individual members of the fund management team. Carried interest (typically up to 20 per cent of the profits of the fund) becomes payable once the investors have achieved repayment of their original investment in the fund plus a defined hurdle rate.

Clawback option — A clawback option requires the general partners in an investment fund to return capital to the limited partners to the extent that the general partner has received more than its agreed profit share. A general partner clawback option ensures that, if an investment fund exits from strong performers early in its life and weaker performers are left at the end, the limited partners get back their capital contributions, expenses and any preferred return promised in the partnership agreement.

Closed-end fund — Fund with a fixed number of shares. These are offered during an initial subscription period. Unlike open-end mutual funds, closed-end funds do not stand ready to issue and redeem shares on a continuous basis.

Closing — A closing is reached when a certain amount of money has been committed to a private equity fund. Several intermediary closings can occur before the final closing of a fund is reached.

Collateral — Assets pledged to a lender until a loan is repaid. If the borrower does not pay back the money owed, the lender has the legal right to seize the collateral and sell it to pay off the loan.

Commitment — A limited partner's obligation to provide a certain amount of capital to a private equity fund when the general partner asks for capital.
See drawdown.

Compliance — The process of ensuring that any other person or entity operating within the financial services industry complies at all times with the regulations currently in force. Many of these regulations are designed to protect the public from misleading claims about returns they could receive from investments, while others outlaw insider trading. Especially in the United Kingdom, regulation of the financial services industry has developed beyond recognition in recent years.

Confidentiality and proprietary rights agreement (or non-disclosure agreement) — An agreement in which an employee, customer or vendor agrees not to disclose confidential information to any third party or to use it in any context other than that of company business. If the agreement is between a company and an employee, the employee typically grants to the company the rights to all inventions he develops while employed by the company and represents that he is not bound by any restrictive obligations to a former employer.

Connected persons — Companies related by ownership or control of each other or common ownership or control by a third person or company, and individuals connected by family relationships or, in some instances, by existing business relationships (such as individuals who are partners).

Contributed capital — Contributed capital represents the portion of capital that was initially raised (committed by investors) which has been drawn down in a private equity fund.

Convertible debt A debt obligation of a company which is convertible into stock under certain circumstances.

Covenants An agreement by a company to perform or to abstain from certain activities during a certain time period. Covenants usually remain in force for the full duration of the time a private equity investor holds a stated amount of securities and may terminate on the occurrence of a certain event such as a public offering. Affirmative covenants define acts that a company must perform and may include payment of taxes, insurance, maintenance of corporate existence and so on. Negative covenants define acts that the company must not perform and can include the prohibition of mergers, sale or purchase of assets, issuing of securities and so on.

Deal flow The number of investment opportunities available to a private equity house.

Debt/equity ratio A measure of a company's leverage, calculated by dividing long-term debt by ordinary shareholders' equity.

Debt financing Financing by selling bonds, notes or other debt instruments.

Debt ratio Debt capital divided by total capital.

Debt service Cash required in a given period to pay interest and matured principal on outstanding debt.

Derivative or derivative security A financial instrument or security whose characteristics and value depend upon the characteristics and value of an underlying instrument or asset (typically a commodity, bond, equity or currency). Examples include futures, options and mortgage-backed securities.

Development capital *See* expansion capital.

Development fund Venture capital fund focused on investing in later-stage companies in need of expansion capital.

Direct public offering A public offering in which shares are sold directly to investors, rather than through an underwriter.

Disbursement (United States) The flow of investment funds from private equity funds into portfolio companies.

Disclosure letter A document disclosing matters which might otherwise amount to a breach of warranties. Matters so disclosed limit the effectiveness of the warranties.

Discounted cash flow (DCF) A method of assessing the value of an investment based on predicted cash flows discounted to take account of the fact that a euro tomorrow is worth less than a euro today.

Distribution The amount disbursed to the limited partners in a private equity fund.

Distribution to paid-in capital (DPI) The DPI measures the cumulative distributions returned to investors (limited partners) as a proportion of the cumulative paid-in capital. DPI is net of fees and carried interest. This is also often called the 'cash-on-cash return'. This is a relative measure of the fund's realised return on investment.
See realisation ratio, residual value, RV/PI and TV/PI.

Divestment *See* exit.

Drag-along rights If the venture capitalist sells his/her shareholding, he/she can require other shareholders to sell their shares to the same purchaser.

Drawdown When investors commit themselves to back a private equity fund, all the funding may not be needed at once. Some is used as drawdown later. The amount that is drawn down is defined as contributed capital.
See commitment, contributed capital.

Early stage Seed and start-up stages of a business.
See seed, start-up, later stage.

Early-stage fund Venture capital fund focused on investing in companies in the early part of their lives.

EBIT Earnings before interest and taxes – a financial measurement often used in valuing a company (price paid expressed as a multiple of EBIT).

EBITDA Earnings before interest, taxes, depreciation and amortisation – a financial measurement often used in valuing a company (price paid expressed as a multiple of EBITDA).

Enterprise DCF model Variant of the DCF model which looks at the company's operations and calculates the present value of future free cash flows by discounting them with the weighted average cost of capital.

Equity kicker In a mezzanine loan, equity warrants payable on exit.

Equity ratio One of the indicators used by banks to calculate debt ceiling. It consists of net equity divided by the company's total assets.

Banks apply yardstick ratios for different industry sectors to arrive at a minimum level of funding that shareholders are required to contribute.

Exit Liquidation of holdings by a private equity fund. Among the various methods of exiting an investment are: trade sale; sale by public offering (including IPO); write-offs; repayment of preference shares/loans; sale to another venture capitalist; sale to a financial institution.

Exiting climates The conditions that influence the viability and attractiveness of various exit strategies.

Exit strategy A private equity house or venture capitalist's plan to end an investment, liquidate holdings and achieve maximum return.

Expansion capital Also called development capital. Financing provided for the growth and expansion of a company, which may or may not break even or trade profitably. Capital may be used to: finance increased production capacity; market or product development; provide additional working capital.

Five-year rolling IRR This shows the development of the five-year horizon IRR, measured at the end of each year.

Follow-on investment An additional investment in a portfolio company that has already received funding from a venture capitalist.
See initial investment.

Fund A private equity investment fund is a vehicle for enabling pooled investment by a number of investors in equity and equity-related securities of companies (investee companies). These are generally private companies whose shares are not quoted on any stock exchange. The fund can take the form either of a company or of an unincorporated arrangement such as a limited partnership.
See limited partnership.

Fund age The age of a fund (in years) from its first drawdown to the time an IRR is calculated.

Fund focus (investment stage) The strategy of specialisation by stage of investment, sector of investment or geographical concentration. This is the opposite of a generalist fund, which does not focus on any specific geographical area, sector or stage of business.

Fund of funds A fund that takes equity positions in other funds. A fund of funds that primarily invests in new funds is a primary fund of funds. One that focuses on investing in existing funds is referred to as a secondary fund of funds.

Fundraising	The process in which venture capitalists themselves raise money to create an investment fund. These funds are raised from private, corporate or institutional investors, who make commitments to the fund which will be invested by the general partner. *See* general partner, limited partner, commitment.
Fund size	The total amount of capital committed by the limited and general partners of a fund.
GAAP (Generally Accepted Accounting Principles)	Rules and procedures generally accepted within the accounting profession.
Gatekeepers	Specialist advisers who provide assistance to institutional and corporate investors when making private equity investments.
Generalist fund	Funds with either a stated focus of investing in all stages of private equity investment, or funds with a broad area of investment activity.
General partner	A partner in a private equity management company who has unlimited personal liability for the debts and obligations of the limited partnership and the right to participate in its management.
General partner's commitment	Fund managers typically invest their personal capital alongside their investors' capital, which often works to instil a higher level of confidence in the fund. The limited partners look for a meaningful general partner investment of 1 per cent to 3 per cent of the fund.
Hands-off	A private equity investment in which the venture capitalist contributes only capital – and not business know-how or management involvement – to the investee company.
Hands-on	A private equity investment in which the venture capitalist adds value by contributing capital, management advice and involvement.
Holding period	The length of time an investment remains in a portfolio. Can also mean the length of time an investment must be held in order to qualify for capital gains tax benefits.
Horizon internal rate of return	An indication of performance trends within an industry sector. Horizon IRR uses the beginning net asset values as an initial cash outflow and net asset values at the period end as the terminal cash flow. Through these values, plus/minus any net interim cash flows, it calculates IRRs for the defined time period. *See* IRR.
Hurdle rate	The IRR that private equity fund managers must return to their investors before they can receive carried interest.

Independent fund One in which the main source of fundraising is from third parties. *See* captive fund, semi-captive fund.

Index A benchmark against which financial or economic performance is measured, (eg, S&P 500, FTSE 100).

Information rights A contractual right to obtain information about a company, including, for example, attending board meetings. Typically granted to venture capitalists investing in privately held companies.

Initial investment First venture-backed investment made in an investee company. *See* follow-up investment.

Initial public offering (IPO) The sale or distribution of a company's shares to the public for the first time. An IPO of the investee company's shares is one of the ways in which a private equity fund can exit from an investment.
See exit.

Insider dealing A range of possible offences centred on the possession of non-public information by a party and the illegal or improper use of that information to deal or encourage others to deal in securities, or to disclose that information to anyone other than in the proper performance of their duties.

Institutional investor An investor, such as an investment company, mutual fund, insurance company, pension fund, or endowment fund, that generally has substantial assets and investment experience. In many countries, institutional investors are not protected as fully by securities laws because it is assumed that they are more knowledgeable and better able to protect themselves.

Internal rate of return (IRR) In a private equity fund, the net return earned by investors from the fund's activity from inception to a stated date. The IRR is calculated as an annualised effective compounded rate of return, using daily or monthly cash flows and annual valuations.

International Accounting Standards (IAS) A series of accounting standards that are to be implemented by businesses by 2005. More information can be obtained from www.iasc.org.uk

Investee company *See* portfolio company.

Investment philosophy The stated investment approach or focus of a management team. *See* fund focus.

J-curve The curve generated by plotting the returns generated by a private equity fund against time (from inception to termination).

The common practice of paying the management fee and start-up costs out of the first drawdowns does not produce an equivalent book value. As a result, a private equity fund will initially show a negative return. When the first realisations are made, the fund returns start to rise quite steeply. After about three to five years the interim IRR will give a reasonable indication of the definitive IRR. This period is generally shorter for buyout funds than for early-stage and expansion funds.

Key-man insurance — A life and/or critical illness insurance policy taken out by a company to provide a cash sum if a key executive dies or becomes ill, thus covering some or all of the resulting financial loss to the business.

Later stage — Expansion, replacement capital and buyout stages of investment. *See* early stage.

Leavers and joiners — The arrangements covering: what happens to the profit interest (through carried interest or ownership of shares) of executives who leave an investee company or a venture capital fund; the provision for making a profit-sharing interest available to rising stars (new or young executives who previously did not have such a profit-sharing interest) or new joiners.

Leveraged buyout (LBO) — A buyout in which the NewCo's capital structure incorporates a particularly high level of debt, much of which is normally secured against the company's assets.

Leveraged recapitalisation — Transaction in which a company borrows a large sum of money and distributes it to its shareholders.

Limited partner — An investor in a limited partnership (ie, private equity fund). *See* general partner.

Limited partnership — The legal structure used by most venture and private equity funds. The partnership is usually a fixed-life investment vehicle, and consists of a general partner (the management firm, which has unlimited liability) and limited partners (the investors, who have limited liability and are not involved with the day-to-day operations). The general partner receives a management fee and a percentage of the profits. The limited partners receive income, capital gains and tax benefits. The general partner (management firm) manages the partnership using policy laid down in a Partnership Agreement. The agreement also covers, terms, fees, structures and other items agreed between the limited partners and the general partner.

Management buy in (MBI) — A buyout in which external managers take over the company. Financing is provided to enable a manager or group of managers from outside the target company to buy into the company with the support of private equity investors.

Management buyout (MBO) A buyout in which the target's management team acquires an existing product line or business from the vendor with the support of private equity investors.

Management fees Compensation received by a private equity fund's management firm. This annual management charge is equal to a certain percentage of investors' initial commitments to the fund.

Mature funds Funds that have been in existence for over two years.

Median IRR The value appearing halfway in a table ranking funds by IRR in descending order.

Memorandum Brochure presented by a general partner in the process of raising funds. This document is dedicated to potential investors (limited partners), and usually contains (amongst other information) a presentation of the management team's track record, terms and conditions and investment strategies.

Mezzanine finance Loan finance that is halfway between equity and secured debt, either unsecured or with junior access to security. Typically, some of the return on the instrument is deferred in the form of rolled-up payment-in-kind (PIK) interest and/or an equity kicker. A mezzanine fund is a fund focusing on mezzanine financing.

Multiples or relative valuation This estimates the value of an asset by looking at the pricing of comparable assets relative to a variable such as earnings, cash flows, book value or sales.
See P/E ratio.

Mutual fund An open-end fund that may sell as many shares as investors demand. As money flows in, the fund grows. If money flows out of the fund, the number of the fund's outstanding shares drops. Open-end funds are sometimes closed to new investors, but existing investors can still continue to invest money in the fund.
See closed-end fund.

Open-end fund A fund which sells as many shares as investors demand.
See closed-end fund, mutual fund.

Overhang Private equity funds still available for investment in the industry.

P/E ratio Price/earnings ratio – the market price of a company's ordinary share divided by earnings per share for the most recent year.

Placement agent A person or entity acting as an agent for a private equity house in raising investment funds.

Pooled IRR

The IRR obtained by taking cash flows from inception together with the residual value for each fund and aggregating them into a pool as if they were a single fund. This is superior to either the average, which can be skewed by large returns on relatively small investments, or the capital-weighted IRR which weights each IRR by capital committed. This latter measure would be accurate only if all investments were made at once at the beginning of the fund's life.

Portfolio company (or investee company)

The company or entity into which a private equity fund invests directly.

Post-money valuation

The valuation made of a company immediately after the most recent round of financing.
See pre-money valuation.

Pre-money valuation

The valuation made of a company prior to a new round of financing.
See post-money valuation.

Present value

Present value is found by dividing the future pay-off by a discount factor which incorporates the interest foregone for not receiving this pay-off at the present time.

Private equity

Private equity provides equity capital to enterprises not quoted on a stock market. Private equity can be used to develop new products and technologies, to expand working capital, to make acquisitions, or to strengthen a company's balance sheet. It can also resolve ownership and management issues. A succession in family-owned companies, or the buyout and buy in of a business by experienced managers may be achieved using private equity funding. Venture capital is, strictly speaking, a sub-set of private equity and refers to equity investments made for the launch, early development, or expansion of a business.
See venture capital, venture capitalist.

Public offering

An offering of stock to the general investing public. The definition of a public offering varies from country to country, but typically implies that the offering is being made to more than a very restricted number of private investors; that roadshows promoting the offering will be open to more than a very restricted audience; or that the offering is being publicised. For a public offering, registration of prospectus material with a national competent authority is generally compulsory.
See initial public offering.

Quartile

The IRR which lies a quarter from the bottom (lower quartile point) or top (upper quartile point) of the table ranking the individual fund IRRs.

Ratchet/sliding scale	A bonus where capital can be reclaimed by managers of investee companies, depending on the achievement of corporate goals.
Realisation ratios	Benchmark measurements of investment performance that complement IRR. Realisation ratios are distributions to paid-in capital (DPI), residual value to paid-in capital (RV/PI) and total value to paid-in (TV/PI). These are measures of returns to invested capital. These measures do not take the time value of money into account.
Residual value	The estimated value of the assets of the fund, net of fees and carried interest.
Residual value to paid-in capital (RV/PI)	A realisation ratio which is a measure of how much of a limited partner's capital is still tied up in the equity of the fund, relative to the cumulative paid-in capital. RV/PI is net of fees and carried interest.
Secondary distribution (or secondary offering)	A public offering of a security by a selling holder of securities, rather than by the issuer. The term secondary offering is also sometimes used more generally in reference to any public offering other than an IPO.
Secondary fund of funds	*See* fund of funds.
Seed stage	Financing provided to research, assess and develop an initial concept before a business has reached the start-up phase. *See* early stage.
Semi-captive fund	A fund in which, although the main shareholder contributes a large part of the capital, a significant share of the capital is raised from third parties. *See* captive fund, independent fund.
Spin-off	Selling off a department, or a division of a company to make it an independent company.
Standard deviation	A statistical parameter: measures how strongly elements in a dataset vary around the mean.
Start-up	Financing provided to companies for product development and initial marketing. Companies may be in the process of being set up or may have been in business for a short time, but have not sold their product commercially. *See* early stage.
Takedown schedule	The plan stated in a private equity fund's memorandum to provide for the actual transfer of funds from the limited partners to the general partner's control.

Terms and conditions	The financial and management conditions under which private equity limited partnerships are structured.
Top quarter	Comprises funds with an IRR equal to or above the upper quartile point.
Total value to paid-in (TV/PI)	A realisation ratio which is the sum of distributions to paid-in capital (DPI) and residual value to paid-in capital (RV/PI). TV/PI is net of fees and carried interest.
Trade sale	The sale of company shares to industrial investors.
Upper half	Comprises funds with an IRR equal to or above the median point.
Valuation and reporting guidelines	Guidelines set by EVCA concerning valuation methodology and reporting practices to investors. Their aim is improve transparency, so that investors are better able to monitor and evaluate the performance of their investments and to make the asset class more accessible and comprehensible to new and existing investors.
Valuation methods	The policy guidelines a management team uses to value the holdings in the fund's portfolio. More generally, valuation is an estimate of the price of an item at a given time, based on a model and comparison with the value of similar items.
Venture capital	Professional equity co-invested with the entrepreneur to fund an early-stage (seed and start-up) or expansion venture. Offsetting the high risk the investor takes is the expectation of higher than average return on the investment. *See* private equity, venture capitalist.
Venture capitalist	The manager of a private equity fund who has responsibility for the management of the fund's investment in a particular portfolio company. In the hands-on approach (the general model for private equity investment), the venture capitalist brings in not only monies as equity capital (ie, without security/charge on assets), but also extremely valuable domain knowledge, business contacts, brand-equity, strategic advice and so on.
Vintage year	The year of fund formation and first drawdown of capital.
Volatility	The volatility of a stock describes the extent of its variance over time. *See* standard deviation.
Write-down	A reduction in the value of an investment.

Write-off The write-down of a portfolio company's value to zero. The value of the investment is eliminated and the return to investors is zero or negative.

Write-up An increase in the value of an investment. An upward adjustment of an asset's value for accounting and reporting purposes.

Bibliography and further reading

Atkins, B. and M. Giannini (2004), 'Risk Management for Private Equity Funds of Funds' in Lars Jaeger (ed.) *The New Generation of Risk Management for Hedge Funds and Private Equity Investments*, New York: Institutional Investor Books, pp. 215–227.

Bauer, M. and H. Zimmermann (2001), *Publicly Traded Private Equity: An Empirical Investigation*, Working Paper No. 5/01, Basel: University of Basel, www.ssrn.com

Blaydon, C., F. Wainwright and R. Hatch (2003), *A Note on Private Equity Allocation: Case Study*, Tuck Business School at Dartmouth: Centre for Private Equity and Entrepreneurship.

Blaydon, C. and M. Horvath (2002), 'GPs Say Valuation Standard Is Important but Can't Agree on One', *Venture Capital Journal*, October, www.venturecapitaljournal.net

Blaydon, C. and M. Horvath (2003), 'Strengthening GP-LP Relationships: The Role of Valuation Reporting', Presentation at Centre for Private Equity and Entrepreneurship, Tuck Business School, November.

Burgel, O. (1999), *UK Venture Capital and Private Equity as an Asset Class for Institutional Investors*, London: London Business School and BVCA Research Report.

BVCA (2003), *Reporting and Valuation Guidelines*, British Venture Capital Association, www.bvca.co.uk.

Bygrave, W., M. Hay and J. Peeters (1999), *The Venture Capital Handbook*, Harrow: Pearson Education Limited.

Chen, P., G. Baierl and P. Kaplan (2002), 'Venture Capital and Its Role in Strategic Asset Allocation: Long Term Risk-Return Characteristics', *The Journal of Portfolio Management*, Vol. 28, No. 2, pp. 83–89.

Cheung, L., V. Kapoor and C. Howley (2003a), *Equity Securitization: Risk and Value*, New York: Standard & Poor's Special Report, October.

Cheung, L., V. Kapoor and C. Howley (2003b), *Rating Private Equity CFOs: Stochastic Market Cash Flows*, New York: Standard & Poor's Special Report, June.

Cochrane, J. (2005), 'The Risk and Return of Venture Capital', *Journal of Financial Economics*, Vol. 75, No.1, pp. 3–52, www.ssrn.com

Cumming, D. and U. Walz (2004), *Private Equity Returns and Disclosure Around the World*, European Finance Association 2004, Maastricht Meetings Paper No. 4233, www.ssrn.com

Das, S., M. Jagannathan and A. Sarin (2002), *The Private Equity Discount: An Empirical Examination of the Exit of Venture Backed Companies*, Social Science Research Network Working Paper Series, January, www.ssrn.com

Diem, G. (2003), *The Information Deficiency Problem of Private Equity Fund-of-Funds: A Risk and Monitoring Management Perspective*, Unpublished MBA Thesis, Birmingham: University of Birmingham.

Dowd, K. (1998), *Beyond Value at Risk: The New Science of Risk Management*, New York: Wiley.

EVCA (2001), *Reporting and Valuation Guidelines*, European Venture Capital Association, www.evca.com

EVCA (2004a), *Why and How to Invest in Private Equity*, Investor Relations Committee Report, www.evca.com

EVCA (2004b), *Performance Measurement and Asset Allocation for European Private Equity Funds*, Research Report, www.evca.com

Fenn, G. W., N. Liang and S. Prowse (1995), *The Economics of the Private Equity Market*, Dallas: Federal Reserve Bank of Dallas.

Fitch Ratings (2002), *Going Public with Private Equity CFOs*, Fitch Report, November.

Frei, A. and M. Studer (2004), 'Quantitative Private Equity Risk Management' in Lars Jaeger (ed.) *The New Generation of Risk Management for Hedge Funds and Private Equity Investments*, New York: Institutional Investor Books, pp. 201–214.

Gockeln, F. (2003), *Measuring the Risk and Return of Venture Capital: A Maximum Likelihood Approach*, Unpublished Diploma Thesis, Frankfurt: Goethe University.

Gompers, P. and J. Lerner (1999), *The Venture Capital Cycle*, Boston: MIT Press.

Gompers, P., J. Lerner and D. Scharfstein (2003), *Entrepreneurial Spawning: Public Corporations and the Genesis of New Ventures, 1986–1999*, Harvard Negotiation, Organizations and Markets Working Paper No. 03-37; MIT Sloan Working Paper No. 4317-03, June, www.ssrn.com

Gottschalg, O., L. Phalippou and M. G. Zollo (2004), *Performance of Private Equity Funds: Another Puzzle?* Paris: INSEAD Working Paper, www.ssrn.com

Hielscher, U., H. Zelger and S. Beyer (2003), 'Performancemessung und Reporting von Venture Capital-/Private Equity-Gesellschaften', *Finanzbetrieb*, No. 7–8/2003, pp. 498ff.

Jaeger, L. (2004), 'Preface' in Lars Jaeger (ed.) *The New Generation of Risk Management for Hedge Funds and Private Equity Investments*, New York: Institutional Investor Books, pp. xxiii–xxv.

Jaffer, S. (1998), *Alternative Investment Strategies*, London: Euromoney Books.

Jones, C. and M. Rhodes-Kropf (2003) 'The Price of Diversifiable Risk in Venture Capital and Private Equity', American Finance Association 2003 Washington DC Meetings, May, www.ssrn.com

Kaneyuki, M. (2003), 'Creative Valuation Techniques for Venture Capital Fund Reporting', *Finanzbetrieb*, No. 7–8, July 2003, pp. 506–511.

Kaplan, S. and A. Schoar (2003), *Private Equity Performance Returns Persistence and Capital*, National Bureau of Economic Research Working Paper, No. w 9807, June, www.ssrn.com

Kaplan, S., B. Sensoy, and P. Strömberg (2002), *How Well Do Venture Capital Databases Reflect Actual Investments?* Unpublished Working Paper, University of Chicago.

Kaserer, C., and C. Diller (2004), *European Private Equity Funds – A Cash Flow Based Performance Analysis*, CEFS Working Paper No. 2004-01, Centre for Entrepreneurial and Financial Studies, Technical University of Munich, May, www.ssrn.com

Kupperman, D. and B. Griffith (2001), 'Historical Distributions of IRR in Private Equity', *Investment Management Research Report*, Goldman Sachs Private Equity Group, November.

Lerner, J. (2000), *Venture Capital and Private Equity: A Casebook*, New York: Wiley.

Ljungqvist, A. and M. Richardson (2003), *The Cash Flow, Return and Risk Characteristics of Private Equity*, New York University Finance Working Paper, No. 03-001, New York, www.ssrn.com

de Malherbe, E. (2004), 'Modelling Private Equity Funds and Private Equity Collateralised Fund Obligations', *International Journal of Theoretical and Applied Finance*, Vol. 7, No. 3, pp. 193–230.

Martin, R. (1995), *Internal Rate Of Return Revisited*, Social Science Research Network Working Paper Series, October, www.ssrn.com

McIntire, G., A. Conner and D. Nevins (2004), 'Portfolio Management Approach to Determining Private Equity Commitments', *Journal of Alternative Investments*, Vol. 6, No. 4, pp. 32–46.

Miller II, W. (1998), 'Alternative Investment Strategies: An Investor's Viewpoint' in Sohail Jaffer (ed.) *Alternative Investment Strategies*, London: Euromoney Books, pp. 3–10.

Moskowitz, T. and A. Vissing-Jorgensen (2000), *The Private Equity Premium Puzzle*, CRSP Working Paper No. 524, November, www.ssrn.com

Peng, L. (2001), *Building a Venture Capital Index*, Yale ICF Working Paper No. 00-51, August, www.ssrn.com

Probitas (2003), *Primary Secondaries: The Emergence of Liquidity for Institutional Private Equity Investors*, Probitas Liquidity Management Report.

Quigley, J. and S. Woodward (2003), *An Index for Venture Capital*, Working Paper No. E03-333, Berkeley: Department of Economics at Berkeley.

Romer, M., M. Moise and R. Hrvatin (2004), 'Hedge Fund and Private Equity Securitisation', in Lars Jaeger (ed.) *The New Generation of Risk Management for Hedge Funds and Private Equity Investments*, New York: Institutional Investor Books, pp. 327–244.

Rouvinez, C. (2003), 'Private Equity Benchmarking with PME+', *Venture Capital Journal*, 1 August, www.venturecapitaljournal.net

Schmidt, D. (2004), *Private Equity-, Stock- and Mixed Asset-Portfolios: A Bootstrap Approach to Determine Performance Characteristics, Diversification Benefits and Optimal Portfolio Allocations*, University of Frankfurt, Centre of Private Equity Research, Working Paper No. 2004-12, www.ssrn.com

Singer, B., R. Staub and K. Terhaar (2003), 'Appropriate Policy Allocation for Alternative Investments', *Journal of Portfolio Management*, Vol. 29, No. 3, pp. 101–110.

Social Science Research Network, Pre-print archive, www.ssrn.com

Swensen, D. (2000), *Pioneering Portfolio Management – An Unconventional Approach to Institutional Investment*, New York: The Free Press.

Takahashi, D. and S. Alexander (2002), 'Illiquid Alternative Asset Fund Modelling', *The Journal for Portfolio Management*, Vol. 28, No. 2, pp. 90–100.

Thatcher, W. (2003), *Time Weighted Return and Internal Rate of Return, What's the Difference*, Report, Commonfound Securities, Inc., www.commonfund.org

Weidig, T. (2002), 'Towards a Risk Model for Venture Capital Funds: Liquidity and Performance Forecasting', www.ssrn.com

Weidig, T. (2003), 'Risk Model for Venture Capital Funds', www.ssrn.com

Weidig, T., A. Kemmerer and B. Born (2004), 'The Risk Profile of Private Equity Fund-of-Funds', www.ssrn.com

Weidig, T. and P. Mathonet (2004), 'The Risk Profile of Private Equity', www.ssrn.com

Weidig, T. and T. Meyer (2003), 'Modelling Venture Capital Funds', *Risk Magazine*, Vol. 16, October, pp. 89–92, www.ssrn.com

Zimmermann, H., S. Bilo, H. Christophers and M. Degosciu (2004), *The Risk and Return of Publicly Traded Private Equity*, WWZ/Department of Finance, Working Paper No. 6/04, Basel: University of Basel.